NATURE WRITING FOR
EVERY DAY OF THE YEAR

NATURE WRITING FOR EVERY DAY
OF THE YEAR

EDITED BY
JANE MCMORLAND HUNTER

–

ILLUSTRATIONS BY
JESSAMY HAWKE

BATSFORD

To Matilda, Tabitha and Tiger, with all my love

First published in the United Kingdom in 2021 by
Batsford
43 Great Ormond Street
London
WC1N 3HZ

ISBN 978-1-84994-605-6

A CIP catalogue record for this book is available from
the British Library.

10 9 8 7 6 5 4 3 2 1

Reproduction by Rival Colour Ltd, UK
Printed and bound by 1010 Printing International Ltd, China

CONTENTS

INTRODUCTION

Nature appears in many unexpected places in books, from Victorian novels and traveller's journals to essays and children's stories. This anthology dips its toe into fact and fiction, letters and diaries, practical field guides and wild imaginings. Following the seasons, day by day, you will find identification notes and musings from bygone times, magical forests and many timely warnings, throughout the ages, of the perils of mistreating nature and taking her riches for granted.

I have compiled two collections of nature poetry and, while doing so, I came to realise that many of the very best nature writers never wrote poetry and that many of the most moving descriptions of the natural world appear as prose rather than verse. Equally, writers such as Jane Austen, Thomas de Quincy, Daphne du Maurier and Samuel Johnson may not be best known for their descriptions of the natural world, but write on nature with great insight and feeling.

Some writers observe the natural world, while others highlight the perils it faces, many much older than we might suspect. In historic times the natural world was linked to the power of God or the gods. Later it was paired with science. Increasingly it became evident that humans wield enormous power over the wild places of the earth. There is then the added problem of how best to safeguard nature: Aldo Leopold, writing in 1949, made the point, 'All conservation of wildness is self-defeating, for to cherish we must see and fondle, and when enough have seen and fondled, there is no wildness left to cherish.' Not all writers even liked the wilderness. Daniel Defoe, while travelling round Britain, went from town to town and deplored the wildness of the Lake District.

This is not intended to be a practical manual, but I have included entries from field guides where the description is particularly beautiful, interesting or humorous. Anne Pratt, Edward Step and Rev. C. A. Johns write so lyrically that their descriptions go far beyond merely useful. Much of the best nature writing allows the imagination to soar, and with this in mind I have included the opinions of witches, griffins and a phoenix. Amongst these pieces you will also find bears (grizzly and duffel-coated), cats, dogs and talking ravens. You will discover how to make a cowslip ball, what advice to offer an oak sapling and the way in which many animals become Real.

Almost every piece here has been taken from a larger work. In each case the original source is given and the date of publication or, if more relevant, the date when the work was written. Placing the pieces in their time is both interesting and often necessary to appreciate the writer's point of view. I have attempted to select extracts that stand alone but I have, where necessary, added a brief introduction to explain the context of the piece or inserted explanations in square brackets. Where a work exists in multiple editions I have chosen the one I particularly like, for example the sixth edition of Charles Darwin's *The Origin of Species* because, in one instance, I preferred the wording. Having chosen that extract I felt it was only logical to keep to the same edition for the other extracts from the book.

This is a very personal selection; readers may be surprised to find the novelist Charles Dickens has more entries than the naturalist W. H. Hudson, and that the probably less well-known Aldo Leopold appears more than Gilbert White. These are the books I love and reread: childhood favourites, moving novels and haunting descriptions of nature. In many cases it was hard to limit the number of extracts, but the book I found hardest to cut was Jean Giono's novella *The Man Who Planted Trees*. Over the years many publishers and readers have taken it to be a true story, and so it should be, a lesson in what one man can achieve in a relatively short space of time. There are many writers who, for reasons of space and copyright, do not have as many entries as I would have liked; my reading life, indeed my life in all respects, would be poorer without the works of John Lewis-Stempel, Robert Macfarlane, H. E. Bates and Roger Deakin. My hope is that many of these excerpts will lead readers to their and other original works.

The aim of this anthology is to bring the wild world into readers' homes and cross the frontier line that Richard Jefferies described in 1879 in his book *Wild Life in a Southern County*. Since then cities have expanded, roads spread and populations grown but the natural world is still there for those who look for it:

> There is a frontier line to civilisation yet,
> and not far outside its great centres we come quickly
> even now on the borderland of nature.

Latin names: the names in this book are those which were in use at the time. Many have since changed.

JANUARY

The Morning Star Glittered Coldly

Crystallized Boughs

From *The Peverel Papers*, January, 1921

This morning, a forgotten milk-can brought me out of bed early. Afterwards, in spite of the rimey tang in the air, I stood at my cottage gate, and was glad of it.

It was a fairy world I looked out upon. During the night, the frost had cast its spell over the woods and glades of the New Forest. This morning, every branch and twig bore a pearly burden of hoar-frost. Over the narrow lane which leads to my retreat, the morning star still glittered coldly; the silence of the dark winter dawn was only broken by the rumbling of wheels upon the frosty ruts, and the *crop, crop* of the forest ponies as they munched their scanty breakfast beside my garden hedge.

At my next appearance, the rose and grey of dawn had given place to high sun and a cloudless blue – a blue so vivid that the crystallized boughs against it had a strange, unearthly splendour.

Such mornings are rare so far south. Mostly, our January days are soft and grey, with, now and again, one borrowed from April or even May amongst them. Days of cloudless beauty – 'weather breeders,' the country people call them, because they are supposed to presage the bad weather we seldom get before the storms of March.

Flora Thompson (1876–1947)

Sounds in Winter

From *Walden or Life in the Woods*, 1854

For sounds in winter nights, and often in winter days, I heard
the forlorn but melodious note of a hooting owl indefinitely
far; such a sound as the frozen earth would yield if struck with
a suitable plectrum, the very *lingua vernacula* of Walden Wood,
and quite familiar to me at last, though I never saw the bird while
it was making it. I seldom opened my door in a winter evening
without hearing it; *Hoo hoo hoo, hoorer, hoo*, sounded sonorously,
and the first three syllables accented somewhat like *how der do*; or
sometimes *hoo hoo* only.

Henry David Thoreau (1817–1862)

The Shivering Sand

From *The Moonstone*, 1868

The sand-hills here run down to the sea, and end in two spits of rock jutting out opposite each other, till you lose sight of them in the water. One is called the North Spit, and one the South. Between the two, shifting backwards and forwards at certain seasons of the year, lies the most horrible quicksand on the shores of Yorkshire. At the turn of the tide, something goes on in the unknown deeps below, which sets the whole face of the quicksand shivering and trembling in a manner most remarkable to see, and which has given to it, among the people in our parts, the name of the Shivering Sand. A great bank, half a mile out, nigh the mouth of the bay, breaks the force of the main ocean coming in from the offing. Winter and summer, when the tide flows over the quicksand, the sea seems to leave the waves behind it on the bank, and rolls its waters in smoothly with a heave, and covers the sand in silence. A lonesome and a horrid retreat, I can tell you! No boat ever ventures into this bay. No children from our fishing-village, called Cobb's Hole, ever come here to play. The very birds of the air, as it seems to me, give the Shivering Sand a wide berth.

Wilkie Collins (1824–1889)

Great Linguists

From *All the Dogs of My Life*, 1936

My third [dog] was Cornelia; a black-backed, brown-bellied dachshund, who only understood German. She it was who taught me my first German words, which were couch – this doesn't sound very German, but it is – *schönmachen,* and *pfui.* The last of these three words I ended by finding most useful. Nearly all my domestic problems in Pomerania, I gradually discovered, could be settled by saying very loudly to recalcitrant, neglectful or erring servants, *Pfui.*

. . . .

We immediately loved. At sight we loved ... . She wimpered round me, in delighted recognition that here at last was a playmate and a friend. Her whole body was one great wag of welcome. She showed off. She did all her tricks. She flung herself on her back, so that I might see for myself how beautiful her stomach was –

'Do not,' interrupted my husband, 'kiss the dog. No dog should be kissed. I have provided you, for kissing purposes, with myself.'

Such was the way he talked. Apophthegms. And I used to listen to them with a kind of respectful amusement, my ear cocked, my head on one side. From the very beginning, I enjoyed and treasured his apophthegms.

. . . .

Dogs being great linguists, she quickly picked up English, far more quickly than I picked up German, so we understood each other very well, and couch, *schönmachen,* and *pfui* continued for a long time to be my whole vocabulary.

Elizabeth von Arnim (1866–1941)

Colder and Colder

From *The Diary of a Country Parson*, 1795

Jan 5, Monday:
In the Afternoon the Weather seemed likely to alter rather Milder if anything than it was. The Horison in the West on the going down of the sun was remarkably red. I thank God!

Jan 15, Thursday:
The Weather Most piercing, severe frost, with Wind and some Snow, the Wind from the East and very rough.

Jan 20, Tuesday:
Last Night was the severest we have had yet. It froze so sharp within doors, that the milk in the Milk-pans in the Dairy, was froze in a mass.

Jan 21, Wednesday:
The last Night, the most severest yet, extreme cold. So cold that the Poultry kept in the Cart-shed and obliged to be driven out to be fed ...

Jan 23, Friday:
The Weather more severe than ever, it froze apples within doors, tho' covered with a thick carpet. The cold to day was the severest I ever felt. The Thermometer in my Study, with a fire, down to No. 46.

Jan 25, Sunday:
The Frost this Morning more severe than yesterday. It froze last Night the Chamber Pots above Stairs. Thermometer in the Study down to No. 40 this Morn. Barometer up high, No. 29 = 16 and very fair. The Cold so severe that it effects me very much.

Feb 4, Wednesday:

As cold a Night last night almost as we have had yet, it froze very sharp within doors, all the Milk and Cream froze. Extreme Cold this Morning with cutting wind, and much Snow besides. Both Barometer and Thermometer very low. Many birds have been found dead, and the Rooks and Crows so tame that they come up to the Kitchen door where I feed my Poultry.

Feb 5, Thursday:

As cold and as severe a Frost as Ever, and now not likely to alter, being very fair above.

Feb 8, Sunday:

Weather much altered, very foggy and a cold Thawe, with very small Rain, all the whole Day. I hope to God that now We shall no more have any very severe Frosts this Year. Barometer fell, Thermometer rose.

James Woodforde (1740–1803)

The Rook (Corvus frugilegus)

From *British Birds in their Haunts*, 1909

There are few English parks that do not boast of their rookery, and few proprietors of modern demesnes pretending to be parks, who would not purchase at a high price the air of antiquity and respectability with an established colony of these birds. Owing to their large size and the familiarity with which they approach the haunts of men, they afford a facility in observing their habits which belongs to no other birds; hence all the treatises on Natural History, and other publications which enter into the details of country life in England, abound in anecdotes of the Rook.

. . . .

I must not conclude this imperfect sketch without noticing a peculiar habit of Rooks, which is said to portend rain. A flock will suddenly rise into the air almost perpendicularly, with great cawing and curious antics, until they have reached a great elevation, and then, having attained their object, whatever that may be, drop with their wings almost folded till within a short distance of the ground, when they recover their propriety, and alight either on trees or on the ground with their customary grave demeanour.

Rev. C. A. Johns (1811–1874)

Witches and Nature

From *Northern Lights*, 1995

The witch, Serafina Pekkala, explains to Lyra:

'We feel the cold, but we don't mind it, because we will not come to harm. And if we wrapped up against the cold, we wouldn't feel other things, like the bright tingle of the stars, or the music of the Aurora, or best of all the silky feeling of moonlight on our skin. It's worth being cold for that.'

Philip Pullman (1946–)

Breeds of the Domestic Pigeon

From *The Origin of Species*, 6th edition, 1872

The diversity of the breeds is something astonishing. Compare the English carrier and the short-faced tumbler, and see the wonderful difference in their beaks, entailing corresponding differences in their skulls. The carrier, more especially the male bird, is also remarkable from the wonderful development of the carunculated skin about the head, and this is accompanied by greatly elongated eyelids, very large external orifices to the nostrils, and a wide gape of mouth. The short-faced tumbler has a beak in outline almost like that of a finch; and the common tumbler has the singular inherited habit of flying at a great height in a compact flock, and tumbling in the air head over heels. The runt is a bird of great size, with long, massive beak and large feet; some of the sub-breeds of runts have very long necks, others very long wings and tails, others singularly short tails. The barb is allied to the carrier, but, instead of a long beak, has a very short and broad one. The pouter has a much elongated body, wings, and legs; and its enormously developed crop, which it glories in inflating, may well excite astonishment and even laughter. The turbit has a short and conical beak, with a line of reversed feathers down the breast; and it has the habit of continually expanding, slightly, the upper part of the oesophagus. The Jacobin has the feathers so much reversed along the back of the neck that they form a hood, and it has, proportionally to its size, elongated wing and tail feathers. The trumpeter and laugher, as their names express, utter a very different coo from the other breeds. The fantail has thirty or even forty tail-feathers, instead of twelve or fourteen, the normal number in all the members of the great pigeon family: these feathers are kept expanded and are carried so erect that in good birds the head and tail touch: the oil-gland is quite aborted. Several other less distinct breeds might be specified.

Charles Darwin (1809–1882)

Arctic Seasons

From *Arctic Dreams*, 1986

Traveling north from the equator you could not help but notice the emergence of recognizable seasons, periods of time characterized by conditions of rising, falling, or relatively stable light, in association with certain ranges of temperature. By the time you entered the Temperate Zone you would find a set of seasons distinct enough to be named and easily separated. Farther north, 'spring' and 'fall' would seem increasingly transitory, until each became a matter of only a few weeks. Winter, you would eventually find, lasted appreciably longer than summer. And together the two would define the final landscape.

The seasons are associated in our minds with the growth of vegetation. Outside of the four primary seasons (a constant referent with us, a ready and seemingly natural way to organize our ideas), we speak of a growing season and of a fallow season, when we picture the earth lying dormant. In the middle of an arctic winter, however, there is such a feeling of a stone crushed beneath iron that it is hard to imagine any organism, even a seed, living, let alone lying fallow. In summer, in the sometimes extravagant light of a July day, one's thoughts are not of growth, of heading wheat and yellowing peaches, but of suspension, as if life had escaped the bounds of earth. In this country, which lacks the prolonged moderations between winter and summer that we anticipate as balmy April mornings and dry Indian summer afternoons, in this two-season country, things grow and die as they do elsewhere, but they are, more deeply than living things anywhere else, seasonal creatures.

Barry Lopez (1945–)

Six Seasons

From *The Pocket Encyclopaedia of Natural Phenomena*, 1827

To me it appears that there are six principal seasons or divisions of the year, to one of which we may venture to refer almost all the wild and most of the hardy herbaceous plants which grow in our climate. This arrangement into six instead of four seasons corresponds better with the actual course of phenomena.

We may consider the first or Primaveral Season as beginning at Candlemas, on the first opening of the early spring flowers; the second or vernal, about old Ladytide; the Solstitial about St. Barnabas; the aestival about St. Swithin; the autumnal about Michaelmas; and the brumal about the Conception.

. . . .

The above arrangement, however defective it may be as to the unequal number of days comprehended by each season, is nevertheless the best division that I can make of the year agreeable to the phenomena of each period.

Thomas Furley Forster (1761–1825)

A Very Rare Sort of Bear

From *A Bear Called Paddington*, 1958

Mr Brown sees a bear on Paddington Station:

Mrs Brown followed the direction of his arm and dimly made out a small, furry object in the shadows. It seemed to be sitting on some kind of suitcase and around its neck there was a label with some writing on it. The suitcase was old and battered and on the side, in large letters were the words WANTED ON VOYAGE.

Mrs Brown clutched at her husband. 'Why, Henry,' she exclaimed. 'I believe you were right after all. It *is* a bear!'

She peered at it more closely. It seemed a very unusual kind of bear. It was brown in colour, a rather dirty brown, and it was wearing a most odd-looking hat, with a wide brim, just as Mr Brown had said. From beneath the brim two large, round eyes stared back at her.

Seeing that something was expected of it the bear stood up and politely raised its hat, revealing two black ears. 'Good afternoon,' it said, in a small, clear voice.

'Er... good afternoon,' replied Mr Brown, doubtfully. There was a moment of silence.

The bear looked at them inquiringly. 'Can I help you?'

Mr Brown looked rather embarrassed. 'Well... no. Er... as a matter of fact, we were wondering if we could help you.'

Mrs Brown bent down. 'You're a very small bear,' she said.

The bear puffed out its chest. 'I'm a very rare sort of bear,' he replied importantly. 'There aren't many of us left where I come from.'

'And where is that?' asked Mrs Brown.

The bear looked round carefully before replying. 'Darkest Peru.'

Michael Bond (1926–2017)

Griffins

From *Pseudodoxia Epidemica*, Chap. XI, Of Griffins, 1650

That there are Griffins in Nature, that is, a mixt and dubious Animall, in the fore-part resembling an Eagle, and behinde the shape of a Lion, with erected eares, four feet, and a long taile, many affirm, and most, I perceive, deny not.

· · · · · · · · · ·

If examined by the doctrine of Animals, the invention is monstrous, nor much inferiour unto the figment of Sphynx, Chimæra, and Harpies. For though some species there be of middle and participating natures, that is, of birds and beasts, as Bats and some few others, yet are their parts so conformed and set together, that we cannot define the beginning or end of either; there being a commixtion of both in the whole, rather then an adaptation or cement of the one unto the other.

Sir Thomas Browne (1605–1682)

The Loon and the Cat

From *The Story of My Boyhood and Youth*, 1913

As soon as the lake ice melted, we heard the lonely cry of the loon, one of the wildest and most striking of all the wilderness sounds, a strange, sad, mournful, unearthly cry, half laughing, half wailing. Nevertheless the great northern diver, as our species is called, is a brave, hardy, beautiful bird, able to fly under water about as well as above it, and to spear and capture the swiftest fishes for food. Those that haunted our lake were so wary none was shot for years, though every boy hunter in the neighborhood was ambitious to get one to prove his skill. On one of our bitter cold New Year holidays I was surprised to see a loon in the small open part of the lake at the mouth of the inlet that was kept from freezing by the warm spring water. I knew that it could not fly out of so small a place, for these heavy birds have to beat the water for half a mile or so before they can get fairly on the wing. Their narrow, finlike wings are very small as compared with the weight of the body and are evidently made for flying through water as well as through the air, and it is by means of their swift flight through the water and the swiftness of the blow they strike with their long, spear-like bills that they are able to capture the fishes on which they feed. I ran down the meadow with the gun, got into my boat, and pursued that poor winter-bound straggler. Of course he dived again and again, but had to come up to breathe, and I at length got a quick shot at his head and slightly wounded or stunned him, caught him, and ran proudly back to the house with my prize. I carried him in my arms; he didn't struggle to get away or offer to strike me, and when I put him on the floor in front of the kitchen stove, he just rested quietly on his belly as noiseless and motionless as if he were a stuffed specimen on a shelf, held his neck erect, gave no sign of suffering from any wound, and though he was motionless, his small black eyes seemed to be ever keenly watchful. His formidable bill, very sharp, three or three and a half inches long, and shaped like a pickaxe, was held perfectly level. But the wonder was that he did not struggle or make the slightest movement. We had a tortoise-shell cat, an old Tom of great experience, who was so fond of lying under the stove in frosty weather that it was difficult even to poke him out with a broom; but when he saw and smelled that strange big fishy, black and white, speckledy bird, the like of which he had never before seen, he rushed wildly to the farther corner of the kitchen, looked back cautiously and suspiciously, and began to make a careful study of the handsome but dangerous-looking stranger. Becoming more and more curious and interested, he at length advanced a step or two for a nearer view and nearer smell; and as the wonderful bird kept absolutely motionless, he was encouraged to venture gradually nearer and nearer until within perhaps five or six feet of its breast. Then the wary loon, not liking Tom's looks in so near a view, which perhaps recalled to his mind the plundering minks and muskrats he had to fight when they approached his nest, prepared to defend himself by slowly, almost imperceptibly drawing back his long pickaxe bill, and without the slightest fuss or stir held it level and ready just over his tail. With that dangerous bill drawn so far back out of the way, Tom's confidence in the stranger's peaceful intentions seemed almost complete, and, thus encouraged, he at last ventured forward with wondering, questioning eyes and quivering nostrils until he was only eighteen or twenty inches from the loon's smooth white breast. When the beautiful bird, apparently as peaceful and inoffensive as a flower, saw that his hairy yellow enemy had arrived at the right distance, the loon, who evidently was a fine judge of the reach of his spear, shot it forward quick as a lightning-flash, in marvelous contrast to the wonderful slowness of the preparatory poising, backward motion. The aim was true to a hair-breadth. Tom was struck right in the centre of his forehead, between the eyes. I thought his skull was cracked. Perhaps it was. The sudden astonishment of that outraged cat, the virtuous indignation and wrath, terror, and pain, are far beyond description. His eyes and screams and desperate retreat told all that. When the blow was received, he made a noise that I never heard a cat make before or since; an awfully deep, condensed, screechy, explosive *Wuck!* as he bounced straight up in the air like a bucking bronco; and when he alighted after his spring, he rushed madly across the room and made frantic efforts to climb up the hard-finished plaster wall. Not satisfied to get the width of the kitchen away from his mysterious enemy, for the first time that cold winter he tried to get out of the house, anyhow, anywhere out of that loon-infested room. When he finally ventured to look back and saw that the barbarous bird was still there, tranquil and motionless in front of the stove, he regained command of some of his shattered senses and carefully commenced to examine his wound. Backed against the wall in the farthest corner, and keeping his eye on the outrageous bird, he tenderly touched and washed the sore spot, wetting his paw with his tongue, pausing now and then as his courage increased to glare and stare and growl at his enemy with looks and tones wonderfully human, as if saying: 'You confounded fishy, unfair rascal! What did you do that for? What had I done to you? Faithless, legless, long-nosed wretch!' Intense experiences like the above bring out the humanity that is in all animals. One touch of nature, even a cat-and-loon touch, makes all the world kin.

John Muir (1838–1914)

Ice in the River

From *Kilvert's Diary*, 1879

14 January

Last night the river rose rapidly and at midnight the
ice was rushing down in vast masses, roaring, cracking
and thundering against the bridge like the rolling of a
hundred waggons. By morning the river had sunk and left
huge piles of ice stranded on the banks.

Francis Kilvert (1840–1879)

A Cat, or a Dog?

From *All the Dogs of My Life*, 1936

It is a bleak business really concentrating on cats. One likes response, and there is very little of that to be got out of them. Lofty and aloof, for ever wrapped in remote, mysterious meditation, they allow themselves to be adored, and give hardly anything back. Except purrs. I admit purrs are enchanting, and I used to long to have one myself, but purrs just don't nourish the hungry human heart in search of something to fill its emptiness; and being to all intents and purposes by this time an only child, and my parents absorbed in their particular interests, and my Mademoiselle on the other side of a barrier in France, I did often feel extraordinarily empty. Besides, how chilling, how snubbing, to be merely looked at when one calls. No blandishments could make those cats stir if they weren't in the mood, and one does want whatever one is calling to *come*. More, one wants it to come enthusiastically, ready for any lark going. One wants, that is, a playfellow, a companion, a friend. One wants, in fact, a dog.

Elizabeth von Arnim (1866–1941)

Outlines

From *The Peverel Papers*, January, 1926

There is no need at this time of year to examine a tree closely in order to identify it. The far-off forms can be distinguished at a glance – the oak, short and massive of trunk and branching at the fork to a spreading head of many boughs; the elm, with a certain resemblance to the oak, but more graceful, dividing at the fork into two or three main limbs, then soaring rather than spreading. Then the ash, with its smoother outline and few, sparsely-set boughs; the beech, like a cathedral pillar; the poplar, pointing skyward, and so on, to that delicate lady of the woods, the silver birch, with its gleaming white stem and tracery of purple twigs.

Flora Thompson (1876–1947)

North-west England

From *A Tour Through the Whole Island of Great Britain*: Letter 10, 1726

Here we were, as it were, locked in between the hills on one side high as the clouds, and prodigiously higher, and the sea on the other, and the sea it self seemed desolate and wild, for it was a sea without ships, here being no sea port or place of trade, especially for merchants; so that, except colliers passing between Ireland and Whitehaven with coals, the people told us they should not see a ship under sail for many weeks together.

Here, among the mountains, our curiosity was frequently moved to enquire what high hill this was, or that. Indeed, they were, in my thoughts, monstrous high; but in a country all mountainous and full of innumerable high hills, it was not easy for a traveller to judge which was highest.

Nor were these hills high and formidable only, but they had a kind of an unhospitable terror in them. Here were no rich pleasant valleys between them, as among the Alps; no lead mines and veins of rich ore, as in the Peak; no coal pits, as in the hills about Hallifax, much less gold, as in the Andes, but all barren and wild, of no use or advantage either to man or beast.

Daniel Defoe (1660–1731)

Seasons

From *Cider with Rosie*, 1959

The seasons of my childhood seemed (of course) so violent, so intense and true to their nature, that they have become for me ever since a reference of perfection whenever such names are mentioned. They possess us so completely they seem to change our nationality; and when I look back to the valley it cannot be one place that I see, but village-winter or village-summer, both separate. It becomes increasingly easy in urban life to ignore their extreme humours, but in those days winter and summer dominated our every action, broke into our houses, conscripted our thoughts, ruled our games, and ordered our lives.

Winter was no more typical of our valley than summer, it was not even summer's opposite; it was merely that other place. And somehow one never remembered the journey towards it; one arrived, and winter was here. The day came suddenly when all details were different and the village had to be rediscovered. One's nose went dead so that it hurt to breathe, and there were jigsaws of frost on the window. The light filled the house with a green polar glow; while outside – in the invisible world – there was a strange hard silence, or a metallic creaking, a faint throbbing of twigs and wires.

Laurie Lee (1914–1997)

A Complete Education

From *Clayhanger*, 1910

For his personal enjoyment of the earth and air and sun and stars, and of society and solitude, no preparation had been made, or dreamt of. The sentiment of nature had never been encouraged in him, or even mentioned. He knew not how to look at a landscape nor at a sky. Of plants and trees he was as exquisitely ignorant as of astronomy. It had not occurred to him to wonder why the days are longer in summer, and he vaguely supposed that the cold of winter was due to an increased distance of the earth from the sun. Still, he had learnt that Saturn had a ring, and sometimes he unconsciously looked for it in the firmament, as for a tea-tray.

. . . .

And now his education was finished.

Arnold Bennett (1867–1931)

Bottomless Ponds

From *Walden or Life in the Woods*, 1854

It is remarkable how long men will believe in the bottomlessness of a pond without taking the trouble to sound it. I have visited two such Bottomless Ponds in one walk in this neighborhood. Many have believed that Walden reached quite through to the other side of the globe. Some who have lain flat on the ice for a long time, looking down through the illusive medium, perchance with watery eyes into the bargain, and driven to hasty conclusions by the fear of catching cold in their breasts, have seen vast holes 'into which a load of hay might be driven,' if there were anybody to drive it, the undoubted source of the Styx and entrance to the Infernal Regions from these parts. Others have gone down from the village with a 'fifty-six' and a wagon load of inch rope, but yet have failed to find any bottom; for while the 'fifty-six' was resting by the way, they were paying out the rope in the vain attempt to fathom their truly immeasurable capacity for marvellousness. But I can assure my readers that Walden has a reasonably tight bottom at a not unreasonable, though at an unusual, depth.

Henry David Thoreau (1817–1862)

Wild Cat (*Felis silvestris*)

From *Animal Life of the British Isles*, 1921

To see the real Wild Cat to-day, we must seek it in Scotland, preferably in the wild, rocky parts from the counties of Ross and Inverness down to central Perthshire, where it is said to have increased its numbers considerably since the Great War. It inhabits the most lonely and inaccessible mountain sides, hiding during the day in some rocky fastness, prowling far and wide at night in search of prey. It is of a general yellowish grey colour, but individuals differ in their dark brown markings, some having vertical stripes running down the sides from a black longitudinal line down the middle of the back; in others these are broken up to form spots. It has a squarish thick head and body, the latter longer than in the Domestic Cat; but the thick bushy tail is relatively shorter, ringed and ending in a long black brush. The limbs, too, are longer than those of a tame cat, so that it stands higher. The fur is long, soft and thick. The average length is about two feet nine inches, of which the tail accounts for eleven inches; but there is a record of a Scottish example measuring three feet nine inches in all.

Edward Step (1855–1931)

The Cat Makes a Bargain

From *Just So Stories*, 1902

He will kill mice and he will be kind to Babies when he is in the
house, just as long as they do not pull his tail too hard. But when
he has done that, and between times, and when the moon gets up
and night comes, he is the Cat that walks by himself, and all places
are alike to him. Then he goes out to the Wet Wild Woods or up
the Wet Wild Trees or on the Wet Wild Roofs, waving his wild tail
and walking by his wild lone.

Rudyard Kipling (1865–1936)

Hoar-frost

From *Our Village*, 1824

January 23rd

At noon to-day I and my white greyhound, Mayflower, set out for a walk into a very beautiful world, – a sort of silent fairyland, – a creation of that matchless magician the hoar-frost. There had been just snow enough to cover the earth and all its covers with one sheet of pure and uniform white, and just time enough since the snow had fallen to allow the hedges to be freed of their fleecy load, and clothed with a delicate coating of rime. The atmosphere was deliciously calm; soft, even mild, in spite of the thermometer; no perceptible air, but a stillness that might almost be felt, the sky, rather grey than blue, throwing out in bold relief the snow-covered roofs of our village, and the rimy trees that rise above them, and the sun shining dimly as through a veil, giving a pale fair light, like the moon, only brighter. There was a silence, too, that might become the moon, as we stood at our little gate looking up the quiet street; a Sabbath-like pause of work and play, rare on a work-day; nothing was audible but the pleasant hum of frost, that low monotonous sound, which is perhaps the nearest approach that life and nature can make to absolute silence. The very waggons as they come down the hill along the beaten track of crisp yellowish frost-dust, glide along like shadows; even May's bounding footsteps, at her height of glee and of speed, fall like snow upon snow.

Mary Russell Mitford (1787–1855)

Wharfe in Flood

From Letter to Miss Susie Beever, written 1875

Bolton Abbey, 24th January:

The black rain, much as I growled at it, has let me see Wharfe in flood; and I would have borne many days in prison to see that.

No one need go to the Alps to see wild water. Seldom, unless in the Rhine or Rhone themselves at their rapids, have I seen anything much grander. An Alpine stream, besides, nearly always has its bed full of loose stones, and becomes a series of humps and dumps of water wherever it is shallow; while the Wharfe swept round its curves of shore like a black Damascus sabre, coiled into eddies of steel. At the Strid, it had risen eight feet, vertical, since yesterday, sheeting the flat rocks with foam from side to side, while the treacherous mid-channel was filled with a succession of boiling domes of water, charged through and through with churning white, and rolling out into the broader stream, each like a vast sea wave bursting on a beach.

There is something in the soft and comparatively unbroken slopes of these Yorkshire shales which must give the water a peculiar sweeping power, for I have seen Tay and Tummel and Ness, and many a big stream besides, savage enough, but I don't remember anything so grim as this.

I came home to quiet tea and a black kitten called Sweep, who lapped half my cream jug-full (and yet I had plenty) sitting on my shoulder.

John Ruskin (1819–1900)

Susie Beever (1805–1893)

Zoos

From *Menagerie Manor*, 1964

I did not want a simple straightforward zoo, with the ordinary run of animals: the idea behind my zoo was to aid the preservation of animal life. All over the world various species are being exterminated or cut down to remnants of their former numbers by the spread of civilisation. Many of the larger species are of commercial or touristic value, and, as such, are receiving the most attention. Yet, scattered about all over the world, are a host of fascinating small mammals, birds and reptiles, and scant attention is being paid to their preservation, as they are neither edible nor wearable, and of little interest to the tourist who demands lions and rhinos. A great number of these are island fauna, and as such their habitat is small. The slightest interference with this, and they will vanish forever: the casual introduction of rats, say, or pigs could destroy one of these island species within a year. One only has to remember the sad fate of the dodo to realise this.

The obvious answer to this whole problem is to see that the creature is adequately protected in the wild state so that it does not become extinct, but this is often easier said than done. However, while pressing for this protection, there is another precaution that can be taken, and that is to build up under controlled conditions breeding stocks of these creatures in parks or zoos, so that, should the worst happen and the species become extinct in the wild state, you have, at least, not lost it forever.

Moreover, you have a breeding stock from which you can glean the surplus animals and reintroduce them into their original homes at some future date. This, it has always seemed to me, should be the main function of any zoo, but it is only recently that the majority of zoos have woken up to this fact and tried to do anything about it. I wanted this to be the main function of my zoo.

Gerald Durrell (1925–1995)

Bull's-eye

From *Oliver Twist*, 1839

In the obscure parlour of a low public-house, in the filthiest part of Little Saffron Hill; a dark and gloomy den, where a flaring gas-light burnt all day in the winter-time; and where no ray of sun ever shone in the summer: there sat, brooding over a little pewter measure and a small glass, strongly impregnated with the smell of liquor, a man in a velveteen coat, drab shorts, half-boots and stockings, whom even by that dim light no experienced agent of the police would have hesitated to recognise as Mr. William Sikes. At his feet, sat a white-coated, red-eyed dog; who occupied himself, alternately, in winking at his master with both eyes at the same time; and in licking a large, fresh cut on one side of his mouth, which appeared to be the result of some recent conflict.

'Keep quiet, you warmint! Keep quiet!' said Mr. Sikes, suddenly breaking silence. Whether his meditations were so intense as to be disturbed by the dog's winking, or whether his feelings were so wrought upon by his reflections that they required all the relief derivable from kicking an unoffending animal to allay them, is matter for argument and consideration. Whatever was the cause, the effect was a kick and a curse, bestowed upon the dog simultaneously.

Dogs are not generally apt to revenge injuries inflicted upon them by their masters; but Mr. Sikes's dog, having faults of temper in common with his owner, and labouring, perhaps, at this moment, under a powerful sense of injury, made no more ado but at once fixed his teeth in one of the half-boots. Having given in a hearty shake, he retired, growling, under a form; just escaping the pewter measure which Mr. Sikes levelled at his head.

'You would, would you?' said Sikes, seizing the poker in one hand, and deliberately opening with the other a large clasp-knife, which he drew from his pocket. 'Come here, you born devil! Come here! D'ye hear?'

The dog no doubt heard; because Mr. Sikes spoke in the very harshest key of a very harsh voice; but, appearing to entertain some unaccountable objection to having his throat cut, he remained where he was, and growled more fiercely than before: at the same time grasping the end of the poker between his teeth, and biting at it like a wild beast.

This resistance only infuriated Mr. Sikes the more; who, dropping on his knees, began to assail the animal most furiously. The dog jumped from right to left, and from left to right; snapping, growling, and barking; the man thrust and swore, and struck and blasphemed; and the struggle was reaching a most critical point for one or other; when, the door suddenly opening, the dog darted out: leaving Bill Sikes with the poker and the clasp-knife in his hands.

Charles Dickens (1812–1870)

Wind in the City

From *In Pursuit of Spring*, 1914

The wind blew from the north-west with such peace and energy together as to call up the image of a good giant striding along with superb gestures – like those of a sower sowing. The wind blew and the sun shone over London. A myriad roofs laughed together in the light. The smoke and the flags, yellow and blue and white, waved tumultuously, straining for joy to leave the chimneys and the flagstaffs, like hounds sighting their quarry. The ranges of cloud bathing their lower slopes in the brown mist of the horizon had the majesty of great hills, the coolness and sweetness and whiteness of the foam on the crests of the crystal fountains, and they were burning with light. The clouds did honour to the city, which they encircled as with heavenly ramparts. The stone towers and spires were soft, and luminous as old porcelain. There was no substance to be seen that was not made precious by the strong wind and the light divine. All was newly built to a great idea. The flags were waving to salute the festal opening of the gates in those white walls to a people that should presently surge in and onward to take possession. Princely was to be the life that had this amphitheatre of clouds and palaces for its display.

Edward Thomas (1878–1917)

Morwenstow Cliff

From *The Vicar of Morwenstow*, 1876

From the cliff an unrivalled view can be had of the Atlantic, from Lundy Isle to Padstow point. Tintagel Rock, with its ancient castle, stands out boldly, as the horn of a vast sweep against glittering water, lit by a passing gleam behind. Gulls, rooks, choughs, wheel and scream around the crag, now fluttering a little way above the head, and then diving down towards the sea, which roars and foams several hundreds of feet below.

The beach is inaccessible save at one point, where a path has been cut down the side of a steep gorse-covered slope, and through slides of ruined slate rock, to a bay, into which the Tonacombe Brook precipitates itself in a broken fall of foam.

The little coves with blue-grey floors wreathed with sea-foam; the splintered and contorted rock; the curved strata, which here bend over like exposed ribs of a mighty mammoth; the sharp skerries that run out into the sea to torment it into eddies of froth and spray – are of rare wildness and beauty.

Rev. Sabine Baring-Gould (1834–1924)

Wilderness Music

From *The Singing Wilderness*, 1956

There are many types of music, each one different from the rest: a pack of coyotes and the wild, beautiful sound of them as they tune up under the moon; the song of a white-throated sparrow, its one clear note so associated with trout streams that whenever I hear one, I see a sunset-tinted pool and feel the water around my boots. The groaning and cracking of forming ice on the lakes, the swish of skis or snowshoes in dry snow – wilderness music, all of it, music for Indians and for those who have ears to hear.

Sigurd F. Olson (1899–1982)

Clouds

From *Hamlet* (1600–1), Act III, scene ii
and *Antony and Cleopatra* (1607–8), Act IV, scene xiv

Hamlet: Do you see yonder cloud that's almost in shape of a camel?

Lord Polonius: By th' mass, and 'tis like a camel, indeed.

Hamlet: Methinks it is like a weasel.

Lord Polonius: It is backed like a weasel.

Hamlet: Or like a whale?

Lord Polonius: Very like a whale.

. . . .

Mark Antony: Sometime we see a cloud that's dragonish;

A vapour sometime like a bear or lion,

A towered citadel, a pendent rock,

A forkèd mountain, or blue promontory

With trees upon't, that nod unto the world,

And mock our eyes with air.

William Shakespeare (1564–1616)

Missel-thrush, or Mistletoe Thrush, or Stormcock *(Turdus viscivorus)*

From *British Birds*, 1930

The missel-thrush is the hardiest of our vocalists, and is better known as a winter than a summer songster. His song may be heard in the autumn but from midwinter until spring his music is most noteworthy. Its loudness and wild character give it a wonderful impressiveness at that season of the year. He is not of the winter singers that wait for a gleam of spring-like sunshine to inspirit them, but is loudest in wet and rough weather; and it is this habit and something in the wild and defiant character of his song, heard above the tumult of nature, which have won for him the proud name of stormcock.

W. H. Hudson (1841–1922)

FEBRUARY

Clouds Gathered and Snow Fell

Ice

From *The Mirror of the Sea*, 1913

At first I saw nothing. The sea was one empty wilderness of black and white hills. Suddenly, half-concealed in the tumult of the foaming rollers I made out awash, something enormous, rising and falling – something spread out like a burst of foam, but with a more bluish, more solid look.

It was a piece of an ice-floe melted down to a fragment, but still big enough to sink a ship, and floating lower than any raft, right in our way, as if ambushed among the waves with murderous intent. There was no time to get down on deck. I shouted from aloft till my head was ready to split. I was heard aft, and we managed to clear the sunken floe which had come all the way from the Southern ice cap to have a try at our unsuspecting lives. Had it been an hour later, nothing could have saved the ship, for no eye could have made out in the dusk that pale piece of ice swept over by the white-crested waves.

Joseph Conrad (1857–1924)

A Winter Display

From *Guide to the Lakes*, 1835

I will take this opportunity of observing, that they who have studied the appearances of nature feel that the superiority, in point of visual interest, of mountainous over other countries – is more strikingly displayed in winter than in summer. This, as must be obvious, is partly owing to the *forms* of the mountains, which, of course, are not affected by the seasons; but also, in no small degree, to the greater variety that exists in their winter than their summer *colouring*. This variety is such, and so harmoniously preserved, that it leaves little cause of regret when the splendour of autumn is passed away. The oak-coppices, upon the sides of the mountains, retain russet leaves; the birch stands conspicuous with its silver stem and puce-coloured twigs; the hollies, with green leaves and scarlet berries, have come forth to view from among the deciduous trees, whose summer foliage had concealed them: the ivy is now plentifully apparent upon the stems and boughs of the trees, and upon the steep rocks. In place of the deep summer-green of the herbage and fern, many rich colours play into each other over the surface of the mountains; turf (the tints of which are interchangeably tawny-green, olive, and brown,) beds of withered fern, and grey rocks, being harmoniously blended together.

William Wordsworth (1770–1850)

Mary Meets the Robin

From *The Secret Garden*, 1911

Ben Weatherstaff introduces Mary to the robin:

To her surprise the surly old weather-beaten face actually changed
its expression. A slow smile spread over it and the gardener looked
quite different. It made her think that it was curious how much nicer
a person looked when he smiled. She had not thought of it before.

He turned about to the orchard side of his garden and began to
whistle – a low soft whistle. She could not understand how such a
surly man could make such a coaxing sound.

Almost the next moment a wonderful thing happened. She
heard a soft little rushing flight through the air – and it was the
bird with the red breast flying to them, and he actually alighted on
the big clod of earth quite near to the gardener's foot.

'Here he is,' chuckled the old man, and then he spoke to the bird
as if he were speaking to a child.

'Where has tha' been, tha' cheeky little beggar?' he said. 'I've not
seen thee before today. Has tha' begun tha' courtin' this early in th'
season? Tha'rt too for'ard.'

The bird put his tiny head on one side and looked up at him
with his soft bright eye which was like a black dewdrop. He
seemed quite familiar and not the least afraid. He hopped about
and pecked the earth briskly, looking for seeds and insects. It
actually gave Mary a queer feeling in her heart, because he was
so pretty and cheerful and seemed so like a person. He had a tiny
plump body and a delicate beak, and slender delicate legs.

'Will he always come when you call him?' she asked almost in a
whisper.

'Aye, that he will. I've knowed him ever since he was a fledgling.
He come out of th' nest in th' other garden an' when first he flew

over th' wall he was too weak to fly back for a few days an' we got friendly. When he went over th' wall again th' rest of th' brood was gone an' he was lonely an' he come back to me.'

'What kind of a bird is he?' Mary asked.

'Doesn't tha' know? He's a robin redbreast an' they're th' friendliest, curiousest birds alive. They're almost as friendly as dogs – if you know how to get on with 'em. Watch him peckin' about there an' lookin' round at us now an' again. He knows we're talkin' about him.'

It was the queerest thing in the world to see the old fellow. He looked at the plump little scarlet-waistcoated bird as if he were both proud and fond of him.

'He's a conceited one,' he chuckled. 'He likes to hear folk talk about him. An' curious – bless me, there never was his like for curiosity an' meddlin'. He's always comin' to see what I'm plantin'. He knows all th' things Mester Craven never troubles hissel' to find out. He's th' head gardener, he is.'

The robin hopped about busily pecking the soil and now and then stopped and looked at them a little. Mary thought his black dewdrop eyes gazed at her with great curiosity. It really seemed as if he were finding out all about her. The queer feeling in her heart increased.

'Where did the rest of the brood fly to?' she asked.

'There's no knowin'. The old ones turn 'em out o' their nest an' make 'em fly an' they're scattered before you know it. This one was a knowin' one an' he knew he was lonely.'

Frances Hodgson Burnett (1849–1924)

Another World

From *Life on Earth*, 1979

Twenty-five years ago I went to the tropics for the first time. I still recall, with great clarity, the shock of stepping out of the plane and into the muggy, perfumed air of West Africa. It was like walking into a steam laundry. Moisture hung in the atmosphere so heavily that my skin and shirt were soaked within minutes. A hedge of hibiscus bordered the airport buildings. Sunbirds, glittering with green and blue iridescence, played around it, darting from one scarlet blossom to another, hanging on beating wings as they probed for nectar. Only after I had watched them for some time, did I notice, clasping a branch within the hedge, a chameleon, motionless except for its goggling eyes which swivelled to follow every passing insect. Beside the hedge, I trod on what appeared to be grass. To my astonishment, the leaflets immediately folded themselves flat against the stem, transforming green fronds into apparently bare twigs. It was sensitive mimosa. Beyond lay a ditch covered with floating plants. In the space between them, the black water wriggled with fish, and over the leaves walked a chestnut-coloured bird, lifting its long-toed feet with the exaggerated care of a man in snow-shoes.

Wherever I looked, I found a prodigality of pattern and colour for which I was quite unprepared. It was a revelation of the splendour and fecundity of the natural world from which I have never recovered.

David Attenborough (1926–)

A Cats' Tea-party

From *Home and Garden*, 1900

Last winter I had a visit of a week or two from my youngest niece, of nine years old. Wishing to have some jollification before she went home, I thought it would be nice to have a pussies' tea-party, and as the prospect delighted her, we set to work to talk it over in earnest. No time was to be lost for it was to be the next afternoon. So we sat down and seriously considered the items of the bill of fare. After some consultation, we decided that the basis of it should be fish, so we sent for some fresh herrings, and they were boiled and held in readiness.

. . . .

In the middle of the sitting-room we placed a small, rather low, round table; and four stools were ranged round for the bigger pussies. As the hour for the feast drew near, much was the wondering as to how the guests would behave. They were to sit on the stools with their fore-paws on the edge of the tablecloth. We decided not to have flowers because it would have overcrowded the spaces, as the two kittens were to be allowed to sit on the table. At last the hour came, and meanwhile the excitement had grown intense. Five grown-ups were present, all as keenly interested as the little girl. The pussies were brought and placed on their stools, and the kittens, Chloe and Brindle, were put up to their saucers on the table. To our great delight they all took in the situation at once; there was only a little hesitation on Maggie's part; she thought it was not manners to put her paws on the tablecloth; but this was soon overcome, and they all set to work as if they were quite accustomed to tea-parties and knew that nice behaviour was expected.

Gertrude Jekyll (1843–1932)

The Object of Books on Birds

From *British Birds*, 1930

It has been remarked more than once that we do not rightly appreciate birds because we do not see them well. In most cases persecution has made them fearful of the human form; they fly from us, and distance obscures their delicate harmonious colouring and blurs the exquisite aerial lines on which they are formed. When we look closely at them, we are surprised at their beauty and indescribable grace of their varied motions. An analogous effect is produced by close examination of their habits or actions, which, seen from afar, may appear few and monotonous. Canon Atkinson, in his *Sketches in Natural History* (1865), has a chapter about the Partridge, prefaced by Yarrell's remark, that of a bird so universally known there was little that was new to be said. While admitting the general truth of this statement, the author goes on to say: 'Still, I have from time to time observed some slight peculiarity in the habits of the partridge that I have not seen in any professed description of the bird, forming certain passages, as it were, of its minute history. It is precisely this 'minute history' that gives so great and enduring a fascination to the study of birds in a state of nature. But it cannot be written, an account of the infinity of 'passages' contained in it, or, in other words, of that element of mind which gives it endless variety.

W. H. Hudson (1841–1922)

Snowdrop *(Galanthus nivalis)*

From *Flowers of the Field*, 1885

Too well known to need any description.

Fl. January–March.

Rev. C. A. Johns (1811–1874)

The Uses of a View

From *Northanger Abbey*, 1817

Catherine takes a walk with Henry and Eleanor Tilney:

They determined on walking round Beechen Cliff, that noble hill whose beautiful verdure and hanging coppice render it so striking an object from almost every opening in Bath.

· · · · · · · · · ·

The Tilneys were soon engaged in another [subject] on which she had nothing to say. They were viewing the country with the eyes of persons accustomed to drawing, and decided on its capability of being formed into pictures, with all the eagerness of real taste. Here Catherine was quite lost. She knew nothing of drawing – nothing of taste: and she listened to them with an attention which brought her little profit, for they talked in phrases which conveyed scarcely any idea to her. The little which she could understand, however, appeared to contradict the very few notions she had entertained on the matter before. It seemed as if a good view were no longer to be taken from the top of an high hill, and that a clear blue sky was no longer a proof of a fine day.

Jane Austen (1775–1817)

Snow-storm

From *Diary*, 1906

February 9:

Snow-storm in the night; this morning we looked out onto a white landscape, this is the first deep snow we have had this winter. I swept a space free on the lawn and strewed it with bread and rice. Crowds of birds came. I counted eight Tits at one time on the cocoa-nut and the tripod of sticks supporting it. There were some terrible battles among the Tits this morning. One tiny Blue-cap took possession of the cocoa-nut, sitting down in the middle of it and bidding defiance to all the others. It was very funny to see him squatting in the shell, sparring and hissing at a Great Tit who came at him with open wings and beak. There was a partial eclipse of the moon visible this morning at 5.57 am. At 8 o'clock in the evening there was a beautiful rainbow-coloured halo round the moon, unusually bright and distinct.

Edith Holden (1871–1920)

Sheep-Bells

From 'Society of the Lakes', August 1840

Passing onwards from Brathay, a ride of about forty minutes
carries you to the summit of a wild heathy tract, along which, even
at noonday, few sounds are heard that indicate the presence of
man, except now and then a woodman's axe in some of the many
coppice-woods scattered about that neighbourhood. In Northern
England there are no sheep-bells; which is an unfortunate defect,
as regards the full impression of wild solitudes, whether amongst
undulating heaths or towering rocks: at any rate, it is so felt by
those who, like myself, have been trained to its soothing effects
upon the hills of Somersetshire – the Cheddar, the Mendip, or
the Quantock – or any other of those breezy downs which once
constituted such delightful local distinctions for four or five
counties in that south-west angle of England. At all hours of day
or night, this silvery tinkle was delightful; but, after sunset, in
the solemn hour of gathering twilight, heard (as it always was)
intermittingly, and at great varieties of distance, it formed the
most impressive incident for the ear, and the most in harmony
with the other circumstances of the scenery, that, perhaps,
anywhere exists – not excepting even the natural sounds, the
swelling and dying intonations of insects wheeling in their vesper
flights. Silence and desolation are never felt so profoundly as when
they are interrupted by solemn sounds, recurring by uncertain
intervals, and from distant places. But in these Westmoreland
heaths, and uninhabited ranges of hilly ground, too often nothing
is heard except occasionally the wild cry of a bird – the plover, the
snipe, or perhaps the raven's croak.

Thomas de Quincey (1785–1859)

Not a Pet

From *A Kestrel for a Knave*, 1968

Billy's teacher comes to see Kes:

'I know, Sir. That's why it makes me mad when I take her out and I'll hear somebody say, "Look there's Billy Casper there wi' his pet hawk." I could shout at 'em; it's not a pet, Sir, hawks are not pets. Or when folks stop me and say, "Is it tame?" Is it heck tame, it's trained that's all. It's fierce, an' it's wild, an' it's not bothered about anybody, not even about me. And that's why it's great,'

'A lot of people wouldn't understand that sentiment though, they like pets they can make friends with; make a fuss of, cuddle a bit, boss a bit; don't you agree?'

'Ye', I suppose so. I'm not bothered about that though. I'd sooner have her, just to look at her, an' fly her. That's enough for me. They can keep their rabbits an' their cats an' their talking budgies, they're rubbish compared wi' her.'

Mr Farthing glanced down at Billy, who was staring at the hawk, breathing rapidly.

'Yes, I think you're right; they probably are.'

'Do you know, Sir, I feel as though she's doin' me a favour just lettin' me stand here.'

Barry Hines (1939– 2016)

Selection

From *The Origin of Species*, 6th edition, 1872

The great power of this principle of selection is not hypothetical. It is certain that several of our eminent breeders have, even within a single lifetime, modified to a large extent their breeds of cattle and sheep. In order fully to realise what they have done it is almost necessary to read several of the many treatises devoted to this subject, and to inspect the animals. Breeders habitually speak of an animal's organisation as something plastic, which they can model almost as they please. If I had space I could quote numerous passages to this effect from highly competent authorities. Youatt, who was probably better acquainted with the works of agriculturalists than almost any other individual, and who was himself a very good judge of animals, speaks of the principle of selection as 'that which enables the agriculturist, not only to modify the character of his flock, but to change it altogether. It is the magician's wand, by means of which he may summon into life whatever form and mould he pleases.'

. . . .

But Natural Selection, we shall hereafter see, is a power incessantly ready for action, and is as immeasurably superior to man's feeble efforts, as the works of Nature are to those of Art.

Charles Darwin (1809–1882)

A Fragile Delicacy

From *Walden or Life in the Woods*, 1854

When the ground was partially bare of snow, and a few warm days had dried its surface somewhat, it was pleasant to compare the first tender signs of the infant year just peeping forth with the stately beauty of the withered vegetation which had withstood the winter, – life-everlasting, golden-rods, pinweeds, and graceful wild grasses, more obvious and interesting frequently than in summer even, as if their beauty was not ripe till then; even cotton-grass, cat-tails, mulleins, johnswort, hard-hack, meadow-sweet, and other strong-stemmed plants, those unexhausted granaries which entertain the earliest birds, – decent weeds, at least, which widowed Nature wears. I am particularly attracted by the arching and sheaf-like top of the wool-grass; it brings back the summer to our winter memories, and is among the forms which art loves to copy, and which, in the vegetable kingdom, have the same relation to types already in the mind of man that astronomy has. It is an antique style older than Greek or Egyptian. Many of the phenomena of Winter are suggestive of an inexpressible tenderness and fragile delicacy. We are accustomed to hear this king described as a rude and boisterous tyrant; but with the gentleness of a lover he adorns the tresses of Summer.

Henry David Thoreau (1817–1862)

The Little Miracle

From *If Only They Could Talk*, 1970

In this extract James Herriot is a recently qualified vet and, after a long, cold struggle, delivers a calf safely:

'I know what this little fellow wants,' I said. I grasped the calf by its fore legs and pulled it up to its mother's head. The cow was stretched out on her side, her head extended wearily along the rough floor. Her ribs heaved, her eyes were almost closed; she looked past caring about anything. Then she felt the calf's body against her face and there was a transformation; her eyes opened wide and her muzzle began a snuffling exploration of the new object. Her interest grew with every sniff and she struggled on to her chest, nosing and probing all over the calf, rumbling deep in her chest. Then she began to lick him methodically. Nature provides the perfect stimulant massage for a time like this and the little creature arched his back as the coarse papillae on the tongue dragged along his skin. Within a minute he was shaking his head and trying to sit up.

I grinned. This was the bit I liked. The little miracle. I felt it was something that would never grow stale no matter how often I saw it.

James Herriot (1916–1995)

The Long Waves

From *Lorna Doone*, 1869

During those two months of fog (for we had it all the winter), the saddest and the heaviest thing was to stand beside the sea. To be upon the beach yourself, and see the long waves coming in; to know that they are long waves, but only see a piece of them; and to hear them lifting roundly, swelling over smooth green rocks, plashing down in the hollow corners, but bearing on all the same as ever, soft and sleek and sorrowful, till their little noise is over.

R. D. Blackmore (1825–1900)

The Wells of Dee

From *The Living Mountain*, 1977

As I stand there [on the plateau] in silence, I become aware that the silence is not complete. Water is speaking. I go towards it, and almost at once the view is lost: for the plateau has its own hollows, and this one slopes widely down to one of the great inward fissures, the Garbh Coire. It lies like a broad leaf veined with watercourses, that converge on the lip of the precipice to drop down in a cataract for 500 feet. This is the River Dee. Astonishingly, up here at 4000 feet, it is already a considerable stream. The immense leaf that it drains is bare, surfaced with stones, gravel, sometimes sand, and in places moss and grass grow on it. Here and there in the moss a few white stones have been piled together. I go to them, and water is welling up, strong and copious, pure cold water that flows away in rivulets and drops over the rock. These are the Wells of Dee. This is the river. Water, that strong white stuff, one of the four elemental mysteries, can be seen here at its origins. Like all profound mysteries, it is so simple that it frightens me. It wells from the rock, and flows away. For unnumbered years it has welled from the rock, and flowed away. It does nothing, absolutely nothing, but be itself.

Nan Shepherd (1893–1981)

The Colours of Winter

From *Chronicles of the Hedges*, 1881

The trunks of the trees vary in hue with the time of year – not quite in so marked a manner as the change from the green to the brown leaf on their branches, but sufficiently to tone the aspect of the field. The darkness of the winter view is chiefly produced by the black timber, and black stems and stoles of the mounds, which, though naturally devoid of colour, appear so at a distance. Meadows remain green all the winter through, yet, looking at the fields from any elevation the green is lost behind the prevailing shadow. This is more singular because when the green leaves appear the grass seems to come again into sight. The driving rain of winter moistens the bark of the elms, and the wetter it is the darker it looks. Oak bark becomes of so dull a grey that a little way off it is almost colourless, and across a field or two fades into the general gloom. Ashes, never very decided a tint, lose what little they possess, and appear yet harder, as if wood and bark contracted, bracing themselves together to face the blows of the wind. Hawthorn stoles and branches, dimly brown at hand, deepen into black afar. Even the reddish bark of the Scotch fir is deadened with drab, and the willow pollards are as dull as the discoloured stream beneath them. All the dead wood and decaying boughs uncovered by the fallen leaves add their grey to these sad hues. As the draughtsman, with innumerable strokes of his pencil, shades his sketch, so the countless branches, side by side and intermingled – the scribbling of the hedges, each, however small, more or less dark, together make the blackness of the winter picture. Thus the trunks, the bark and branches – that is, the wood itself apart from foliage – rule, as it were, the landscape, and from these the eye derives its impression.

Richard Jefferies (1848–1887)

A Surprising Talent for a Raven

From *Barnaby Rudge*, 1841

Grip the Raven surprises Gabriel Varden the locksmith and
Edward Chester:

'Halloa!' cried a hoarse voice in his ear. 'Halloa, halloa, halloa! Bow
wow wow. What's the matter here! Hal-loa!'

The speaker – who made the locksmith start as if he had been
some supernatural agent – was a large raven, who had perched
upon the top of the easy-chair, unseen by him and Edward,
and listened with a polite attention and a most extraordinary
appearance of comprehending every word, to all they had said
up to this point; turning his head from one to the other, as if his
office were to judge between them, and it were of the very last
importance that he should not lose a word.

'Look at him!' said Varden, divided between admiration of the
bird and a kind of fear of him. 'Was there ever such a knowing imp
as that! Oh he's a dreadful fellow!'

The raven, with his head very much on one side, and his bright
eye shining like a diamond, preserved a thoughtful silence for
a few seconds, and then replied in a voice so hoarse and distant,
that it seemed to come through his thick feathers rather than out
of his mouth.

'Halloa, halloa, halloa! What's the matter here! Keep up your
spirits. Never say die. Bow wow wow. I'm a devil, I'm a devil, I'm a
devil. Hurrah!' – And then, as if exulting in his infernal character,
he began to whistle.

Charles Dickens (1812–1870)

Becoming Real

From *The Velveteen Rabbit*, 1922

The Skin Horse had lived longer in the nursery than any of the others. He was so old that his brown coat was bald in patches and showed the seams underneath, and most of the hairs in his tail had been pulled out to string bead necklaces. He was wise, for he had seen a long succession of mechanical toys arrive to boast and swagger, and by-and-by break their mainsprings and pass away, and he knew that they were only toys, and would never turn into anything else. For nursery magic is very strange and wonderful, and only those playthings that are old and wise and experienced like the Skin Horse understand all about it.

'What is REAL?' asked the Rabbit one day, when they were lying side by side near the nursery fender, before Nana came to tidy the room. 'Does it mean having things that buzz inside you and a stick-out handle?'

'Real isn't how you are made,' said the Skin Horse. 'It's a thing that happens to you. When a child loves you for a long, long time, not just to play with, but REALLY loves you, then you become Real.'

'Does it hurt?' asked the Rabbit.

'Sometimes,' said the Skin Horse, for he was always truthful.

'When you are Real you don't mind being hurt.'

'Does it happen all at once, like being wound up,' he asked, 'or bit by bit?'

'It doesn't happen all at once,' said the Skin Horse. 'You become. It takes a long time. That's why it doesn't happen often to people who break easily, or have sharp edges, or who have to be carefully kept. Generally, by the time you are Real, most of your hair has been loved off, and your eyes drop out and you get loose in the joints and very shabby. But these things don't matter at all, because once you are Real you can't be ugly, except to people who don't understand.'

'I suppose you are Real?' said the Rabbit. And then he wished he had not said it, for he thought the Skin Horse might be sensitive. But the Skin Horse only smiled.

'The Boy's Uncle made me Real,' he said. 'That was a great many years ago; but once you are Real you can't become unreal again. It lasts for always.'

Margery Williams (1881–1944)

Winter Drifts Away

From *The White Peacock*, 1911

At last, winter began to gather her limbs, to rise, and drift with saddened garments northwards.

. . . .

The birds fluttered and dashed; the catkins on the hazel loosened their winter rigidity, and swung soft tassels. All through the day sounded long, sweet whistlings from the bushes; then later, loud, laughing shouts of bird triumph on every hand.

D. H. Lawrence (1885–1930)

The Winter Night

From *Ethan Frome*, 1911

At sunset the clouds gathered again, bringing an earlier night, and the snow began to fall straight and steadily from a sky without wind, in a soft universal diffusion more confusing than the gusts and eddies of the morning. It seemed to be a part of the thickening darkness, to be the winter night itself descending on us layer by layer.

Edith Wharton (1862–1937)

A Beautiful Fungus

From *The South Country*, Chapter II, Suffolk, 1909

Rain and wind cease together, and here on the short grass at the cliff's edge is a strange birth – a gently convex fungus about two inches broad, the central boss of it faintly indented, the surface not perfectly regular but dimpled so as to break the light, and the edge wavering away from the pure circular form; in hue a pale chestnut paling to a transparent edge of honey colour; and the whole surface so smooth and polished by rain as to seem coated in ice. What a thought for the great earth on such a day!

Edward Thomas (1878–1917)

A Lunar Halo

From *Journal*, 1872

Feb 23:

A lunar halo: I looked at it from the upstairs library window. It was a grave grained sky, the strands rising a little from left to right. The halo was not quite round, for in the first place it was a little pulled and drawn below, by the refraction of the lower air perhaps, but what is more it fell in on the nether left hand side to rhyme the moon itself, which was not quite at full. I could not but strongly feel in my fancy the odd instress of this, the moon leaning on her side, as if fallen back, in the cheerful light floor within the ring, after with magical rightness and success tracing round her the ring the steady copy of her own outline. But this sober grey darkness and pale light was happily broken through by the orange pealing of Mitton bells.

Gerard Manley Hopkins (1844–1889)

Pincher

From *All the Dogs of My Life*, 1936

It wasn't till more than four years after Coco's death that Pincher appeared – so true that if you love a dog very much, and lose him, you cannot bear the thought of having another. Yet the only real cure for one's distress is another – I am told this also applies to lovers, – and the sooner you get him the better.

But I, obstinately mourning, spent the best part of five years without the simple comfort of a dog. Please God it shall never happen again. And I dare say the idiotic abstinence would have lasted even longer if an observant friend, opining that I badly needed something, and knowing it couldn't be a husband, since, from my second, I had fled, decided it must be a dog, and packed up Pincher and sent him off.

I was living in a tiny cottage in the New Forest – sulking, it now seems to me, though then I called it by a grander name, – and hardly anybody ever came along my lane; so that when I saw the carrier's cart drawing up at my garden gate I was sure he had made a mistake, and that the box he presently brought up the path couldn't be for me.

'Live dog,' he said, putting it down carefully.

Live dog? No live dog was expected, and I told him he had come to the wrong address.

'You're 'er, ain't you?' he said, turning up the label for me to look.

'Yes, I am she,' I answered, being all for grammar when it happens to be the bits I know.

'Then I should let 'im out and give 'im a drink,' said the carrier, preparing to depart. 'Name of Pincher,' he added, coming back to point to a corner of the label; and, climbing into his cart, was gone.

Pincher, hearing this conversation, had begun making a great to-do in his box, for he was thirsty, and knew the word drink as well as anybody. Whoever had sent him, and for whatever reason he was there, obviously he must be let out and given water; so I called the woman who did for me, and we opened the box and let him out, – or rather he squeezed himself out before half the lid was off; and there is no getting away from it, I am made for dogs and dogs for me, because the instant I saw him I began to cheer up.

Sitting on the floor, I watched with admiration as he rushed round the room sniffing at everything, and making friends even with the chairs. On them he leaped, to leap off again the next minute and investigate the sofa. To finish up with he leaped onto me, sniffing my hair and my clothes, and wriggling all over with excitement.

'O, but aren't you a dear, funny little thing,' I laughed, trying to hug his woolly body – he was a very woolly dog, – but not succeeding, because he was off round the room again.

. . . .

Never was a dog more full of eager life and insatiable curiosity. He couldn't keep still; and even when night came, and like the rest of us he had to go to bed, I believe one eye stayed awake just so as not to miss anything, just so as to be instantly ready for anything that might happen to come along.

Elizabeth von Arnim (1866–1941)

Swallows

From *Survey of Cornwall*, 1602

In the West parts of Cornwall, during the Winter season, Swallowes are found sitting in old deepe Tynne-workes, and holes of the sea Cliffes: but touching their lurking places, Olaus Magnus maketh a farre stranger report. For he saith, that in the North parts of the world, as Summer weareth out, they clap mouth to mouth, wing to wing, and legge in legge, and so after a sweete singing, fall downe into certaine great lakes or pooles amongst the Canes, from whence at the next Spring, they receive a new resurrection; and hee addeth for proofe hereof, that the Fishermen, who make holes in the Ice, to dip up such fish with their nets, as resort thither for breathing, doe sometimes light on these Swallowes, congealed in clods, of a slymie substance, and that carrying them home to their Stoves, the warmth restoreth them to life and flight: this I have seene confirmed also, by the relation of a Venetian Ambassadour, employed in Poland, and heard avowed by travaylers in those parts: Wherethrough I am induced to give it a place of probabilitie in my mind, and of report in this treatise.

Richard Carew (1555–1620)

Windermere

From *Guide to the Lakes*, 1835

Windermere ought to be seen both from its shores and from its surface. None of the other Lakes unfold so many fresh beauties to him who sails upon them. This is owing to its greater size, to the islands, and to its having *two* vales at the head, with their accompanying mountains of nearly equal dignity. Nor can the grandeur of these two terminations be seen at once from any point, except from the bosom of the Lake. The Islands may be explored at any time of the day; but one bright unruffled evening, must, if possible, be set apart for the splendour, the stillness, and solemnity of a three hour's voyage upon the higher division of the Lake, not omitting, towards the end of the excursion, to quit the expanse of water, and peep into the close and calm River at the head; which, in its quiet character, at such a time, appears rather like an overflow of the peaceful Lake itself, than to have any more immediate connection with the rough mountains whence it has descended, or the turbulent torrents by which it is supplied.

William Wordsworth (1770–1850)

Winter Memories

From *O Pioneers!*, 1913

Winter has settled down over the Divide again; the season in which nature recuperates, in which she sinks to sleep between the fruitfulness of autumn and the passion of spring. The birds have gone. The teeming life that goes on down in the long grass is exterminated. The prairie dog keeps his hole. The rabbits run shivering from one frozen garden patch to another and are hard put to it to find frostbitten cabbage-stalks. At night the coyotes roam the wintry waste, howling for food. The variegated fields are all one color now; the pastures, the stubble, the roads, the sky are the same leaden gray. The hedgerows and trees are scarcely perceptible against the bare earth, whose slaty hue they have taken on. The ground is frozen so hard that it bruises the foot to walk in the roads or in the ploughed fields. It is like an iron country, and the spirit is oppressed by its rigor and melancholy. One could easily believe that in that dead landscape the germs of life and fruitfulness were extinct forever.

Willa Cather (1873–1947)

Willows

From *The History of the Worthies of England*, Cambridgeshire, 1662

A sad tree, whereof such who have lost their love make their mourning garlands; and we know what exiles hung up their harps upon such doleful supporters. The twigs hereof are physic, to drive out the folly of children. This tree delighteth in moist places, and is triumphant in the Isle of Ely, where the roots strengthen their banks, and lop affords fuel for their fire. It groweth incredibly fast; it being a by-word in this county, 'that the profit by willows will buy the owner a horse, before that by other trees will pay for his saddle.' Let me add, that if green ash may burn before a queen, withered willows may be allowed to burn before a lady.

Thomas Fuller (1608–1661)

The Turn of the Year

From *The Peverel Papers*, February, 1924

The turn of the year is certainly behind us: a thousand sights, scents, and sounds declare the fact. But exactly at what moment the mystic change took place and Nature, writing 'Finis' to the tale of last year, started without pause Chapter I of this, is a mystery. Officially, I suppose, the turn of the year is at midnight on the shortest day, when the earth starts spinning the 580 odd million miles yearly trip round the sun again. But Nature knows no calendar; and long before that moment came sap was rising, buds were swelling, and this year's shoots pushing upwards from the soil. Earlier still, the last leaves of last year were thrust from the bough by the rising life of this. So there seems to be no definite beginning: the seasons move in a circle.

Flora Thompson (1876–1947)

MARCH

The Spring Plumage of a Jay

The Coming of Spring

From *Nature Rambles*, 1930

How long the winter has been in going! Winters are always long; but some of them seem to us much longer than they ought to be, owing to a lengthy spell of north-east winds filling the sky with dark, heavy cloud, when we are longing to see the swaying tassels of the hazel, the golden stars of lesser celandine and the haloes of the leafless coltsfoot; to hear the welcome call of cuckoo and the rippling song of nightingale.

To town-folk the winter always appears much longer than it does to dwellers in the country; these, being on the spot, can take a fair ramble during the eight or nine hours of daylight, making up for the scarcity of flowers and insects by watching for those birds that are with us only during the winter. There are, also, the shrews and mice of the hedge-bottom, and their hunters the stoat and weasel, to take note of; as well as glimpses of squirrels and the occasional bat that has woken up for a brief flight. There are almost endless treasures to be found in the pond, as soon as the thick ice has melted and made them easy to see and reach; and there are some things, such as many of the mosses, that can be found in full beauty during the cooler, moister months only.

Edward Step (1855–1931)

Summer and Winter

From *Great Expectations*, 1861

It was one of those March days when the sun shines hot and the wind blows cold: when it is summer in the light, and winter in the shade.

Charles Dickens (1812–1870)

A Sloe-wind

From *Ask the Fellows Who Cut the Hay: Old Words and Old Sayings*, 1956

The phrase a sloe-wind, meaning a cold wind, gives the clue to an old belief which is mentioned every year in this village. The belief is enshrined in the proverb: 'Sloe-hatching time is the coldest time in the year'. This is the time when the blackthorn breaks into its spectacular blossom; and, strangely enough, within the writer's experience, this period often coincides with a cold spell distinguished by east or north-east winds. It is likely, however, that the coming together of the cold and the blackthorn blossom is one of accident; and it is probable that the belief is another vestige of the primitive form of reasoning displayed in the examples already given of homeopathic or imitative magic. Like produces like: the blackthorn in spring simulates the depths of winter – A blackthorn hedge in full bloom does, in fact, look as if it is covered with snow, or a thick hoarfrost – therefore according to the old principle cold weather is an inevitable and logical consequence.

George Ewart Evans (1909–1988)

Sloe or Blackthorn (Prunus spinosa)

From *Flowers of the Field*, 1885

A well-known thorny bush, which presumably derived its name Blackthorn from the hue of its bark, which is much darker than that of the Hawthorn. The flowers appear in March and April, and usually before the leaves have begun to expand. The latter are used to adulterate tea. The fruit is small, nearly round, and so austere that a single drop of its juice placed on the tongue will produce a roughness on the throat and palate which is perceptible for a long time. It enters largely into the composition of spurious port wine.

Fl. March–May.

Rev. C. A. Johns (1811–1874)

Tarka's Birth

From *Tarka the Otter*, 1927

The eldest and the biggest of the litter was a dog-cub, and when he drew his first breath he was less than five inches long from his nose to where his wee tail joined his backbone. His fur was soft and grey as the buds of the willow before they open at Eastertide. He was called Tarka, which was the name given to otters many years ago by men dwelling in hut circles on the moor. It means Little Water Wanderer, or, Wandering as Water.

With his two sisters he mewed when hungry, seeking the warmth of his mother, who uncurled and held up a paw whenever tiny pads would stray in her fur, and tiny noses snuffle against her. She was careful that they should be clean, and many times in the nights and days of their blind helplessness she rolled on her back, ceasing her kind of purr to twist her head and lick them. And sometimes her short ears would stiffen as she started up, her eyes fierce with a tawny glow and the coarse hair of her neck bristling, having heard some danger sound. By day the dog [otter] was far away sleeping in a holt by the weir-pools which had its rocky entrance underwater, but in the darkness his whistle would move the fierceness from her eyes, and she would lie down to sigh happily as her young struggled to draw life from her.

This was her first litter, and she was overjoyed when Tarka's lids ungummed, and his eyes peeped upon her, blue and wondering. He was then eleven days old. Before the coming of her cubs, her world had been a wilderness, but now her world was in the eyes of her firstborn.

Henry Williamson (1895–1977)

Sturton's Hatt

From *The Natural History of Wiltshire*, 1656–1691

About the middle of Groveley Forest was a fair wood of oakes, which was called Sturton's Hatt. It appeared a good deale higher than the rest of the forest (which was most coppice wood), and was seen over all Salisbury plaines. In the middle of this hatt of trees (it resembled a hatt) there was a tall beech, which overtopt all the rest.

John Aubrey (1626–1697)

Planting Oak Trees

From *Sylva*, 1664

Some advise, that in planting of *Oaks*, &c. *four* or *five* be suffer'd
to stand very neer to one another, and then to leave the most
prosperous, when they find the rest to disturb his growth; but
I conceive it were better to plant them at such *distances*, as they
may least incommode one another: For Timber-trees, I would have
none neerer than *forty* foot where they stand *closest*; especially of
the spreading kind.

John Evelyn (1620–1706)

A Singing Mouse

From Letter to Miss Susie Beever, written 1877

Venice, 8th March:

That is entirely new and wonderful to me about the singing
mouse*. Douglas (was it the Douglas?) saying 'he had rather
hear the lark sing than the mouse squeak' needs revision. It is a
marvellous fact in natural history.

*A pleasant story that a friend sent me from France. The mouse
often came into their sitting-room and actually sang to them, the
notes being a little like a canary's. S. B.

John Ruskin (1819–1900)
Susie Beever (1805–1893)

The Dryads Awake

From *Far From the Madding Crowd*, 1874

It was now early spring – the time of going to grass with the sheep, when they have the first feed of the meadows, before these are laid up for mowing. The wind, which had been blowing east for several weeks, had veered to the southward, and the middle of spring had come abruptly – almost without a beginning. It was that period in the vernal quarter when we may suppose the Dryads to be waking for the season. The vegetable world begins to move and swell and the saps to rise, till in the completest silence of lone gardens and trackless plantations, where everything seems helpless and still after the bond and slavery of frost, there are bustlings, strainings, united thrusts, and pulls – altogether, in comparison with which the powerful tugs of cranes and pulleys in a noisy city are but pigmy efforts.

Thomas Hardy (1840–1928)

A Spring Pic-nic

From *Diary*, 1906

March 10:

When I got to the bottom of the lane, I set my bicycle against a bank and pic-niced on a fence. A beautiful Jay in all the glory of his spring plumage flew screaming across the lane into a spinney of larch trees opposite. He seemed to resent the intrusion of a human being in such an unfrequented spot. I was glad to find the white Periwinkle still 'trailing its wreathes' on the bank, but the flowers were only in bud, and the Violets too, were just uncurling their buds under their fresh green leaves. Among the notes of the numerous birds I recognised those of the Thrush, Blackbird, Hedge Sparrow, Sky-lark, Wren, Great Tit, Chaffinch, Green-finch, Pied Wagtail and Yellow Bunting. The latter was especially conspicuous, perched high up on the hedge with his bright yellow plumage, repeating his cry – one can hardly call it a song – with its last, peculiar, long drawn out note, over and over again. 'A little bit of bread and no che-ese' the country people liken it to. In Cumberland they say it says 'Devil, devil dinna touch me-e'. This bird is called Yeldrin and Yellow Yowlie in Scotland. I noticed that the white Periwinkle blossoms have five petals, while the blue have only four. I wonder if this is always so.

Edith Holden (1871–1920)

The Last of the Fine Weather

From *Wuthering Heights*, 1847

That Friday made the last of our fine days for a month. In the
evening the weather broke; the wind shifted from south to
north-east, and brought rain first, and then sleet and snow.
On the morrow one could hardly imagine that there had been
three weeks of summer; the primroses and crocuses were hidden
under wintry drifts; the larks were silent, the young leaves of the
early trees smitten and blackened.

Emily Brontë (1818–1848)

Sun and Sunset

From *Journal*, 1870

March 12:

A fine sunset: the higher sky dead clear blue bridged by a broad slant causeway rising from right to left of wisped or grass cloud, the wisps lying across; the sundown yellow, moist with light but ending at the top in a foam of delicate white pearling and spotted with big tufts of cloud in colour russet between brown and purple but edged with brassy light. But what I note it all for is this: before I had always taken the sunset and the sun as quite out of gauge with each other, as indeed physically they are, for the eye after looking at the sun is blunted to everything else and if you look at the rest of the sunset you must cover the sun, but today I inscaped them together and made the sun the true eye and ace of the whole, as it was. It was all active and tossing out light and started as strongly forward from the field as a long stone or a boss in the knop of the chalice-stem: it is indeed by stalling it so that it falls into scape with the sky.

Gerard Manley Hopkins (1844–1889)

A Divided Empire

From *Cock-A-Doodle-Doo!*, 1853

It was a cool and misty, damp, disagreeable air. The country looked underdone, its raw juices squirting out all round. I buttoned out this squitchy air as well as I could with my lean, double-breasted dress-coat – my over-coat being so long-skirted I only used it in my wagon – and spitefully thrusting my crab-stick into the oozy sod, bent my blue form to the steep ascent of the hill. This toiling posture brought my head pretty well earthward, as if I were in the act of butting it against the world. I marked the fact, but only grinned at it with a ghastly grin.

All round me were tokens of a divided empire. The old grass and the new grass were striving together. In the low wet swales the verdure peeped out in vivid green; beyond, on the mountains, lay light patches of snow, strangely relieved against their russet sides; all the humped hills looked like brindled kine in the shivers. The woods were strewn with dry dead boughs, snapped off by the riotous winds of March, while the young trees skirting the woods were just beginning to show the first yellowish tinge of the nascent spray.

Herman Melville (1819–1891)

Snowy Mountains

From *Kilvert's Diary*, 1871

14 March

The afternoon had been stormy but it cleared towards sunset. Gradually the heavy rain clouds rolled across the valley to the foot of the opposite mountains and began climbing up their sides wreathing in rolling masses of vapour. One solitary cloud still hung over the brilliant sunlit town, and that whole cloud was a rainbow. Gradually it lost its bright prismatic hues and moved away up the Cusop Dingle in the shape of a pillar and of the colour of golden dark smoke. The Black Mountains were invisible, being wrapped in clouds, and I saw one very white brilliant dazzling cloud where the mountains ought to have been. This cloud grew more white and dazzling every moment, till a clearer burst of sunlight scattered the mists and revealed the truth. This brilliant white cloud that I had been looking and wondering at was the mountain in snow. The last cloud and mist rolled away over the mountain tops and the mountains stood up in the clear blue heaven, a long rampart line of dazzling glittering snow so as no fuller on earth can white them. I stood rooted to the ground, struck with amazement and over-whelmed at the extraordinary splendour of this marvellous spectacle. I never saw anything to equal it I think, even among the high Alps.

Francis Kilvert (1840–1879)

The Primrose Tribe

From *Flowers of the Field*, 1885

Herbaceous plants, mostly of humble growth, inhabiting, principally, the colder regions of the northern hemisphere, and in lower latitudes ascending to the confines of perpetual snow. In this order are found several of our most favourite British plants. The Primrose, as its name indicates (*prima rosa*, the first rose) is the most welcome harbinger of spring; the Cowslip is scarcely less prized for its pastoral associations than for its elegance and fragrance; Pimpernel, or 'Poor man's weather-glass', is as trusty a herald of summer weather as the Primrose is of spring.

Nor is it only as *Flowers of the Field* that the plants of this tribe are valued. The Polyanthus and Auricula equally grace the cottager's garden, and the collections of the florist; and several species of Cyclamen are commonly found in conservatories. Some species possess active medicinal properties; the flowers of the Cowslip are made into a pleasant soporific wine, and the leaves of the Auricula are used in the Alps as a remedy for coughs.

Rev. C. A. Johns (1811–1874)

Hares Drumming

From *Wild Life in a Southern County*, 1879

When startled by a passer-by the hare – unless there is a dog – goes off in a leisurely fashion, doubtless feeling quite safe in the length of his legs, and after getting a hundred yards or so sits upon his haunches and watches the intruder. Their runs or paths are rather broader than a rabbit's, and straighter – the rabbit does not ramble so far from home; he has his paths across the meadow to the hedge on the other side, but no farther. The hare's track may be traced for a great distance crossing the hills; but while the roads are longer they are much fewer in number. The rabbit makes a perfect network of runs, and seems always to feed from a regular path; the hare apparently feeds anywhere, without much reference to the runs, which he uses simply to get from one place to another in the most direct line, and also, it may be suspected, as a promenade on which to meet the ladies of his acquaintance by moonlight.

It is amusing to see two of these animals drumming each other; they stand on their hind legs (which are very long) like a dog taught to beg, and strike with the fore-pads as if boxing, only the blow is delivered downwards instead of from the shoulder. The clatter of their pads may be heard much farther than would be supposed. Round and round they go like a couple waltzing; now one giving ground and then the other, the fore-legs striking all the while with marvellous rapidity. Presently they pause – it is to recover breath only; and, 'time' being up, to work they go again with renewed energy, dancing round and round, till the observer cannot choose but smile. This trick they will continue till you are weary of watching.

Richard Jefferies (1848–1887)

From Barnacles to Birds

From *Survey of Cornwall*, 1602

It is held, that the Barnacle breedeth under water on such ships sides, as have beene verie long at Sea, hanging there by the Bill, untill his full growth dismisse him to be a perfect fowle: and for proofe hereof, many little things like birds, are ordinarily found in such places, but I cannot heare any man speake of having seene them ripe.

Richard Carew (1555–1620)

Shells

From *Survey of Cornwall*, 1602

The sea strond is also strowed with sundry fashioned & coloured shels, of so diversified and pretty workmanship, as if nature were for her pastime disposed to shew her skil in trifles.

Richard Carew (1555–1620)

The Kaatskill Mountains

From 'Rip Van Winkle', 1819

Whoever has made a voyage up the Hudson must remember the Kaatskill Mountains. They are a branch of the great Appalachian family, and are seen away to the west of the river, swelling up to a noble height, and lording it over the surrounding country. Every change of season, every change of weather, indeed, every hour of the day, produces some change in the magical hues and shapes of these mountains, and they are regarded by all the good wives, far and near, as perfect barometers. When the weather is fair and settled, they are clothed in blue and purple, and print their bold outlines on the clear evening sky; but, sometimes, when the rest of the landscape is cloudless, they will gather a hood of gray vapors about their summits, which, in the last rays of the setting sun, will glow and light up like a crown of glory.

Washington Irving (1783–1859)

The Lambs' Race-track

From *A Country Child*, 1931

Every year, for two hundred years at least, lambs ran the same race in Whitewell field. In other fields they had their odd games, but here it was always the same.

By the side of one of the paths stood the oak tree, with the seat under it, and a short distance away stood the great spreading ash. The lambs formed up in a line at the oak, and at some signal they raced to the ash, as fast as their tiny legs would go; then they wheeled round and tore back again. They held a little talk, a consultation, with nose-rubbing, friendly pushes, and then off they went again on their race-track.

Alison Uttley (1884–1976)

Sand Martins

From *In Pursuit of Spring*, 1914

A thrush and several larks were singing, and through their songs I heard a thin voice that I had not heard for six months, very faint yet unmistakable, though I could not at once see the bird – a sand martin. I recognized the sound, as I always recognize at their first autumnal ascent above the horizon the dim small cluster of the Pleiades on a September evening. On such a morning one sand martin seems enough to make a summer, and here were six, flitting in narrow circles like butterflies with birds' voices.

Edward Thomas (1878–1917)

Animals in Church

From *The Vicar of Morwenstow*, 1876

He was usually followed to church by nine or ten cats, which entered the chancel with him and careered about it during service. Whilst saying prayers Mr. Hawker would pat his cats, or scratch them under their chins. Originally ten cats accompanied him to church; but one, having caught, killed and eaten a mouse on a Sunday, was excommunicated, and from that day was not allowed again within the sanctuary.

A friend tells me that on attending Morwenstow Church one Sunday morning, nothing amazed him more than to see a little dog sitting upon the altar step behind the celebrant, in the position which is usually attributed to a deacon or a server. He afterwards spoke to Mr. Hawker on the subject, and asked him why he did not turn the dog out of the chancel and church.

'Turn the dog out of the ark!' he exclaimed: 'all animals, clean and unclean, should find there a refuge.'

Rev. Sabine Baring-Gould (1834–1924)

The Enjoyment of Loving Flowers

From *Northanger Abbey*, 1817

Catherine tells Henry she has learnt to love a hyacinth:

'What beautiful hyacinths! I have just learnt to love a hyacinth.'

'And how might you learn? By accident or argument?'

'Your sister taught me; I cannot tell how. Mrs. Allen used to take pains, year after year, to make me like them; but I never could, till I saw them the other day in Milsom Street; I am naturally indifferent about flowers.'

'But now you love a hyacinth. So much the better. You have gained a new source of enjoyment, and it is well to have as many holds upon happiness as possible. Besides, a taste for flowers is always desirable in your sex, as a means of getting you out of doors, and tempting you to more frequent exercise than you would otherwise take: and though the love of a hyacinth may be rather domestic, who can tell, the sentiment once raised, but you may in time come to love a rose?'

Jane Austen (1775–1817)

The Struggle for Existence

From *The Origin of Species*, 6th edition, 1872

I should premise that I use this term in a large and metaphorical sense, including dependence of one being on another, and including (which is more important) not only the life of the individual, but success in leaving progeny. Two canine animals, in a time of dearth, may be truly said to struggle with each other which shall get food and live. But a plant on the edge of a desert is said to struggle for life against the drought, though more properly it should be said to be dependent on the moisture. A plant which annually produces a thousand seeds, of which only one of an average comes to maturity, may be more truly said to struggle with the plants of the same and other kinds which already clothe the ground. The mistletoe is dependent on the apple and a few other trees, but can only in a far-fetched sense be said to struggle with these trees, for, if too many of these parasites grow on the same tree, it languishes and dies. But several seedling mistletoes, growing close together on the same branch, may more truly be said to struggle with each other. As the mistletoe is disseminated by birds, its existence depends on them; and it may metaphorically be said to struggle with other fruit-bearing plants, in tempting the birds to devour and thus disseminate its seeds. In these several senses, which pass into each other, I use for convenience sake the general term of Struggle for Existence.

Charles Darwin (1809–1882)

Buck and the Timber Wolf

From *The Call of the Wild*, 1903

One night he sprang from sleep with a start, eager-eyed, nostrils quivering and scenting, his mane bristling in recurrent waves. From the forest came the call (or one note of it, for the call was many noted), distinct and definite as never before, – a long-drawn howl, like, yet unlike, any noise made by husky dog. And he knew it, in the old familiar way, as a sound heard before. He sprang through the sleeping camp and in swift silence dashed through the woods. As he drew closer to the cry he went more slowly, with caution in every movement, till he came to an open place among the trees, and looking out saw, erect on haunches, with nose pointed to the sky, a long, lean, timber wolf.

He had made no noise, yet it ceased from its howling and tried to sense his presence. Buck stalked into the open, half crouching, body gathered compactly together, tail straight and stiff, feet falling with unwonted care. Every movement advertised commingled threatening and overture of friendliness. It was the menacing truce that marks the meeting of wild beasts that prey. But the wolf fled at sight of him. He followed, with wild leapings, in a frenzy to overtake. He ran him into a blind channel, in the bed of the creek where a timber jam barred the way. The wolf whirled about, pivoting on his hind legs after the fashion of Joe and of all cornered husky dogs, snarling and bristling, clipping his teeth together in a continuous and rapid succession of snaps.

Buck did not attack, but circled him about and hedged him in with friendly advances. The wolf was suspicious and afraid; for Buck made three of him in weight, while his head barely reached Buck's shoulder. Watching his chance, he darted away, and the chase was resumed. Time and again he was cornered, and the thing repeated, though he was in poor condition, or Buck could not so easily have overtaken him. He would run till Buck's head was even with his flank, when he would whirl around at bay, only to dash away again at the first opportunity.

But in the end Buck's pertinacity was rewarded; for the wolf, finding that no harm was intended, finally sniffed noses with him. Then they became friendly, and played about in the nervous, half-coy way with which fierce beasts belie their fierceness. After some time of this the wolf started off at an easy lope in a manner that plainly showed he was going somewhere. He made it clear to Buck that he was to come, and they ran side by side through the sombre twilight.

Jack London (1876–1916)

The Responsibilities and Joys of Botanizing

From *The Concise British Flora in Colour*, 1965

We should like to make two suggestions about gathering flowers: first that it should be done sparingly, and secondly that collectors should be fully courteous to the owner of enclosed land.

We have tried to take care of the flowers, and only to gather rare species very sparingly or not at all. Often we have hidden them with foliage from less scrupulous fingers. And when leading walks or expeditions of field clubs, we have tried to persuade others to do the same. Unfortunately there was sometimes one in the party, who thought it his special privilege to pick the only specimen seen or even to come back afterwards and do so! It really is important that we should preserve rare and interesting flowers for future generations. Real botanists understand this. Gathering the flower prevents the casting of seed. Even for drawing these figures we have sometimes been content with two florets from a good spike with an upper and a lower leaf. We have walked miles in mountain mist and rain to restore a small rare plant to its own niche.

W. Keble Martin (1877–1969)

Sweet Violet (Viola odorata)

From *Wild Flowers*, 1855

The sweet Violet is a native of every part of Europe. Lane, in his Arabian Nights, says sherbet is made of the Violet by pounding the flowers and boiling them with sugar. In Palestine it blooms with the Narcissus as early as the twentieth of January; and it is in full flower during winter, in the palm groves of Barbary, and in Japan and China.

This flower was formerly cultivated, for medicinal uses, in great quantities at Stratford-upon-Avon, and the syrup of Violets is still used by chemists, to detect the presence of an acid or alkali.

The scentless species called the Dog-violet has a much larger and brighter flower, which grows on longer stalks, so that, instead of hiding itself among the leaves, it often renders the bank of a lilac tint by its blossoms. It begins to bloom in March or April, and remains in flower long after the sweet species has disappeared. There are six other kinds of wild violet, including the little Pansy or Heartsease; and so numerous are violets in other lands, that more than a hundred species have been recorded. None of them, however, has a sweeter scent than the fragrant flower of our woodlands.

Anne Pratt (1806–1893)

Is Spring Coming?

From *The Secret Garden*, 1911

Mary tells Colin about the secret garden:

'What are bulbs?' he put in quickly.

'They are daffodils and lilies and snowdrops. They are working in the earth now – pushing up pale green points because the spring is coming.'

'Is the spring coming?' he said. 'What is it like? You don't see it in rooms if you are ill.'

'It is the sun shining on the rain and the rain falling on the sunshine, and things pushing up and working under the earth,' said Mary.

. . . .

'I think it has been left alone so long – that it has grown all into a lovely tangle. I think the roses have climbed and climbed and climbed until they hang from the branches and walls and creep over the ground – almost like a strange grey mist. Some of them have died but many – are alive and when the summer comes there will be curtains and fountains of roses. I think the ground is full of daffodils and snowdrops and lilies and iris working their way out of the dark. Now the spring has begun – perhaps – perhaps –'

The soft drone of her voice was making him stiller and stiller and she saw it and went on.

'Perhaps they are coming up through the grass – perhaps there are clusters of purple crocuses and gold ones – even now. Perhaps the leaves are beginning to break out and uncurl – and perhaps – the grey is changing and a green gauze veil is creeping – and creeping over – everything. And the birds are coming to look at it – because it is – so safe and still. And perhaps – perhaps – perhaps–' very softly and slowly indeed, 'the robin has found a mate – and is building a nest.'

Frances Hodgson Burnett (1849–1924)

Common Yet Perfect

From *Down to Earth*, Part II, The Wood, 1947

We call wild flowers common because of their quantity. But this is just where we strike the great difference between productions of Nature and the productions of Man. When we produce many samples of the same thing they are of poor quality and we speak of them as mass-produced. The mass productions of Nature do not fail at all in terms of quality. Take the bluebell. There indeed is quantity. Yet every single year we are freshly struck by their quality. Only a flower-snob could fail to see that any one of those bells on the uplifted belfry is as delicate a construction as any tulip or rose. I will not say more beautiful, or less, for in this realm of flowers we actually are in the presence of abundant examples of – perfection. I think that perfection is the key to the emotion that flowers cause in us. When a thing is perfect the problem of its existence is solved. Gazing at flowers in a wood an unexpected signal seems to go up; we feel a movement of happiness and hope about everything, there is a suggestion that all is really well, all is right with the world, regardless of the geographical situation of the Deity. It is because of this that all men, even ruffians, feel attracted to flowers. For they do intimate to us that, in spite of everything, all is well.

John Stewart Collis (1900–1984)

A Basket of Violets

From *All the Dogs of My Life*, 1936

Pincher, a woolly dog, and Knobbie, a fox terrier:

I thought the basket had violets in it. It was March, and everywhere in London were violets. The shops were full of them; the street corners were massed with them; and I called my maid to bring a bowl and water, while I cut the string and opened the lid.

But this wasn't violets. Curled up snugly, its head between its paws, and looking at me with great gravity out of the corner of one lifted eye, was a smooth white creature, with a card tied round its neck on which was written: *I am Knobbie. A young lady three months old. Try me on Pincher.*

. . . .

Pincher took me to London, and Knobbie brought me away.
It looked as if I were beginning to be led about by dogs.

Elizabeth von Arnim (1866–1941)

Beavers

From *The Itinerary of Archbishop Baldwin Through Wales*, Book II, Chapter III, c. 1188
Translated by Sir Richard Colt Hoare (1758–1838)

The beavers, in order to construct their castles in the middle
of rivers, make use of the animals of their own species instead
of carts, who, by a wonderful mode of carnage, convey the
timber from the woods to the rivers. Some of them, obeying the
dictates of nature, receive on their bellies the logs of wood cut
off by their associates, which they hold tight with their feet, and
thus with transverse pieces placed in their mouths, are drawn
along backwards, with their cargo, by other beavers, who fasten
themselves with their teeth to the raft. The moles use a similar
artifice in clearing out the dirt from the cavities they form by
scraping. In some deep and still corner of the river, the beavers
use such skill in the construction of their habitations, that not a
drop of water can penetrate, or the force of storms shake them;
nor do they fear any violence but that of mankind, nor even that,
unless well armed. They entwine the branches of willows with
other wood, and different kinds of leaves, to the usual height of the
water, and having made within-side a communication from floor
to floor, they elevate a kind of stage, or scaffold, from which they
may observe and watch the rising of the waters. In the course of
time, their habitations bear the appearance of a grove of willow
trees, rude and natural without, but artfully constructed within.

Giraldus Cambrensis / Gerald of Wales (c. 1146–1223)

APRIL

Daffodils Laughing in the Wind

A Mad Cat

From *Alice's Adventures in Wonderland*, 1865

Alice was a little startled by seeing the Cheshire Cat sitting on a bough of a tree a few yards off.

The Cat only grinned when it saw Alice. It looked good-natured, she thought: still it had very long claws and a great many teeth, so she felt that it ought to be treated with respect.

'Cheshire Puss,' she began, rather timidly, as she did not at all know whether it would like the name: however, it only grinned a little wider. 'Come, it's pleased so far,' thought Alice, and she went on. 'Would you tell me, please, which way I ought to go from here?'

'That depends a good deal on where you want to get to,' said the Cat.

'I don't much care where – ' said Alice.

'Then it doesn't matter which way you go,' said the Cat.

' – so long as I get *somewhere*,' Alice added as an explanation.

'Oh, you're sure to do that,' said the Cat, 'if you only walk long enough.'

Alice felt that this could not be denied, so she tried another question. 'What sort of people live about here?'

'In *that* direction,' the Cat said, waving its right paw round, 'lives a Hatter: and in *that* direction,' waving the other paw, 'lives a March Hare. Visit either you like: they're both mad.'

'But I don't want to go among mad people,' Alice remarked.

'Oh, you can't help that,' said the Cat: 'we're all mad here. I'm mad. You're mad.'

'How do you know I'm mad?' said Alice.

'You must be,' said the Cat, 'or you wouldn't have come here.'

Alice didn't think that proved it at all; however, she went on 'And how do you know that you're mad?'

'To begin with,' said the Cat, 'a dog's not mad. You grant that?'

'I suppose so,' said Alice.

'Well, then,' the Cat went on, 'you see, a dog growls when it's angry, and wags its tail when it's pleased. Now *I* growl when I'm pleased, and wag my tail when I'm angry. Therefore I'm mad.'

'*I* call it purring, not growling,' said Alice.

'Call it what you like,' said the Cat.

. . . .

'I wish you wouldn't keep appearing and vanishing so suddenly: you make one quite giddy.'

'All right,' said the Cat; and this time it vanished quite slowly, beginning with the end of the tail, and ending with the grin, which remained some time after the rest of it had gone.

Lewis Carroll (1832–1898)

2 APRIL

The Cavern

From *The Books That Bind*, 2018

In the basement of Hatchards Bookshop:

There's a wooden door in the wall. Slide back the lock and open it. Watch out for the gust of dust and the slightly sulphurous smell. Can you see the silence? Can you hear the darkness? If you dare enter a little way you will now be standing underneath Piccadilly. Now, I have no idea how big this cavern is or indeed where it leads, for it stretches off into the darkness. But (and this can't be true but think on it anyway) ...

It might lead to a distant forest. Picture it – a vast forest of huge trees that have slowly risen out of the ground, their branches shattering and cracking the sky, emerging out of the trunks like slow lightning, like an estuary of dry riverbeds. In the autumn the leaves burn a mad glow of orange and ochre and magenta, a quilt of gems, a million embers that buzz and spark like the neurons in the brain. Then they fall and carpet the forest floor. Ashes to ashes ... The trees stand naked and silent and wait, like their ancestors standing on the shelves. And they will wait for you. Because we've been here before, remember? When we were stardust. Beyond before. We, the imagination of the universe.

If a tree falls in the forest does it make a sound? Yes, the sound of a bird taking flight in slow motion, a massively decelerated round of applause. And as new trees rise up around you so too the seeds of imagination are sown in the mind, to flourish. We all came from something, and the bookshop came from here. Here, where the trees help us breathe, under a canopy of stars.

Mark Staples (1980–)

Walling in the Cuckoo

From *Yorkshire Legends and Traditions*, 1889

The well-worn legend, common to so many places, of an attempt to 'wall in' the cuckoo, is related to the inhabitants of Austwick, but with the additional credit that they not only attempted the task, but that they were the *first* villagers to make the attempt. Theirs is a grazing district, and much of the year's success depends upon there being suitable weather for the growth of grass in spring and early summer. Noticing that such weather always came with the cuckoo, they determined on the next occasion to surround the bird with a high wall, and by this means secure her permanent residence among them. The work was begun, and carried on, up to the point when success was all but certain – but then, alas! the bird took fright, and soaring, with her mocking cry, 'Cuckoo, cuckoo,' above their highest effort, they saw her no more until her return in nature's course another year.

Rev. Thomas Parkinson (1864–1922)

Unfulfilled Promise

From *This Side of Paradise*, 1920

Summer is only the unfulfilled promise of spring, a charlatan in place of the warm balmy nights I dream of in April. It's a sad season of life without growth.

F. Scott Fitzgerald (1896–1940)

The Snow Ceases

From *The South Country*, Chapter III, Spring, 1909

Next day the wind has flown and the snow is again almost rain: there is ever a hint of pale sky above, but it is not as luminous as the earth. The trees over the road have a beauty of darkness and moistness. Beyond them the earth is a sainted corpse, with a blue light over it that is fast annihilating all matter and turning the landscape to a spirit only. Night and the snow descend upon it, and at dawn the nests are full of snow. The yews and junipers on a league of Downs are chequered white upon white slopes, and the green larches support cirrus clouds of snow. In the garden the daffodils bend criss-cross under snow that cannot quite conceal the yellow flowers. But the snow has ceased. The sky is at first pale without a cloud and tender as from a long imprisonment; it deepens in hue as the sun climbs and gathers force. The crooked paths up the Downs begin to glitter like streaks of lightning. The thrushes sing. From the straight dark beeches the snow cannot fall fast enough in great drops, in showers, in masses that release the boughs with a quiver and a gleam. The green leaves close to the ground creep out, and against them the snow is blue. A little sighing wind rustles ivy and juniper and yew. The sun mounts, and from his highest battlement of cloud blows a long blast of light over the pure land. Once more the larch is wholly green, the beech rosy brown with buds.

Edward Thomas (1878–1917)

Wild Hyacinth (*Hyacinthus non-scriptus*)

From *Wild Flowers*, 1855

Every child who has wandered in the woods in the sweet months of April and May, knows the Blue-bell, or Wild Hyacinth. Scarcely a copse can be found throughout our land which is not then blue with its flowers, for it is to the woodland and the green lane, in Spring, what the buttercup is to the meadow. Growing near it we often find the beautiful pinkish-white blossoms of the wood-anemone, and before it fades away the hedges are getting white, and becoming fragrant with wreaths of the blooming May; but the primroses have almost departed; and the violets are daily more rare.

The root of the Wild Hyacinth is round, and full of a poisonous, clammy juice; indeed every part of the plant gives out more or less of this juice if we bruise it. Though the root is unfit for food, and is useless to us now, yet in former times it was much prized. In days when very stiff ruffs were worn, the juice was made into starch, and employed to stiffen linen. It served the bookbinder, too, as glue, to fasten the covers of books.

Anne Pratt (1806–1893)

The Garden of England

From *Emma*, 1815

Mrs Elton silences Emma:

'When you have seen more of this country, I am afraid you will think you have overrated Hartfield. Surry is full of beauties.'

'Oh! yes, I am quite aware of that. It is the garden of England, you know. Surry is the garden of England.'

'Yes; but we must not rest our claims on that distinction. Many counties, I believe, are called the garden of England, as well as Surry.

'No, I fancy not,' replied Mrs. Elton, with a most satisfied smile. 'I never heard any county but Surry called so.'

Emma was silenced.

Jane Austen (1775–1817)

When the Water Found Us

First published 2021

The day the water found us the house brooded silently: we rattled within its confines (dry pebbles inside a hollow gourd).

Only later did we draw ourselves to its purpose: fingers vinelike, tongues outstretched to lap better the falling rain.

Joel Knight (1975–)

A Mouse

From *Kilvert's Diary*, 1873

9 April

While we were sitting at supper this evening we were startled by a sound under the sideboard as if a rat were tearing and gnawing at the wainscot or skirting board. The noise ceased and then began again. Suddenly Dora uttered an exclamation and a strange look came over her face. She seized the lamp and went to the sideboard pointing to a white handled knife which lay under the sideboard and which she said she had seen a moment before crawling and wriggling along the floor-cloth by itself and making the tearing, gnawing, rending noise we had heard. No one knew how the knife had got under the sideboard. As four of us stood round looking at the knife lying on the floorcloth suddenly the knife leaped into the air and fell back without anyone touching it. It looked very strange and startled us a good deal. We thought of spirit agency and felt uncomfortable and compared the time expecting to hear more of the matter, until Dora observed a very tiny grey mouse taking the buttered point of the knife in his mouth and dragging it along and walking backwards. Then all was explained.

Francis Kilvert (1840–1879)

Plum Blossom

From *The Rainbow*, 1915

She drew up her blind and saw the plum trees in the garden below all glittering and snowy and delighted with the sunshine, in full bloom under a blue sky. They threw out their blossom, they flung it out under the blue heavens, the whitest blossom! How excited it made her.

She had to hurry through her dressing to go and walk in the garden under the plum trees, before anyone should come and talk to her. Out she slipped, and paced like a queen in fairy pleasaunces. The blossom was silver-shadowy when she looked up from under the tree at the blue sky. There was a faint scent, a faint noise of bees, a wonderful quickness of happy morning.

D. H. Lawrence (1885–1930)

Sky Dance

From *A Sand County Almanac and Sketches Here and There*, April, 1949

I owned my farm for two years before learning that the sky dance is to be seen over my woods every evening in April and May. Since we discovered it, my family and I have been reluctant to miss even a single performance.

The show begins on the first warm evening in April at exactly 6:50 p.m. The curtain goes up one minute later each day until 1 June, when the time is 7:50. This sliding scale is dictated by vanity, the dancer demanding a romantic light intensity of exactly 0.05 foot-candles. Do not be late, and sit quietly, lest he fly away in a huff.

The stage props, like the opening hour, reflect the temperamental demands of the performer. The stage must be an open amphitheatre in woods or brush, and in its center there must be a mossy spot, a streak of sterile sand, a bare outcrop of rock, or a bare roadway. Why the male woodcock should be such a stickler for a bare dance floor puzzled me at first, but now I think it is a matter of legs. The woodcock's legs are short, and his strutting cannot be executed to advantage in dense grass or weeds, nor could his lady see them there. I have more woodcocks than most farmers because I have more mossy sand, too poor to support grass.

Knowing the place and the hour, you seat yourself under a bush to the east of the dancefloor and wait, watching against the sunset for the woodcock's arrival. He flies in low from some neighbouring thicket, alights on the bare moss, and at once begins the overture: a series of queer throaty peents spaced about two seconds apart, sounding much like the summer call of the nighthawk.

Suddenly the peenting ceases and the bird flutters skyward in a series of wide spirals, emitting a musical twitter. Up and up he goes, the spirals steeper and smaller, the twittering louder and louder, until the performer is only a speck in the sky. Then, without warning, he tumbles like a crippled plane, giving voice in a soft liquid warble that a March bluebird might envy. A few feet from the ground he levels off and returns to his peenting ground, usually to the exact spot where the performance began, and there resumes his peenting.

It is soon too dark to see the bird on the ground, but you can see his flights against the sky for an hour, which is the usual duration of the show. On moonlit nights, however, it may continue, at intervals, as long as the moon continues to shine.

At daybreak the whole show is repeated. In early April the final curtain falls at 5:15 a.m.; the time advances two minutes a day until June, when the performance closes for the year at 3:15. Why the disparity in sliding scale? Alas, I fear that even romance tires, for it only takes a fifth as much light to stop the dance at dawn as suffices to start it at sunset.

Aldo Leopold (1887–1948)

The Birds of the Sand Counties

From *A Sand County Almanac and Sketches Here and There*, Wisconsin, 1949

There are birds that are found only in the Sand Counties, for reasons sometimes easy, sometimes difficult to guess. The clay-coloured sparrow is there, for the clear reason that he is enamored of the jackpines, and jackpines of sand. The sandhill crane is there, for the clear reason that he is enamored of solitude, and there is none left anywhere else. But why do woodcocks prefer to nest in sandy regions? Their preference is rooted in no such mundane matter as food, for earthworms are far more abundant on better soils. After years of study, I now think I know the reason. The male woodcock, while doing his peenting prologue to the sky dance, is like a short lady in high heels: he does not show up to advantage in dense tangled ground cover. But on the poorest sand-streak of the poorest pasture or meadow of the Sand Counties, there is, in April at least, no ground cover at all, save only moss. Draba, Cardamine, sheep-sorrel, and Antennaria, all negligible impediments to a bird with short legs. Here the male woodcock can puff and strut and mince, not only without let or hindrance, but in full view of his audience, real or hoped-for. This little circumstance, important for only an hour a day, for only one month of the year, perhaps only for one of the two sexes, and certainly wholly irrelevant to economic standards of living, determines the woodcock's choice of home.

The economists have not yet tried to resettle woodcocks.

Aldo Leopold (1887–1948)

The First Morning

From *The Enchanted April*, 1922

Mrs Wilkins opens the shutters and looks out:

All the radiance of April in Italy lay gathered together at her feet. The sun poured in on her. The sea lay asleep in it, hardly stirring. Across the bay the lovely mountains, exquisitely different in colour, were asleep too in the light; and underneath her window, at the bottom of the flower-starred grass slope from which the wall of the castle rose up, was a great cypress, cutting through the delicate blues and violets and rose-colours of the mountains and the sea like a great black sword.

She stared. Such beauty; and she there to see it. Such beauty; and she alive to feel it. Her face was bathed in light. Lovely scents came up to the window and caressed her. A tiny breeze gently lifted her hair. Far out in the bay a cluster of almost motionless fishing boats hovered like a flock of white birds on the tranquil sea. How beautiful, how beautiful. Not to have died before this ... to have been allowed to see, breathe, feel this ... She stared, her lips parted. Happy? Poor, ordinary, everyday word. But what could one say, how could one describe it? It was as though she could hardly stay inside herself, it was as though she were too small to hold so much of joy, it was as though she were washed through with light.

Elizabeth von Arnim (1866–1941)

Cuckoo (*Cuculus canorus*)

From *British Birds*, 1930

'Perhaps no bird,' says Yarrell, 'has attracted so much attention, while of none have more idle tales been told.' And he might have added, that of no other bird so much remains to be known. Our cuckoo interests us in two distinct ways: he charms us, and he affects the mind with his strangeness. He is a visitor of the early spring, with a far-reaching, yet soft and musical, voice, full of beautiful associations, prophetic of the flowery season. To quote Sir Philip Sidney's words, applying them to a feathered instead of a human troubadour: 'He cometh to you with a tale to hold both children from their play and old men from the chimney-corner.' Seen, this melodist has the bold figure, rough, feathered legs, and barred plumage of a hawk. This fierce, predacious aspect is deceptive: he is a timid bird, with the climbing feet of the wood-pecker and the wryneck. Strangest of all, the female has the habit of placing her eggs in other birds' nests, forgetting her mother-hood, a proceeding which, being contrary to nature's use, seems unnatural. It reads like a tale from the *Thousand and One Nights*, in which we sometimes encounter human beings, good, or bad, or merely fantastic, who wander about the world disguised as birds. Only when we see and handle the cuckoo's egg placed in the hedge-sparrow's, or pipit's, or wagtail's nest, when we see the large hawk-like young cuckoo being fed and tenderly cared for by its diminutive foster-parent, do we realise the extraordinary nature of such an instinct.

W. H. Hudson (1841–1922)

Daffodils

From *The Grasmere Journals*, 1802

Thursday 15th April

When we were in the woods beyond Gowbarrow Park we saw a few daffodils close to the water-side. We fancied that the sea had floated the seeds ashore, and that the little colony had so sprung up. But as we went along there were more and yet more; and at last, under the boughs of the trees, we saw that there was a long belt of them along the shore, about the breadth of a country turnpike road. I never saw daffodils so beautiful. They grew among the mossy stones about and above them; some rested their heads upon these stones, as on a pillow, for weariness; and the rest tossed and reeled and danced, and seemed as if they verily laughed with the wind, that blew upon them over the lake; they looked so gay, ever glancing, ever changing. This wind blew directly over the lake to them. There was here and there a little knot, and a few stragglers higher up; but they were so few as not to disturb the simplicity, unity, and life of that one busy highway.

Dorothy Wordsworth (1771–1855)

Piggs and Beer

From *The Diary of a Country Parson*, 1778

April 15

Brewed a vessel of strong Beer today. My two large Piggs, by drinking some Beer grounds taking out of one of my Barrels today, got so amazingly drunk by it, that they were not able to stand and appeared like dead things almost, and so remained all night from dinner time today. I never saw Piggs so drunk in my life ...

April 16

... My 2 Piggs are still unable to walk yet, but they are better than they were yesterday. They tumble about the yard and can by no means stand at all steady yet. In the afternoon my 2 Piggs were tolerably sober.

James Woodforde (1740–1803)

Nightingales

From *The Woodlanders*, 1887

Spring weather came on rather suddenly, the unsealing of buds that had long been swollen accomplishing itself in the space of one warm night. The rush of sap in the veins of the trees could almost be heard. The flowers of late April took up a position unseen, and looked as if they had been blooming a long while, though there had been no trace of them the day before yesterday; birds began not to mind getting wet. In-door people said they had heard the nightingale, to which out-door people replied contemptuously that they had heard him a fortnight before.

Thomas Hardy (1840–1928)

The Arrival of the Nightingale

From *Chronicles of the Hedges*, 1886

The nightingales have arrived. They have already been heard, and early notice of the fact has been duly and promptly made. There is always someone ready to chronicle this event, and many who believe that the precise period is of importance. Scientific men seem now to have decided that no particular significance is to be attached to early or late arrivals. Head winds are quite sufficient to explain a delay of a few days, which is the greatest interval between an early and a very early return. A family of the name of Massham, living in the neighbourhood of Norwich, kept for four generations a chronicle of the dates of arrival. The first entry was made in the spring of 1736, and the series was left unbroken till April 1810, after which it was allowed to drop. It was, however, resumed in 1836, and the returns duly entered up to 1874. These 110 cases give every variety of premature and belated arrival of the nightingales, and showed that the dates were quite useless as a weather guide.

Richard Jefferies (1848–1887)

A Song of Spring

From *The Charm of Birds*, 1927

Of all the bird songs or sounds known to me there is none that
I would prefer to the spring notes of the curlew. I have seen
the bird finish its notes on the ground after alighting, but I
have not observed if it ever gives them without any flight. As a
rule the wonderful notes are uttered on the wing, and are the
accompaniment of a graceful flight that has motions of evident
pleasure. The notes do not sound passionate: they suggest peace,
rest, healing, joy, an assurance of happiness past, present and to
come. To listen to curlews on a bright, clear April day, with the
fullness of spring still in anticipation, is one of the best experiences
that a lover of birds can have. On a still day one can almost hear
the air vibrating with the blessed sound. There is no rarity about it
where curlews breed: it is to be heard through long days in April,
May and far into June. In autumn and winter curlews resort to
estuaries and the seashore, and the call note is melancholy; but
even at this season on a mild day one may be surprised to hear
a single bird give a few of the joy notes, just enough to revive
memory of the past spring and to stir anticipation of the next one.

Sir Edward Grey (1862–1933)

Bracken in Spring

From *Through the Woods*, 1936

From this angle, the wood looks not only solid, but awake. It is almost the best time to come to it; the between time, half bud, half leaf. The leaves will never show up again with the same brilliance, except in autumn. And there is something else that will never show up again until autumn, as it shows up now: the big spread of bracken that is really the beginning of the wood. It begins at the very angle of the road and comes down to the edge of it, bordered by a hawthorn hedge that is so thin that it is not really a hedge at all. This bracken is dead and it has been dead for six months. There are no trees on it except some misshapen gorse bushes, some odd oaks and two sallow trees, now green with catkins that are past their best. So the bracken stretches openly for about fifty yards until there comes a point which it fuses with the wood. It is in reality a point of overlapping, birches overlapping bracken, bracken running under birches, the trees at first thin and small, then gradually thicker and taller, until they annihilate the bracken and rise in a solid mass of white trunks that are brilliant in their own shadows. I have described this bracken because, though it stands dead and dry and ready for the complete annihilation by its own leaves, it stands as a perfect foil for the wood. Its pale fox-colour shows up the trees in a wonderful way. They are thick and sweet with the life the bracken has lost. Even so the bracken is not as dead as it looks. It holds another life, a little paradise of small bird life.

H. E. Bates (1905–1974)

The Tortoise

From *The Natural History and Antiquities of Selborne*, Letter L to
The Honourable Daines Barrington

Selborne, April 21, 1780

The old Sussex tortoise, that I have mentioned to you so often, is
become my property. I dug it out of its winter dormitory in March
last, when it was enough awakened to express its resentments by
hissing; and, packing it in a box with earth, carried it eighty miles
in post-chaises. The rattle and hurry of the journey so perfectly
roused it that, when I turned it out on a border, it walked twice
down to the bottom of my garden; however, in the evening,
the weather being cold, it buried itself in the loose mould, and
continues still concealed.

As it will be under my eye, I shall now have an opportunity of
enlarging my observations on its mode of life, and propensities;
and perceive already that, towards the time of coming forth, it
opens a breathing place in the ground near its head, requiring,
I conclude, a freer respiration, as it becomes more alive. This

creature not only goes under the earth from the middle of November to the middle of April, but sleeps great part of the summer; for it goes to bed in the longest days at four in the afternoon, and often does not stir in the morning till late. Besides, it retires to rest for every shower; and does not move at all in wet days.

When one reflects on the state of this strange being, it is a matter of wonder to find that Providence should bestow such a profusion of days, such a seeming waste of longevity, on a reptile that appears to relish it so little as to squander more than two-thirds of its existence in a joyless stupor, and be lost to all sensation for months together in the profoundest of slumbers.

Gilbert White (1720–1793)

The River Bank

From *The Wind in the Willows*, 1908

The Mole takes a break from spring-cleaning:

He thought his happiness was complete when, as he meandered aimlessly along, suddenly he stood by the edge of a full-fed river. Never in his life had he seen a river before – this sleek, sinuous, full-bodied animal, chasing and chuckling, gripping things with a gurgle and leaving them with a laugh, to fling itself on fresh playmates that shook themselves free, and were caught and held again. All was a-shake and a-shiver – glints and gleams and sparkles, rustle and swirl, chatter and bubble. The Mole was bewitched, entranced, fascinated. By the side of the river he trotted as one trots, when very small, by the side of a man who holds one spellbound by exciting stories; and when tired at last, he sat on the bank, while the river still chattered on to him, a babbling procession of the best stories in the world, sent from the heart of the earth to be told at last to the insatiable sea.

As he sat on the grass and looked across the river, a dark hole in the bank opposite, just above the water's edge, caught his eye, and dreamily he fell to considering what a nice, snug dwelling-place it would make for an animal with few wants and fond of a bijou riverside residence, above flood level and remote from noise and dust. As he gazed, something bright and small seemed to twinkle down in the heart of it, vanished, then twinkled once more like a tiny star. But it could hardly be a star in such an unlikely situation; and it was too glittering and small for a glow-worm. Then, as he looked, it winked at him, and so declared itself to be an eye; and a small face began gradually to grow up round it, like a frame round a picture.

A brown little face, with whiskers.

A grave round face, with the same twinkle in its eye that had first attracted his notice.

Small neat ears and thick silky hair.

It was the Water Rat!

Kenneth Grahame (1859–1932)

The Caterpillar

From *The Compleat Angler*, Part I, 1653–1676

His lips and mouth somewhat yellow; his eyes black as Jet; his forehead purple; his feet and hinder parts green; his tail two-forked and black; the whole body stained with a kind of red spots, which run along the neck and shoulder-blade, not unlike the form of St. Andrew's Cross, or the letter X, made thus cross-wise, and a white line drawn down his back to his tail; all which add much beauty to his whole body. And it is to me observable, that at a fixed age this Caterpillar gives over to eat, and towards Winter comes to be covered over with a strange shell or crust, called an Aurelia, and so lives a kind of dead life, without eating all the Winter; (and as others of several kinds turn to be several kinds of flies and vermin the Spring following) so this Caterpillar then turns to be a painted Butter-fly.

Izaak Walton (1593–1683)

About Wrens

From Letter to John Ruskin, 1887

This year I have seen wrens' nests in three different kinds of places
– one built in the angle of a doorway, one under a bank, and a
third near the top of a raspberry bush; this last was so large that
when our gardener first saw it, he thought it was a swarm of bees.
It seems a pleasure to this active bird to build; he will begin to
build several nests sometimes before he completes one for Jenny
Wren to lay her eggs and make her nursery. Think how busy both
he and Jenny are when the sixteen young ones come out of their
shells – little helpless gaping things wanting feeding in their turns
the livelong summer day! What hundreds and thousands of small
insects they devour! they catch flies with good-sized wings. I have
seen a parent wren with its beak so full that the wings stood out at
each side like the whiskers of a cat.

Susie Beever (1805–1893)
John Ruskin (1819–1900)

The Traveller's View

From *Adam Bede*, 1859

High up against the horizon were the huge conical masses of hill, like giant mounds intended to fortify this region of corn and grass against the keen and hungry winds of the north; not distant enough to be clothed in purple mystery, but with sombre greenish sides visibly specked with sheep, whose motion was only revealed by memory, not detected by sight; wooed from day to day by the changing hours, but responding with no change in themselves – left for ever grim and sullen after the flush of morning, the winged gleams of the April noonday, the parting crimson glory of the ripening summer sun. And directly below them the eye rested on a more advanced line of hanging woods, divided by bright patches of pasture or furrowed crops, and not yet deepened into the uniform leafy curtains of high summer, but still showing the warm tints of the young oak and the tender green of the ash and lime. Then came the valley, where the woods grew thicker, as if they had rolled down and hurried together from the patches left smooth on the slope, that they might take the better care of the tall mansion which lifted its parapets and sent its faint blue summer smoke among them. Doubtless there was a large sweep of park and a broad glassy pool in front of that mansion, but the swelling slope of meadow would not let our traveller see them from the village green. He saw instead a foreground which was just as lovely – the level sunlight lying like transparent gold among the gently curving stems of the feathered grass and the tall red sorrel, and the white umbels of the hemlocks lining the bushy hedgerows.

George Eliot (1819–1880)

The Colouring of Eggs

From *The Charm of Birds*, 1927

An interesting question, but one for which Sir Edward Grey manages to find no definite answer:

Eggs are fragile things. It is therefore necessary for birds to place them where they will be protected from accidents: eggs are also greatly desired by ground vermin and by some kinds of predatory birds; it is therefore necessary for birds to endeavour to conceal their eggs. The shell, judging from the substance of which it is made, would naturally be white; in some cases it is so, but in others there is an infinite variety of colour. It would be reasonable to suppose that this variety of colour has been evolved to help in concealing the egg. That protective colouration exists in some insects is an irresistible conclusion: why should this theory not apply to the colouring of eggs of birds?

Sir Edward Grey (1862–1933)

Geese

From *Walden or Life in the Woods*, 1854

In the morning I watched the geese from the door through the mist, sailing in the middle of the pond, fifty rods off, so large and tumultuous that Walden appeared like an artificial pond for their amusement. But when I stood on the shore they at once rose up with a great flapping of wings at the signal of their commander, and when they had got into rank circled about over my head, twenty-nine of them, and then steered straight to Canada, with a regular honk from the leader at intervals, trusting to break their fast in muddier pools. A 'plump' of ducks rose at the same time and took the route to the north in the wake of their noisier cousins.

Henry David Thoreau (1817–1862)

Primroses in a Wild Country

From *English Hours*, English Vignettes I, 1870

Toward the last of April, in Monmouthshire, the primroses were as big as your fist. I say in Monmouthshire, because I believe that a certain grassy mountain which I gave myself the pleasure of climbing and to which I took my way across the charming country, through lanes where the hedges were perched upon blooming banks, lay within the borders of this ancient province.

. . . .

I say the roads were empty, but they were peopled with the big primroses I just now spoke of – primroses of the size of ripe apples and yet, in spite of their rank growth, of as pale and tender a yellow as if their gold had been diluted with silver. It was indeed a mixture of gold and silver, for there was a wealth of the white wood-anemone as well, and these delicate flowers, each of so perfect a coinage, were tumbled along the green wayside as if a prince had been scattering largess.

Henry James (1843–1916)

A Long Spring Month

From *Lorna Doone*, 1869

After the long dry skeltering wind of March and part of April, there had been a fortnight of soft wet; and when the sun came forth again, hill and valley, wood and meadow, could not make enough of him. Many a spring have I seen since then, but never yet two springs alike, and never one so beautiful. Or was it that my love came forth and touched the world with beauty?

The spring was in our valley now; creeping first for shelter shyly in the pause of the blustering wind. There the lambs came bleating to her, and the orchis lifted up, and the thin dead leaves of clover lay for the new ones to spring through. There the stiffest things that sleep, the stubby oak, and the stunted beech, dropped their brown defiance to her, and prepared for a soft reply. While her over-eager children (who had started forth to meet her, through the frost and shower of sleet), catkin'd hazel, gold-gloved withy, youthful elder, and old woodbine, with all the tribe of good hedge-climbers (who must hasten, while haste they may) – was there one of them, that did not claim the merit of coming first?

There she stayed, and held her revel, as soon as the fear of frost was gone; all the air was a fount of freshness, and the earth of gladness, and the laughing waters prattled of the kindness of the sun.

R. D. Blackmore (1825–1900)

Tabby Cats

From *Home and Garden*, 1900

Gertrude Jekyll, better-known as a gardener, always had four or five cats:

I much prefer cats of the common short-haired kind. They are stronger and hardier than the long-haired breeds, and the short fur always looks and feels much cleaner and brighter, and they can keep it nice themselves without any need of adventitious grooming; and there are never those long periods – nine months out of the twelve it always seems to me – when the owner is apologising for a ragged ruff or a wispy tail. And the short coat allows one to see the beautiful structure, and every detail of lithe bound and lively caper, and all the infinitely varied and graceful movements that are so pleasant to watch.

Tabby and white is my favourite colouring. I have two all tabby without white, and dear pussies they are; but for appearance I like them better with white fronts and paws; it makes them look so clean and well-dressed. The word 'tabby' has an interesting etymology; coming from an Arabic root, and always signifying something striped or waved or brindled, whether of animal's coat or of woven fabric. Hence also the word 'tabinet' for a woven stuff of striated surface; and doubtless the same word corrupted is the 'tabouret' of the modern upholsterer, the name of a woven silk stuff whose design is always in stripes. It was much in use at the beginning of the century, and has been reproduced and now again finds favour.

Gertrude Jekyll (1843–1932)

MAY

Enveloped in a Cloud of Green

The Pleasures of Spring

From *Mansfield Park*, 1814

It was sad to Fanny to lose all the pleasures of spring. She had
not known before what pleasures she had to lose in passing
March and April in a town. She had not known before how much
the beginnings and progress of vegetation had delighted her.
What animation, both of body and mind, she had derived from
watching the advance of that season which cannot, in spite of its
capriciousness, be unlovely, and seeing its increasing beauties from
the earliest flowers in the warmest divisions of her aunt's garden,
to the opening of leaves of her uncle's plantations, and the glory of
his woods.

Jane Austen (1775–1817)

Sunset

From *Our Village*, 1824

May 2nd

What a sunset! how golden! how beautiful! The sun just disappearing, and the narrow liny clouds, which a few minutes ago lay like soft vapoury streaks along the horizon, lighted up with a golden splendour that the eye can scarcely endure, and those still softer clouds which floated above them wreathing and curling into a thousand fantastic forms, as thin and changeful as summer smoke, now defined and deepened into grandeur, and edged with ineffable, insufferable light! Another minute and the brilliant orb totally disappears, and the sky above grows every moment more varied and more beautiful as the dazzling golden lines are mixed with glowing red and gorgeous purple, dappled with small dark specks, and mingled with such a blue as the egg of the hedge-sparrow. To look up at that glorious sky, and then to see that magnificent picture reflected in the clear and lovely Loddon water, is a pleasure never to be described and never forgotten. My heart swells and my eyes fill as I write of it, and think of the immeasurable majesty of nature, and the unspeakable goodness of God, who has spread an enjoyment so pure, so peaceful, and so intense before the meanest and the lowliest of His creatures.

Mary Russell Mitford (1787–1855)

Corncrakes

From *Findings*, 2005

I want to see a corncrake. So I sit on a bench and watch the lacy heads of cow parsley waft in the breeze. I'm thinking about corncrakes, as though thinking about them could summon one up. A glimpse is all I'll be granted – maybe a female darting from one patch of cover to another, or rival males so forgetting themselves as to have a quick squabble in public view. The corncrake has become a Hebridean bird, part of the Hebridean summer along with the blue windswept skies, the surf and rain, the wild flowers on machair, the skylarks and the empty, cream-pale beaches. Its decline is doubtless bad for the corncrake, but there's an interesting side effect. In this age of supposed homogeneity and sameness everywhere, as naturalist Richard Mabey put it, 'the differences between native and stranger are fading', we have driven the birds away. Once-common species, like the corncrake, are becoming more localised, more specialised. But, as they do, it seems that people are learning a new identification with the birds of their patch. Mull makes much of its sea eagle, a species that was hunted to extinction, then reintroduced.

On Coll everyone knows about corncrakes – they're adopting them as their own, like totems of Neolithic tribes. On Coll, it's corncrakes that are good for business. Summer visitors themselves, they beget others. Birdwatchers come especially – Sarah tells us of an old lady who sat quiet and demure on this very viewing bench for an hour, two hours ... then there was a whoop, and Sarah turned to see the old lady leaping around, punching the air like a footballer, just for a glimpse of an elusive brown bird. I sit on the bench, looking at the long grass, but it's beginning to rain, and though there are geese and lapwings and redshanks, a flock of noisy starlings, and a laverock rising, I see no corncrake. Maybe it's just as well. In Shetland they held it very bad luck, actually to clap eyes on the thing.

When, later that day, I do see one, it's scuttering away from the wheels of the car. Like a miniature road-runner, a slender upright hen with hunched shoulders and strong, pinkish legs, it squeezes under a wire fence, and with relief vanishes among the irises, even as I brake. It's the colour of slipware and looks, in that glimpse, like an elegant ceramic water jug suddenly come to life. That's that. I do not punch the air.

Kathleen Jamie (1962–)

Evening in the Forest

From *Brendon Chase*, 1944

The sunlight of late afternoon illuminated the tops of the oak trees. Every ride, every rabbit track, was wrapped in cool shade; scarce a breath of wind stirred the million, million leaves.

In the very heart of this magnificent forest which covered an area of eleven thousand undulating acres, in a little green clearing hedged around with fern and sallow, grew a massive oak tree. It was not very tall, indeed it was considerably lower than many of the other oaks round about, for centuries since its top had decayed away only the massive rough trunk remained. But thick healthy foliage grew from the gnarled and knotted crown, and these new branches spread wide like a vast, deep green umbrella for many yards on all sides.

The roughened trunk was covered with excrescences and bulges, its total girth must have been nearly twenty-five feet. At its base, on the western side, was a small aperture not more than two feet wide by three height, like the opening to a little black cave or a postern door.

In the quiet of evening the nightingales were singing, whitethroats were bubbling their merry woodland music from the depths of the hazels and sallows, and now and then a pigeon passed over, high in the sunlight, its breast lit by the low rays of the setting sun.

B. B. / Denys Watkins-Pitchford (1905–1990)

Valleys

From 'Recollections of Grasmere', September 1839

It is the character of all the northern English valleys, as I have already remarked – and it is a character first noticed by Wordsworth – that they assume, in their bottom areas, the level, floor-like shape, making every-where a direct angle with the surrounding hills, and definitely marking out the margin of their outlines; whereas the Welch valleys have too often the glaring imperfection of the basin shape, which allows no sense of any flat area or valley surface: the hills are already commencing at the very centre of what is called the level area.

Thomas de Quincey (1785–1859)

Cowslip or Paigle *(Primula veris)*

From *Flowers of the Field*, 1885

Among the many pleasing purposes to which these favourite
flowers are applied by children, none is prettier than the making
of Cowslip Balls. The method, which may not be known to all my
readers, is as follows:

The umbels are picked off as close as possible to the top of
the main stalk, and from fifty to sixty are made to hang across a
string stretched between the backs of two chairs. The flowers are
then carefully pressed together, and the string tied tightly so as to
collect them in a ball. Care should be taken to choose such heads
or umbels only as have all the flowers open, or the surface of the
ball will be uneven.

Fl. April, May.

Rev. C. A. Johns (1811–1874)

Spring Happiness

From *Elizabeth and Her German Garden*, 1898

I am always happy (out of doors be it understood, for indoors there are servants and furniture) but in quite different ways, and my spring happiness bears no resemblance to my summer or autumn happiness, though it is not more intense, and there were days last winter when I danced for sheer joy out in my frost-bound garden, in spite of my years and children. But I did it behind a bush, having a due regard for the decencies.

There are so many bird-cherries round me, great trees with branches sweeping the grass, and they are so wreathed just now with white blossoms and tenderest green that the garden looks like a wedding. I never saw such masses of them; they seemed to fill the place. Even across a little stream that bounds the garden on the east, and right in the middle of the cornfield beyond, there is an immense one, a picture of grace and glory against the cold blue of the spring sky.

My garden is surrounded by cornfields and meadows, and beyond are great stretches of sandy heath and pine forests, and where the forests leave off the bare heath begins again; but the forests are beautiful in their lofty, pink-stemmed vastness, far overhead the crowns of softest gray-green, and underfoot a bright green wortleberry carpet, and everywhere the breathless silence; and the bare heaths are beautiful too, for one can see across them into eternity almost, and to go out on to them with one's face towards the setting sun is like going into the very presence of God.

Elizabeth von Arnim (1866–1941)

An Ancient Trap

From *The Tree*, 1979

I came on my first Soldier Orchid, a species I had long wanted to encounter, but hitherto never seen outside a book. I fell on my knees before it in a way that all botanists will know. I identified, to be quite certain, with Professors Clapham, Tutin and Warburg in hand (the standard British *Flora*), I measured, I photographed, I worked out where I was on the map, for future reference. I was excited, very happy, one always remembers one's 'firsts' of the rarer species. Yet five minutes after my wife had finally (other women are not the only form of adultery) torn me away, I suffered a strange feeling. I realized I had not actually seen the three plants in the little colony we had found. Despite all the identifying, measuring, photographing, I had managed to set the experience in a kind of present past, a having-looked, even as I was temporarily and physically still looking. If I had the courage, and my wife the patience, I would have asked her to turn and drive back, because I knew I had just fallen, in the stupidest possible way, into an ancient trap. It is not necessarily too little knowledge that causes ignorance; possessing too much, or wanting to gain too much, can produce the same result.

John Fowles (1926–2005)

Oak Saplings

From *The Journal of a Disappointed Man*, 1908

May 9

Among the Oak saplings we seemed enveloped in a cloud of green.
The tall green grasses threw up a green light against the young
green of the Oaks, and the sun managed to trickle through only
here and there. Bevies of swinging bluebells grew in patches among
the grass. Overhead in the oaks I heard secret leaf whispers – those
little noiseless noises. Birds and trees and flowers were secretive
and mysterious like expectant motherhood. All the live things
plotted together, having the same big business in hand. Out in
the sunlit meadows, there was a different influence abroad. Here
everything was gay, lively, irresponsible. The brook prattled like
an inconsequential schoolgirl. The Marsh Marigolds in flamboyant
yellow sunbonnets played ring-a-ring-a-roses.

An Oak sapling should make an elderly man avuncular. There
are so many tremendous possibilities about a well-behaved young
oak that it is tempting to put a hand upon its shoulder and give
some seasoned, timberly advice.

W. N. P. Barbellion (1889–1919)

Early Risers

From *The Adventures of Tom Sawyer*, 1876

Tom, Huck and Joe camp:

When Tom awoke in the morning, he wondered where he was. He sat up and rubbed his eyes and looked around; then he comprehended. It was the cool gray dawn, and there was a delicious sense of repose and peace in the deep pervading calm and silence of the woods. Not a leaf stirred; not a sound obtruded upon great Nature's meditation. Beaded dewdrops stood upon the leaves and grasses. A white layer of ashes covered the fire, and a thin blue breath of smoke rose straight into the air. Joe and Huck still slept. Now, far away in the woods a bird called; another answered; presently the hammering of a woodpecker was heard. Gradually the cool dim gray of the morning whitened, and as gradually sounds multiplied and life manifested itself. The marvel of Nature shaking off sleep and going to work unfolded itself to the musing boy. A little green worm came crawling over a dewy leaf, lifting two-thirds of his body into the air from time to time and 'sniffing around,' then proceeding again – for he was measuring, Tom said; and when the worm approached him, of its own accord, he sat as still as a stone, with his hopes rising and falling, by turns, as the creature still came toward him or seemed inclined to go elsewhere; and when at last it considered a painful moment with its curved body in the air and then came decisively down upon Tom's leg and began a journey over him, his whole heart was glad – for that meant that he was going to have a new suit of clothes – without the shadow of a doubt a gaudy piratical uniform. Now a procession of ants appeared, from nowhere in particular, and went about their labors; one struggled manfully by with a dead spider five times as big as itself in its arms, and lugged it straight up a tree-trunk. A brown spotted lady-bug climbed the dizzy height of a grass blade, and Tom bent down close to it and said,

'Lady-bug, lady-bug, fly away home,
Your house is on fire, your children's alone,'

and she took wing and went off to see about it – which did not surprise the boy, for he knew of old that this insect was credulous about conflagrations, and he had practised upon its simplicity more than once. A tumblebug came next, heaving sturdily at its ball, and Tom touched the creature, to see it shut its legs against its body and pretend to be dead. The birds were fairly rioting by this time. A catbird, the Northern mocker, lit in a tree over Tom's head, and trilled out her imitations of her neighbors in a rapture of enjoyment; then a shrill jay swept down, a flash of blue flame, and stopped on a twig almost within the boy's reach, cocked his head to one side and eyed the strangers with a consuming curiosity; a gray squirrel and a big fellow of the 'fox' kind came scurrying along, sitting up at intervals to inspect and chatter at the boys, for the wild things had probably never seen a human being before and scarcely knew whether to be afraid or not. All Nature was wide awake and stirring, now; long lances of sunlight pierced down through the dense foliage far and near, and a few butterflies came fluttering upon the scene.

Mark Twain (1835–1910)

On a Monument to the Pigeon

From *A Sand County Almanac and Sketches Here and There*, Wisconsin, 1949

We have erected a monument to commemorate the funeral of a species. It symbolizes our sorrow. We grieve because no living man will see again the onrushing phalanx of victorious birds, sweeping a path for spring across the March skies, chasing the defeated winter from all the woods and prairies of Wisconsin.

Men still live who, in their youth, were shaken by a living wind. But a decade hence only the oldest oaks will remember, and at long last only the hills will know.

There will always be pigeons in books and in museum, but these are effigies and images, dead to all hardships and to all delights. Book-pigeons cannot dive out of a cloud to make the deer run for cover, or clap their wings in thunderous applause of mast-laden woods. Book-pigeons cannot breakfast on new-mown wheat in Minnesota, and dine on blueberries in Canada. They know no urge of seasons; they feel no kiss of sun, no lash of wind and weather. They live forever by not living at all.

Our grandfathers were less well-housed, well-fed, well-clothed than we are. The strivings by which they bettered their lot are also those which deprived us of pigeons. Perhaps now we grieve because we are not sure, in our hearts, that we have gained by the exchange. The gadgets of industry bring us more comforts than the pigeon did, but do they add as much to the glory of the spring?

(The monument to the Passenger Pigeon, placed in Wyalusing State Park, Wisconsin, by the Wisconsin Society for Ornithology. Dedicated 11 May 1947.)

Aldo Leopold (1887–1948)

Passenger Pigeons

From *Ornithological Biography*, 1831

The breeding of the Wild Pigeons, and the places chosen for that purpose, are points of great interest. The time is not much influenced by season, and the place selected is where food is most plentiful, and always at a convenient distance from water. Forest-trees of great height are those in which Pigeons form their nests. Thither the countless myriads resort, and prepare to fulfil one of the great laws of nature. At this period the note of the Pigeon is a soft coo-coo-coo-coo, much shorter than that of the domestic species. The common notes resemble the monosyllables kee-kee-kee-kee, the first being the loudest, the others gradually diminishing in power. The male assumes a pompous demeanour, and follows the female whether on the ground, or on the branches, with spread tail and drooping wings, which it rubs against the part over which it is moving. The body is elevated, the throat swells, the eyes sparkle. He continues his notes, and now and then rise on the wing, and flies a few yards to approach the fugitive and timorous female. Like the domestic Pigeon and other species, they caress each other by billing, in which action, the bill of the one is introduced transversely into that of the other, and both parties alternately disgorge the contents of their crop by repeated efforts. These preliminary affairs are soon settled, and the Pigeons commence their nests in general peace and harmony. They are composed of a few dry twigs, crossing each other, and are supported by forks of the branches. On the same tree from fifty to a hundred nests may frequently be seen: – I might say a much greater number, were I not anxious, kind reader, that however wonderful my account of the Wild Pigeon is, you may not feel disposed to refer it to the marvellous.

John James Audubon (1785–1851)

Kittens

From *Chia the Wildcat*, 1971

The kittens had opened their eyes and Chia knew them well. The smallest, a little tom, was also the fiercest, and his quick hiss and snarl greeted any strange noise long before he could see.

The second tom was larger and lazier, except when he was hungry. Then he shouldered and hissed and butted, and tried to bite his sisters as he struggled to get the most milk. His brother was more cunning and knew how to wait his time, ousting another of the litter.

The three females were all of a size. The first was gentle, anxious for love, needing her mother's tongue on her head before she settled to feed, eager to greet Chia before the others; the second was curious, alert for every sound, her ears listening constantly to birdcall and wind song and the thrill of running water. The third wanted nothing from the world but the infinite satisfaction of food.

. . . .

The kittens had not yet ventured outside the tree. They were unable to run. They staggered when they walked, tumbling over one another on unsteady legs. When they fell, as they often did, they were astounded and mewed plaintively, annoyed by legs that would not obey their brains. Though so small, the threat of intrusion from the outside world transformed them into scratching, spitting demons. Inside the lair they were balls of fluff, gentle and wide-eyed, with all the charm of domestic kits.

Joyce Stranger (1924–2007)

The Sheep-washing

From *Far From the Madding Crowd*, 1874

The sheep-washing pool was a perfectly circular basin of brickwork in the meadows, full of the clearest water. To birds on the wing its glassy surface, reflecting the light sky, must have been visible for miles around as a glistening Cyclops' eye in a green face. The grass about the margin at this season was a sight to remember long – in a minor sort of way. Its activity in sucking the moisture from the rich damp sod was almost a process observable by the eye. The outskirts of this level water-meadow were diversified by rounded and hollow pastures, where just now every flower that was not a buttercup was a daisy, losing their character somewhat as they sank to the verge of the intervening river. This slid along noiselessly as a shade – the swelling reeds and sedge forming a flexible palisade upon its moist brink. To the north of the mead were trees, the leaves of which were new, soft, and moist, not yet having stiffened and darkened by summer sun and drought, their colour being yellow beside anything green – green beside anything yellow. From the recesses of this knot of foliage the loud notes of three cuckoos were at the present moment resounding through the still air.

Thomas Hardy (1840–1928)

The House-martin's Nest

From *The Natural History and Antiquities of Selborne*, Letter XVI to The Honourable Daines Barrington

Selborne, Nov. 20, 1773

About the middle of May, if the weather be fine, the martin begins to think in earnest of providing a mansion for its family. The crust or shell of this nest seems to be formed of such dirt or loam as comes most readily to hand, and is tempered and wrought together with little bits of broken straws to render it tough and tenacious. As this bird often builds against a perpendicular wall without any projecting ledge under, it requires its utmost efforts to get the first foundation firmly fixed, so that it may safely carry the superstructure. On this occasion the bird not only clings with its claws, but partly supports itself by strongly inclining its tail against the wall, making that a fulcrum; and thus steadied it works and plasters the materials into the face of the brick or stone. But then, that this work may not, while it is soft and green, pull itself down by its own weight, the provident architect has prudence and forbearance enough not to advance her work too fast; but by building only in the morning, and by dedicating the rest of the day to food and amusement, gives it sufficient time to dry and harden. About half an inch seems to be a sufficient layer for a day. Thus careful workmen when they build mud-walls (informed at first perhaps by this lithe bird) raise but a moderate layer at a time, and then desist; lest the work should become top-heavy, and so be ruined by its own weight. By this method in about ten or twelve days is formed an hemispheric nest with a small aperture towards the top, strong, compact, and warm; and perfectly fitted for all the purposes for which it was intended.

Gilbert White (1720–1793)

The Knepp Oak

From *Wilding: The Return of Nature to a British Farm*, 2018

An oak tree's view of history on the Knepp Estate in Sussex:

Its girth made it about 550 years old. Most likely, it had started life during the Wars of the Roses, nearly three centuries before my husband's family, the Burrells, had arrived at Knepp. It would have germinated when 'Knap' was a thousand-acre deer park owned by the Dukes of Norfolk, its acorns fodder – or 'pannage' – for wild boar and fallow deer. As a fine young tree only a hundred years old, it would have welcomed the arrival of the Carylls, Catholic ironmasters, owners of Knepp for over a hundred and seventy years. In the mid-seventeenth century it would have witnessed the Civil War, the assault on Knepp by Parliamentary troops and counter-assaults by Royalists. It had lived and breathed what we can only absorb from history books.

. . . .

One of our longest-lived trees, the oak – so the saying goes – grows for 300 years, rests for another 300 years and spends the last 300 gracefully declining.

Isabella Tree (1964–)

A Sea of Gold

From *Kilvert's Diary*, 1874

17 May

We shall not have a more lovely Sunday than this has been. The hawthorn bushes were loaded with their sweet May snow, and in the glowing afternoon sun the sheets of buttercups stretched away under the bright elms like a sea of gold.

Francis Kilvert (1840–1879)

The Company of Birds

From *A New Orchard and Garden*, 1618

The Black-bird and Threstle (for I take it, the Thrush sings not, but devours) sing loudly in a *May* morning, and delights the eare much and you need not want their company, if you have ripe Cherries or Berries, and would as gladly as the rest doe your pleasure: but I had rather want their company than my fruit.

William Lawson (c. 1554–1635)

Spring Comes to Lowood

From *Jane Eyre*, 1847

April advanced to May: a bright serene May it was; days of blue
sky, placid sunshine, and soft western or southern gales filled
up its duration. And now vegetation matured with vigour;
Lowood shook loose its tresses; it became all green, all flowery;
its great elm, ash, and oak skeletons were restored to majestic life;
woodland plants sprang up profusely in its recesses; unnumbered
varieties of moss filled its hollows, and it made a strange ground-
sunshine out of the wealth of its wild primrose plants: I have seen
their pale gold gleam in overshadowed spots like scatterings of the
sweetest lustre.

Charlotte Brontë (1816–1855)

Landscapes and Gardens

From *Second Nature*, 1996

A woodchuck lays waste the newly planted vegetable garden:

The reader might reasonably wonder at this point why it was that I had no fence. I was asked this question several times after the woodchuck struck and never came up with an entirely satisfactory answer. I could offer a few trivial explanations, having to do with economy and competence. But I suspect my reluctance to put up a fence was a more visceral matter. Fences just didn't accord with my view of gardening. A garden should be continuous with the natural landscape, I felt, in harmony with its surroundings. The idea that a garden might actually require *protection* from nature seemed absurd. Somewhere along the line I had been convinced that a fence bespoke disharmony, even alienation, from nature.

I suspect I had also absorbed the traditional American view that fences were Old World, out of place in the American landscape. The notion turns up repeatedly on nineteenth-century American writing about the landscape. One author after denounces 'the Englishman's insultingly inhospitable brick wall, topped with broken bottles'.

. . . .

We may no longer spell it out, but most of us still believe the landscape is somehow sacred, and to meddle with it sacrilegious. And to set up hierarchies within it – to set off a garden from the surrounding countryside – well, that makes no sense at all.

Michael Pollan (1955–)

A Conceited Tarrier

From *The Torrington Diaries*, A Tour of Bedfordshire, 1794

Wednesday May 21:

On Wednesday 21st I was abroad at an early hour, to take out my new dog; but he is no hunter, but a conceited tarrier as most of them are, (I want a busy, bold, cocking spaniel, who will endure travell, range wide, and thread a brake – poor Jock, thy equal in, sense, steadiness – endurance, and courage, is rarely to be found.)

John Byng (1743–1813)

A Swan

From *The Ugly Duckling*, 1843
Translated by M. R. James (1862–1936)

One evening, when there was a lovely sunset, a whole flock of beautiful great birds rose out of the bushes. The Duckling had never seen any so handsome. They were brilliantly white, with long supple necks. They were swans, and they uttered a strange sound and spread their splendid long wings and flew far away from the cold region to warmer lands, and unfrozen lakes. They mounted so high, so high that the ugly little Duckling was strangely moved; he whirled himself round in the water like a wheel, he stretched his neck straight up into the air after them and uttered such a loud cry, so strange, that he was quite frightened at it himself. Oh, he could not forget those beautiful birds, those wonderful birds! And the moment they were out of sight he dived right down to the bottom of the water, and when he came up again he was almost beside himself. He didn't know what the birds were called or which way they were flying, but he loved them as he had never loved anything yet. He was not envious of them – how could it enter his mind to wish for such beauty for himself – he would have been happy if even the ducks had let him into their company – poor ugly creature.

. . . .

It would be too sad to tell of all the hardships and miseries which he had to go through in that hard winter. When the sun began once more to shine out warm and the larks to sing, he was lying among the reeds in the marsh, and it was the beautiful spring.

Then all at once he lifted his wings, and they rustled more strongly than before, and bore him swiftly away; and before he knew it he was in a spacious garden where were apple trees in blossom, and sweet-smelling lilacs hung on long green boughs right down to the winding moat. Oh, it was lovely here, and fresh with spring; and straight in front of him, out of the shadows, came three beautiful white swans with rustling plumage floating lightly on the water. The Duckling recognized the splendid creatures, and a strange sorrowfulness came over him.

'I will fly to them, these royal birds, and they will peck me to death because I, who am so ugly, dare to approach them; but it doesn't matter; it's better to be killed by them than to be snapped at by the ducks and pecked at by hens and kicked by the servant who looks after the poultry-yard, and suffer all the winter.' So he flew out into the open water and swam towards the stately swans, and they saw him and hastened with swelling plumage to meet him. 'Yes, kill me,' the poor creature said, bowing his head down to the water, and waited for death. But what did he see in the clear water? He beheld his own image, but it was no longer that of a clumsy dark grey bird, ugly and repulsive. He was a swan himself.

Hans Christian Andersen (1805–1875)

Grizzly Bears

From A Sand County Almanac and Sketches Here and There, Wilderness for Wildlife, 1949

The National Parks do not suffice as a means of perpetuating the larger carnivores; witness the precarious status of the grizzly bear, and the fact that the park system is already wolfless. Neither do they suffice for mountain sheep; most sheep herds are shrinking.

The reasons for this are clear in some cases and obscure in others. The parks are certainly too small for such a far-ranging species as the wolf. Many animal species, for reasons unknown, do not seem to thrive as detached islands of population.

The most feasible way to enlarge the area available for wilderness fauna is for the wilder parts of the National Forests, which usually surround the Parks, to function as parks in respect of threatened species. That they have not so functioned is tragically illustrated in the case of the grizzly bear.

In 1909, when I first saw the West, there were grizzlies in every major mountain mass, but you could travel for months without meeting a conservation officer. Today there is some kind of conservation officer 'behind every bush,' yet as wildlife bureaus grow, our most magnificent mammal retreats steadily towards the Canadian border. Of the 6,000 grizzlies officially reported as remaining in areas owned by the United States, 5,000 are in Alaska. Only five states have any at all. There seems to be a tacit assumption that if grizzlies survive in Canada and Alaska, that is good enough. It is not good enough for me. The Alaskan bears are a distinct species. Relegating grizzlies to Alaska is about like relegating happiness to heaven; one may never get there.

Aldo Leopold (1887–1948)

Spring in Scotland

From *The Thirty-Nine Steps*, 1915

Richard Hannay's first days in Scotland, on the run:

It was a gorgeous spring evening, with every hill showing as clear as a cut amethyst. The air had the queer, rooty smell of bogs, but it was as fresh as mid-ocean, and it had the strangest effect on my spirits. I actually felt light-hearted. I might have been a boy out for a spring holiday tramp, instead of a man of thirty-seven very much wanted by the police. I felt just as I used to feel when I was starting for a big trek on a frosty morning on the high veld. If you believe me, I swung along that road whistling. There was no plan of campaign in my head, only just to go on and on in this blessed, honest-smelling hill country, for every mile put me in better humour with myself.

In a roadside planting I cut a walking-stick of hazel, and presently struck off the highway up a by-path which followed the glen of a brawling stream.

John Buchan (1875–1940)

Lily of the Valley

From *The English Physician*, 1653

It is under the dominion of Mercury, and therefore strengthens the brain, recruits a weak memory, and makes it strong again: The distilled water dropped into the eyes, helps inflammations there; as also that infirmity which they call the pin and web. The spirit of the flowers distilled in wine, restoreth lost speech, helps the palsy, and is exceedingly good in the apoplexy, comforts the heart and vital spirits. Gerrard saith, that the flowers being close stopped up in a glass, put into an ant-hill, and taken away again a month after, ye shall find liquor in the glass, which, being outwardly applied, helps the gout.

Nicholas Culpeper (1616–1654)

Dragon-flies

From *Our Village*, 1824

May 26th

Walking along these meadows one bright sunny afternoon, a year
or two back, and rather later in the season, I had an opportunity
of noticing a curious circumstance in natural history. Standing
close to the edge of the stream, I remarked a singular appearance
on a large tuft of flags. It looked like bunches of flowers, the
leaves of which seemed dark, yet transparent, intermingled with
brilliant tubes of bright blue or shining green. On examining this
phenomenon more closely, it turned out to be several clusters of
dragon-flies, just emerged from their deformed chrysalis state, and
still torpid and motionless from the wetness of their filmy wings.
Half an hour later we returned to the spot and they were gone.

Mary Russell Mitford (1787–1855)

An Unusual Foster-mother

From *A Shepherd's Life*, 1910

The shepherd remembered another curious incident in Rough's career. At one time when she had a litter of pups at home she was yet compelled to be a great part of the day with the flock of ewes as they could not do without her. The boys just then were bringing up a motherless lamb by hand and they would put it with the sheep, and to feed it during the day were obliged to catch a ewe with milk. The lamb trotted at Caleb's heels like a dog, and one day when it was hungry and crying to be fed, when Rough happened to be sitting on her haunches close by, it occurred to him that Rough's milk might serve as well as a sheep's. The lamb was put to her and took very kindly to its canine foster-mother, wriggling its tail and pushing vigorously with its nose. Rough submitted patiently to the trial, and the result was that the lamb adopted the sheep-dog as its mother and sucked her milk several times every day, to the great admiration of all who witnessed it.

W. H. Hudson (1841–1922)

The Midland Landscape

From *Middlemarch*, 1871

The ride to Stone Court, which Fred and Rosamond took the next morning, lay through a pretty bit of midland landscape, almost all meadows and pastures, with hedgerows still allowed to grow in bushy beauty and to spread out coral fruit for the birds. Little details gave each field a particular physiognomy, dear to the eyes that have looked on them from childhood: the pool in the corner where the grasses were dank and trees leaned whisperingly; the great oak shadowing a bare place in mid-pasture; the high bank where the ash-trees grew; the sudden slope of the old marl-pit making a red background for the burdock; the huddled roofs and ricks of the homestead without a traceable way of approach; the grey gate and fences against the depths of the bordering wood; and the stray hovel, its old, old thatch full of mossy hills and valleys with wondrous modulations of light and shadow such as we travel far to see in later life, and see larger, but not more beautiful. These are the things that make the gamut of joy in landscape to midland-bred souls – the things they toddled among, or perhaps learned by heart standing between their father's knees while he drove leisurely.

George Eliot (1819–1880)

The Importance of Climate

From *The Origin of Species*, 6th edition, 1872

Each species, even where it most abounds, is constantly suffering enormous destruction at some period of its life, from enemies or from competitors for the same place and food; and if these enemies or competitors be in the least degree favoured by any slight change of climate, they will increase in numbers; and as each area is already fully stocked with inhabitants, the other species must decrease. When we travel southward and see a species decreasing in numbers, we may feel sure that the cause lies quite as much in other species being favoured, as in this one being hurt. So it is when we travel northward, but in a somewhat lesser degree, for the number of species of all kinds, and therefore of competitors, decreases northward; hence in going northward, or in ascending a mountain, we far oftener meet with stunted forms, due to the *directly* injurious action of climate, than we do in proceeding southward or in descending a mountain. When we reach the Arctic regions, or snow-capped summits, or absolute deserts, the struggle for life is almost exclusively with the elements.

That climate acts in main part indirectly by favouring other species we clearly see in the prodigious number of plants which in our gardens can perfectly well endure our climate, but which never become naturalised, for they cannot compete with our native plants nor resist destruction by our native animals.

Charles Darwin (1809–1882)

Proportion and Beauty in Plants

From *A Philosophical Enquiry into the Origin of Our Ideas of the Sublime and Beautiful*, 1757

Turning our eyes to the vegetable creation, we find nothing there so beautiful as flowers; but flowers are almost of every sort of shape, and of every sort of disposition; they are turned and fashioned into an infinite variety of forms; and from these forms botanists have given them their names, which are almost as various. What proportion do we discover between the stalks and the leaves of flowers, or between the leaves and the pistils? How does the slender stalk of the rose agree with the bulky head under which it bends? but the rose is a beautiful flower; and can we undertake to say that it does not owe a great deal of its beauty even to that disproportion; the rose is a large flower, yet it grows upon a small shrub; the flower of the apple is very small, and grows upon a large tree; yet the rose and the apple blossom are both beautiful, and the plants that bear them are most engagingly attired, notwithstanding this disproportion. What by general consent is allowed to be a more beautiful object than an orange-tree, nourishing at once with its leaves, its blossoms, and its fruit? but it is in vain that we search here for any proportion between the height, the breadth, or anything else concerning the dimensions of the whole, or concerning the relation of the particular parts to each other.

Edmund Burke (1729–1797)

Upland Country

From *The Thirty-Nine Steps*, 1915

I sat down on the very crest of the pass and took stock of my position.

Behind me was the road climbing through a long cleft in the hills, which was the upper glen of some notable river. In front was a flat space of maybe a mile, all pitted with bog-holes and rough with tussocks, and then beyond it the road fell steeply down another glen to a plain whose blue dimness melted into the distance. To left and right were round-shouldered green hills as smooth as pancakes, but to the south – that is, the left hand – there was a glimpse of high heathery mountains, which I remembered from the map as the big knot of hill which I had chosen for my sanctuary. I was on the central boss of a huge upland country, and could see everything moving for miles. In the meadows below the road half a mile back a cottage smoked, but it was the only sign of human life. Otherwise there was only the calling of plovers and the tinkling of little streams.

John Buchan (1875–1940)

JUNE

A Kingfisher Darting Blue

The Colours of Summer

From *The Real Charlotte*, 1894

It was the first of June, and the gaiety of the spring was nearly gone. The flowers had fallen from the hawthorn, the bluebells and primroses were vanishing as quietly as they came, the meadows were already swarthy, and the breaths of air that sent pale shimmers across them, were full of the unspeakable fragrance of the ripening grass. Under the trees, near Rosemount, the shadowing greenness had saturated the daylight with its gloom, but out among the open pastures and meadows the large grey sky seemed almost bright, and, in the rich sobriety of tone, the red cattle were brilliant spots of colour.

Somerville & Ross
(Edith Somerville, 1858–1949,
and Martin Ross / Violet Florence Martin, 1862–1915)

Delight or Use

From *The Englishman's Flora*, 1958

A delight in plants, above all when their flowers are out (so we talk of 'wild flowers', the part for the whole), seems to us the most natural – and most innocent – and inevitable of emotions. In earlier centuries delight was an ingredient not always present by any means, it was one item in a more practical response. The nature of the response is often revealed in the prosaic names for a beautiful species, or the entire neglect of a beautiful species which did not happen to be useful. Plants (or some plants) were necessary to a degree that we are forgetting. They were not only givers of food, they were nine-tenths of that specialized food we call medicine, they were nine-tenths of all cosmetics and colourings: they possessed, or certain kinds possessed, a powerful *mana*. They could keep malignant influences and weapons of disease from your body, or they could expel them from your body; they could keep malignant beings from your house, your cow-shed, your milk and butter animals – or your god's temple. It was necessary to have a knowledge of the kinds, of when it was right or wrong to collect them, and of the ways and blends in which they were to be employed. So the physic garden was no fancy, no idle fun, but a need of life. Until the end of the Middle Ages, gardens, first of all, were utilitarian. Delight they gave, but incidentally. And beyond the hedges or the walls of the garden, the countryside, again, was not so enjoyable for itself: it was the world's surface which provided grain and leaf and fruit and timber, and many more plants to be collected for the health and protection of the body and spirit, since the garden could not contain all the plants of virtue.

Geoffrey Grigson (1905–1985)

The Prime of the Year

From *Oliver Twist*, 1839

Spring flew swiftly by, and summer came. If the village had been beautiful at first it was now in the full glow and luxuriance of its richness. The great trees, which had looked shrunken and bare in the earlier months, had now burst into strong life and health; and stretching forth their green arms over the thirsty ground, converted open and naked spots into choice nooks, where was a deep and pleasant shade from which to look upon the wide prospect, steeped in sunshine, which lay stretched beyond. The earth had donned her mantle of brightest green; and shed her richest perfumes abroad. It was the prime and vigour of the year; all things were glad and flourishing.

Charles Dickens (1812–1870)

Tree-climbers

From *Wild Life in a Southern County*, 1879

The bark of some of the apple trees peels of itself – that is, the thin outer skin – and insects creep under these brown scales curled at the edges. If you sit down on the elm butt placed here as a seat and watch quietly, before long the little tree-climber will come. He flies to the trunk of the apple tree (other birds fly to the branches), and then proceeds to ascend it, going round it as he rises in a spiral. His claws cling tenaciously to the bark, his tail touches the tree, and seems to act as a support – like what I think the carpenters call a 'knee' – and his head is thrown back so as to enable him to spy into every cranny he passes. After a few turns round the trunk he is off to another tree, to resume the same restless spiral ascent there; and in a minute or so off again to a third; for he never apparently examines one-half of the trunk, though, probably, his eyes, accustomed to the work, see farther than we may imagine. The orchard is never long without a tree-climber: it seems a favourite resort of these birds. They have a habit of rushing quickly a little way up; then pausing, and again creeping swiftly another foot or so, and are so absorbed in their pursuit that they are easily approached and observed.

Richard Jefferies (1848–1887)

A Clear Sky

From *The Vicar of Morwenstow*, 1876

The moist air from the ocean condenses over the land, and envelops it in fine fog or rain. But when the sky is clear, with only floating clouds drifting along it, the sunlight and shadows that fall over the landscape through the vaporous air are exquisite in their delicacy of colour; the sun-gleams soft as primrose, the shadows pure cobalt, tenderly laid on as the bloom on the cheek of a plum.

Rev. Sabine Baring-Gould (1834–1924)

Birds and Rabbits

From *Little House on the Prairie*, 1935

All day long, after their chores were done, Laura and Mary were busy:

In the tall grass they lay still as mice and watched flocks of little prairie chickens running and pecking around their anxiously clucking, smooth brown mothers. They watched striped snakes rippling between the grass stems or lying so still that only their tiny flickering tongues and glittering eyes showed that they were alive. They were garter snakes and would not hurt anybody, but Laura and Mary did not touch them. Ma said snakes were best left alone, because some snakes would bite, and it was better to be safe than sorry.

And sometimes there'd be a great grey rabbit, so still in the lights and shadows of a grass clump that you were near enough to touch him before you saw him. Then, if you were very quiet, you might stand a long time looking at him. His round eyes stared at yours without meaning anything. His nose wiggled, and sunlight was rosy through his long ears, that had delicate veins in them and the softest short fur on their outsides. The rest of his fur was so thick and soft that at last you couldn't help trying, very carefully, to touch it.

Then he was gone in a flash and the place where he had been sitting was hollowed and smooth and still warm from his warm behind.

Laura Ingalls Wilder (1867–1957)

Moths

From *The Peverel Papers*, June 1923

There are other winged things besides nightingales and bats abroad these summer nights. Moths, so silent and ghostly they can scarce be distinguished from the petals of white flowers, float here and there about the garden beds. All day they have each of them slept in some tiny crevice, under stone or leaf, or between the furrows of some rough-barked tree. At night they awake and seek nutriment for themselves, performing at the same time their allotted task in the scheme of things by fertilising night-blooming plants.

The moth is a creature little considered except by collectors. Butterflies are known to all; yet there are many more species of moths than of butterflies in this country, and the study of their dim, mysterious lives is most fascinating.

A common sight at this time of year is the Ghost Moth, which hovers above the fields and hedges at dusk – at one moment a pale, floating shape flitting across our path, then suddenly vanishing. It is usually still within reach of our hand, although invisible, for it only has to alight and fold its wings to disappear in the half-light. The upper side of its wings is mealy-white and glimmering, coming into view when poised, a most perfect disguise of brownish grey.

Some of the day-flying moths are so royally marked and richly coloured as to pass with the casual observer for butterflies. The difference can readily be distinguished by the shape of the body. The butterfly has a waist like a wasp, the moth has none.

Flora Thompson (1876–1947)

Nature's Vistas

From *Observations on the River Wye, and Several Parts of South Wales, &c. Relative Chiefly to Picturesque Beauty; made in the Summer of the Year 1770*

The vistas of art are tame, and formal. They consist of streets; or of trees planted nicely in rows; or some other species of regularity. Nature's vistas are of a different cast. She forms them sometimes of mountains, sometimes of rocks, and sometimes of woods. But all her works even of this formal kind, are the works of a master. If the idea of regularity be impressed on the *general form*, the *parts* are broken with a thousand varieties. Her vistas are models to paint from. In *this*, both the mountains themselves are beautiful; and the perspective combination of them.

William Gilpin (1724–1804)

The Creek

From *Frenchman's Creek*, 1941

Dora discovers the Frenchman's hiding-place:

She followed the track that she had found in the morning, but this time plunging down deep into the woods without hesitation. The birds were astir again, after their noonday silence, and the silent butterflies danced and fluttered, while drowsy bumble bees hummed in the warm air, winging their way to the topmost branches of the trees. Yes, there once again was the glimmer of water that had surprised her. The trees were thinning, she was coming to the bank – and there, suddenly before her for the first time, was the creek, still and soundless, shrouded by the trees, hidden from the eyes of men. She stared at it in wonder, for she had had no knowledge of its existence, this stealthy branch of the parent river creeping into her own property, so sheltered, so concealed by the woods themselves. The tide was ebbing, the water oozing away from the mud flats, and here where she stood was the head of the creek itself, for the stream ended in a trickle, and the trickle in a spring. The creek twisted round a belt of trees, and she began to walk along the bank, happy, fascinated, forgetting her mission, for this discovery was a pleasure quite unexpected, this creek was a source of enchantment, a new escape, better than Navron itself, a place to drowse and sleep, a lotus-land. There was a heron standing in the shadows, solemn and grey, his head sunk in his hooded shoulders, and beyond him a little oyster-catcher pattered in the mud, and then, weird and lovely, a curlew called, and rising from the bank, flew away from her down the creek.

Daphne du Maurier (1907–1989)

The Brock or Badger

From *Pseudodoxia Epidemica*, Chap. V, Of the Badger, 1650

That a Brock or Badger hath the legs on one side shorter then of the other, though an opinion perhaps not very ancient, is yet very generall; received not only by theorists and unexperienced beleevers, but assented unto by most who have the opportunity to behold and hunt them daily. Which notwithstanding upon enquiry I find repugnant unto the three determinators of truth, Authority, Sense, and Reason. For first, Albertus *magnus* speaks dubiously, confessing he could not confirm the verity hereof; but Aldrovand affirmeth plainly, there can be no such inequality observed. And for my own part, upon indifferent enquiry, I cannot discover this difference, although the regardable side be defined, and the brevity by most imputed unto the left.

Again, It seems no easie affront unto reason, and generally repugnant unto the course of nature; for if we survey the totall set of animals, we may in their legs, or organs of progression, observe an equality of length, and parity of numeration; that is, not any to have an odde leg, or the supporters and movers of one side not exactly answered by the other. Although the hinder may be unequal unto the fore and middle legs, as in Frogs, Locusts, and Grasshoppers; or both unto the middle, as in some beetles and spiders, as is determined by Aristotle, *de incessu animalium.* Perfect and viviparous quadrupeds, so standing in their position of pronenesse, that the opposite joints of neighbour legs consist in the same plane; and a line descending from their navell intersects at right angles the axis of the Earth.

Sir Thomas Browne (1605–1682)

Forget-Me-Not *(Myosotis palustris)*

From *Wild Flowers*, 1855

The various traditions which give rise to the popular name of this bright flower throughout Europe, are told by poets and historians. Agnes Strickland says, that Henry of Lancaster, when in exile, gave it to the Duchess of Bretagne, and by placing it on his collar of S. S. with the initial latter of his mot or watchword, 'Souveigne youe de moy,' rendered it the symbol of remembrance. Bishop Mant gives us the traditionary creed more generally received, though certainly less entitled to belief. A lady and a knight were sitting by a river side, when the former wished for the bright blue blossoms to braid among her hair. The knight dashed into the water to gratify her wishes, and gathered the flowers, but was overborne by the strength of the current.

> Then the blossoms blue to the bank he threw
>> Ere he sank in the eddying tide;
> And 'Lady, I'm gone, thine own knight true,
>> Forget me not,' he cried.
> The farewell pledge the lady caught,
>> And hence, as legends say,
> The flower is a sign to awaken thought
>> Of friends who are far away.

Thus say the poets, but the philosophers believe them not; and so one of our great botanists suggests, that after all the flowers owes its name to the beautiful blue petals, which once looked upon are not likely to be forgotten.

Anne Pratt (1806–1893)

Ducks in Society

From *The Devoted Friend*, 1888

The little ducks were swimming about in the pond, looking just like a lot of yellow canaries, and their mother, who was pure white with real red legs, was trying to teach them how to stand on their heads in the water.

'You will never be in the best society unless you can stand on your heads,' she kept saying to them; and every now and then she showed them how it was done. But the little ducks paid no attention to her. They were so young that they did not know what an advantage it is to be in society at all.

Oscar Wilde (1854–1900)

A Vast Museum

From *The Origin of Species*, 6th edition, 1872

The crust of the earth is a vast museum; but the natural collections have been imperfectly made, and only at long intervals of time.

Charles Darwin (1809–1882)

The Story of Elzéard Bouffier

From *The Man Who Planted Trees*, written 1953
Translated by Barbara Bray (1924–2010)

The narrator walks through an 'expanse of bare and monotonous
moorland', 'a landscape of unparalleled desolation', where he meets
the shepherd Elzéard Bouffier:

1913:

When he reached the place he was aiming for, he began making
holes in the ground with his rod, putting an acorn in each and then
covering it up again. He was planting oak trees. I asked him if the
land was his. He said it wasn't. Did he know who the owner was?
No, he didn't. He thought it must be common land, or perhaps
it belonged to people who weren't interested in it. He wasn't
interested in who they were. And so, with great care, he planted
his hundred acorns.

After the midday meal he started sorting more acorns to sow.
I must have been very pressing with my questions, because he
answered them. He'd been planting trees in this wilderness for
three years. He'd planted a hundred thousand of them. Out of
those twenty thousand had come up. Of the twenty thousand he
expected to lose half, because of rodents or the unpredictable ways
of Providence. That still meant ten thousand oaks would grow
where before there had been nothing.

. . . .

1920:

By this time the 1910 oaks were ten years old and taller than both
him and me. They were an impressive sight. I was left literally

speechless, and as he didn't speak either we spent the whole day walking silently through his forest. It was in three sections, and measured eleven kilometres across at its widest point. When you remembered that it had all emerged from the hands and spirit of this one man, without any technical aids, you saw that men could be as efficient as God in other things beside destruction.

. . . .

1933:
He [the shepherd] had a visit from a shocked forest warden who told him he mustn't light fires out of doors in case he endangered the 'natural forest'.

. . . .

1945:
But now all was changed, even the air. Instead of the rough and arid gusts that I had met with before, there was a soft and scented breeze. A sound like water drifted down from the heights: it was the wind in the forests. But the most astonishing thing of all was the sound of water actually flowing into a basin. I saw that the people in the village had built a fountain: it was gushing forth in abundance, and – this was what moved me most – beside it they had planted a lime tree which must have been about four years old. It was already quite sturdy – an indisputable symbol of resurrection.

Jean Giono (1895–1970)

Hungry Fledgelings

From *Diary*, 1906

June 15:

The birds still sing morning and evening, but there is not nearly such a full choir as there was a month ago. The cares and responsibilities of large families of hungry fledgelings make too many demands on the time and attention of the anxious parents.

It is very pretty to see the House Martins sitting in the roadway, collecting mud for their nests. Their short feathered legs look as if they had little white socks on.

I was quite surprised to come upon a bank of beautiful Foxgloves today. These the first I have seen in flower.

Edith Holden (1871–1920)

The Nautilus

From *The Innocents Abroad*, 1869

We saw the usual sharks, blackfish, porpoises, etc., of course, and by and by large schools of Portuguese men-of-war were added to the regular list of sea wonders. Some of them were white and some of a brilliant carmine color. The nautilus is nothing but a transparent web of jelly that spreads itself to catch the wind, and has fleshy-looking strings a foot or two long dangling from it to keep it steady in the water. It is an accomplished sailor and has good sailor judgment. It reefs its sail when a storm threatens or the wind blows pretty hard, and furls it entirely and goes down when a gale blows. Ordinarily it keeps its sail wet and in good sailing order by turning over and dipping it in the water for a moment. Seamen say the nautilus is only found in these waters between the 35th and 45th parallels of latitude.

Mark Twain (1835–1910)

Dawn in the Rookery

From *Wildwood: A Journey Through Trees*, 2007

The sky can seem very pale in summer once you've grown accustomed to the darkness. I could make out the silhouettes of the trees, but the rooks and their nests melted into the general blackness. In the wood, complete silence apart from the occasional rustling further off. Starlight filtered down, strained through the black leaves. Then I heard a tawny owl enter and traverse the wood calling to other, more distant owls, which called back. Even the cuckoo was singing in the dark for a while. As I began to drift in and out of sleep, drugged by bluebells, I felt doubly submerged, a long way beneath the surface on the sea floor of the wood. Once I was woken with a jolt by a sudden mad commotion in the rookery caused, I suppose, by a bad bird dream: a pouncing fox in the skull of a rook that sent a wave of alarm through the canopy. Some rooks took flight and circled briefly in the dark before they settled back. Do birds fly in their sleep? I heard the whisper of wood-pigeon wings as a pair slipped away into the darkness.

Hours later, while the sun was still in the horizon, I drifted back into consciousness to the most raucous of dawn choruses. It was still only ten past four. Rooks are early risers but not as early as crows, which are often already on the wing above my meadows in the hour before dawn. From my rabbit's perspective I was aware that in the birdsong, as in the physical zoning of the wood, there was an under-storey. The sweetness of robins and chiffchaffs descanted subtly from hazel or elder beneath the harsh, relentless chorus of the rooks in the ash-tops. Blackbirds arrowed silently through the shadows. Mist swam into the deep green of my glade through the waving seaweed of nettles, goosegrass, pink campion, bluebells, grasses and ferns. In the foreground, burdock, ground ivy, self-heal and bugle. Further off, layers of vapour hung in the new shoots of the hazel coppice.

Roger Deakin (1943–2006)

Magic

From *The Rainbow*, 1915

She [Ursula] loved the little brooks. Wherever she found a little running water, she was happy. It seemed to make her run and sing in spirit along with it. She could sit for hours by a brook or stream, on the roots of the alders, and watch the water hasten dancing over the stones, or among the twigs of a fallen branch. Sometimes, little fish vanished before they had become real, like hallucinations, sometimes wagtails ran by the water's brink, sometimes other little birds came to drink. She saw a kingfisher darting blue – and then she was very happy. The kingfisher was the key to the magic world: he was witness of the border of enchantment.

D. H. Lawrence (1885–1930)

Eve's Flowers

From 'Carnation', 1918

On those hot days Eve – curious Eve – always carried a flower. She snuffed it, twirled it in her fingers, laid it against her cheek, held it to her lips, tickled Katie's neck with it, and ended, finally, by pulling it to pieces and eating it, petal by petal.

'Roses are delicious, my dear Katie,' she would say, standing in the dim cloak room, with a strange decoration of flowery hats on the hat pegs behind her – 'but carnations are simply divine! They taste like – like – ah well!' And away her little thin laugh flew, fluttering among those huge, strange flower heads on the wall behind her. (But how cruel her little thin laugh was! It had a long sharp beak and claws and two bead eyes, thought fanciful Katie.)

To-day it was a carnation. She brought a carnation to the French class, a deep, deep red one, that looked as though it had been dipped in wine and left in the dark to dry. She held it on the desk before her, half shut her eyes and smiled.

'Isn't it a darling?' said she.

Katherine Mansfield (1888–1923)

Caves

From *The Diary of John Evelyn*, 1644

June: 20

We took hors and rid to see certaine natural Caves, calld Goutiere, neere Colombieres, where there is a spring within the bowels of the Earth very deepe, so excessive cold, that the dropps, meeting with some lapidescent matter, converts them into a hard stone, which hangs about it like Isicles; having many others in the forme of Comfitures and sugar plumms as wee call them.

John Evelyn (1620–1706)

A Caravan of Shrews

From *Meadowland*, 2014

Shrews mate from March, and up to four litters are produced in a year. By sixteen days old the young begin to emerge from the nest, and are said to sometimes follow their mother around in a 'caravan', whereby a young shrew grabs the tail of the shrew in front of it, so the mother takes the lead and her offspring follow in a train.

I would like to see such a caravan. I never have.

John Lewis-Stempel (1961–)

Grip the Raven

From *Barnaby Rudge*, 1841

Grip was by no means an idle or unprofitable member of the humble household. Partly by dint of Barnaby's tuition, and partly by pursuing a species of self-instruction common to his tribe, and exerting his powers of observation to the utmost, he had acquired a degree of sagacity which rendered him famous for miles round. His conversational powers and surprising performances were the universal theme: and as many persons came to see the wonderful raven, and none left his exertions unrewarded – when he condescended to exhibit, which was not always, for genius is capricious – his earnings formed an important item in the common stock. Indeed, the bird himself appeared to know his value well; for though he was perfectly free and unrestrained in the presence of Barnaby and his mother, he maintained in public an amazing gravity, and never stooped to any other gratuitous performances than biting the ankles of vagabond boys (an exercise in which he much delighted), killing a fowl or two occasionally, and swallowing the dinners of various neighbouring dogs, of whom the boldest held him in great awe and dread.

Charles Dickens (1812–1870)

Summer Rain

From *The South Country*, Chapter III, Hampshire, 1909

June puts bronze and crimson on many of her leaves. The maple-leaves and many of the leaves of thorn and bramble and dogwood are rosy; the hazel-leaves are rosy-brown; the herb-robert and parsley are rose-red; the leaves of ash and holly are dark lacquered. The copper beeches, opulently sombre under a faintly yellowed sky, seem to be the sacred trees of the thunder that broods above. Presently the colour of the threat is changed to blue, which soiled white clouds pervade until the whole sky is woolly white and grey and moving north. There is no wind, but there is a roar as of a hurricane in the trees far off; soon it is louder, in the trees not so remote; and in a minute the rain has traversed half-a-mile of woods, and the distant combined roar is swallowed up by the nearer pattering on roof and pane and leaf, the dance of leaves, the sway of branches, the trembling of whole trees under the flood. The rain falls straight upon the hard road, and each drop seems to leap upward from it barbed. Great drops dive among the motionless, dusty nettles. The thunder unloads its ponderous burden upon the resonant floor of the sky; but the sounds of the myriad leaves and grass-blades drinking all but drowns the boom, the splitting roar, and the echo in the hills. When it is over it has put a final sweetness into the blackbird's voice and into the calm of the evening garden when the voice of a singer does but lay another tribute at the feet of the enormous silence.

Edward Thomas (1878–1917)

Jackdaw (Corvus monedula)

From *British Birds*, 1930

The jackdaw is probably just as common as he ever was, while
the chough is rapidly dying out, and the crow and jay and
pie are yearly diminishing in numbers, and the raven, driven
from its inland haunts clings to existence in the wildest and
most inaccessible parts of the coast. The reason of this is that
the jackdaw is more adaptive than other species. He has been
compared in this respect to the house-sparrow, for he can exist
in town as well as country, and readily adapts himself to new
surroundings. The variety of sites he uses for breeding purposes
shows how plastic are his habits. He builds in hollow trees in
woods and parks, in rabbit-burrows, in ruins, church-towers, and
buildings of all kinds; and in holes and crevices in cliffs, whether
inland or facing the sea, where he lives in company with the rock-
pigeon and the puffin.

· · · · · · · · · ·

The social disposition of the jackdaw, and its friendliness towards
other species of its family, is no doubt favourable in the long
run to it; for by mixing with the rooks, both when feeding and
roosting, he comes in for a share of the protection extended to that
bird in most districts. There is also a sentiment favourable to the
jackdaw on account of its partiality for churches and castles: the
'ecclesiastical' daws are safe and fearless of man while soaring and
playing around the sacred buildings in villages and towns; when
they go abroad to forage, and are not with the rooks, there is a
danger for them, and they are, accordingly, wary and shy of man.

W. H. Hudson (1841–1922)

The Crimson Rose

From *The Nightingale and the Rose*, 1888

And when the moon shone in the heavens the nightingale flew to the rose tree, and set her breast against the thorn. All night long she sang with her breast against the thorn, and the cold crystal moon leaned down and listened. All night long she sang, and the thorn went deeper and deeper into her breast, and her life-blood ebbed away from her.

She sang first of the birth of love in the heart of a boy and a girl. And on the topmost spray of the rose tree there blossomed a marvellous rose, petal following petal, as song followed song. Pale was it, at first, as the mist that hangs over the river – pale as the feet of the morning, and silver as the wings of the dawn. As the shadow of a rose in a mirror of silver, as the shadow of a rose in a water-pool, so was the rose that blossomed on the topmost spray of the tree.

But the tree cried to the nightingale to press closer against the thorn. 'Press closer, little nightingale,' cried the tree, 'or the day will come before the rose is finished.'

So the nightingale pressed closer against the thorn, and louder and louder grew her song, for she sang of the birth of passion in the soul of a man and a maid.

And a delicate flush of pink came into the leaves of the rose, like the flush in the face of the bridegroom when he kisses the lips of the bride. But the thorn had not yet reached her heart, so the rose's heart remained white, for only a nightingale's heart's-blood can crimson the heart of a rose.

And the tree cried to the nightingale to press closer against the thorn. 'Press closer, little nightingale,' cried the tree, 'or the day will come before the rose is finished.'

So the nightingale pressed closer against the thorn, and the thorn touched her heart, and a fierce pang of pain shot through her. Bitter, bitter was the pain, and wilder and wilder grew her song, for she sang of the love that is perfected by death, of the love that dies not in the tomb.

And the marvellous rose became crimson, like the rose of the eastern sky. Crimson was the girdle of petals, and crimson as a ruby was the heart.

But the nightingale's voice grew fainter, and her little wings began to beat, and a film came over her eyes. Fainter and fainter grew her song, and she felt something choking her in her throat.

Then she gave one last burst of music. The white moon heard it, and she forgot the dawn, and lingered on in the sky. The red rose heard it, and it trembled all over with ecstasy, and opened its petals to the cold morning air. Echo bore it to her purple cavern in the hills, and woke the sleeping shepherds from their dreams. It floated through the reeds of the river, and they carried its message to the sea.

'Look, look!' cried the tree, 'the rose is finished now;' but the nightingale made no answer, for she was lying dead in the long grass, with the thorn in her heart.

Oscar Wilde (1854–1900)

Mole (*Talpa europaea*)

From *Animal Life of the British Isles*, 1921

However slight may be their personal acquaintance with the Mole himself, his engineering work is only too evident to every possessor of a garden. He may, perchance, live in a neighbour's land, but from time to time we shall find some morning that he has driven a tunnel right across the lawn or the tennis-court, marring its hitherto fair surface with an ugly ridge, and at intervals a little heap of raw earth. If we are sufficiently self-controlled to dissemble our inward rage, we may get some countervailing good out of the calamity. If we bring a garden chair and sit quietly within the range of the newest heap, our quiet watching may be rewarded by sight of the clever little engineer, and we may be restrained from throwing stones at him by the thought that he is seeking to reduce the number of those worm-casts on the lawn that have annoyed us so much.

If the tunnelling work is not yet completed, we shall see a heaving of the fresh heap of soil, and after a short interval the short, black snout of the Mole will be pushed up from the centre to sniff the air and ascertain if it is safe for him to make a fuller appearance. Satisfied that it is so, he exhibits his shoulders and the broad shovel-shaped hands with which he has accomplished all this navigator's work. Now he is right out, even to his ridiculous little tail, and so to speak swimming over the turf – for he cannot walk on his fore-feet, the hands being set sideways for his shovelling work.

Edward Step (1855–1931)

The Breath of Flowers

From *The Essays or Counsels, Civil and Moral*, Of Gardens, 1625

And because the breath of flowers is far sweeter in the air (where it comes and goes like the warbling of music) than in the hand, therefore nothing is more fit for that delight, than to know what be the flowers and plants that do best perfume the air. Roses, damask and red, are fast flowers of their smells; so that you may walk by a whole row of them, and find nothing of their sweetness; yea, though it be in a morning's dew. Bays, likewise, yield no smell as they grow. Rosemary little, nor sweet marjoram. That which above all others yields the sweetest smell in the air, is the violet, especially the white double violet, which comes twice a year, about the middle of April, and about Bartholomew-tide. Next to that is the musk-rose. Then the strawberry-leaves dying, which yield a most excellent cordial smell. Then the flower of the vines; it is a little dust, like the dust of a bent, which grows upon the cluster in the first coming forth. Then sweet-briar. Then wall-flowers, which are very delightful to be set under a parlour or lower chamber window. Then pinks and gilliflowers, specially the matted pink and clove gillyflower. Then the flowers of the lime-tree. Then the honeysuckles, so they be somewhat afar off. Of bean-flowers I speak not, because they are field flowers. But those which perfume the air most delightfully, not passed by as the rest, but being trodden upon and crushed, are three; that is, burnet, wild-thyme, and watermints. Therefore you are to set whole alleys of them, to have the pleasure when you walk or tread.

Francis Bacon (1561–1626)

The Jungle

From *Brazilian Adventure*, 1933

In June 1932 Peter Fleming joined an expedition to solve the
mystery of Colonel Fawcett's disappearance seven years earlier:

We came into Rio at sunset. This must surely be the best time
to do it.

For some hours Brazil had been in sight, a dark-green
formidable outline, a coast (as far as we could see) almost
unscathed by man. The huge cliffs slanted a little backwards, as if
the land had been reined in sharply on the brink of salt perdition.
The charging jungle stopped short only at the sea. I got the
impression of a sub-continent with imperfect self-control.

Peter Fleming (1907–1971)

Man's Precarious Hold

From 'The Empire of the Ants', 1905

Holroyd [the Lancashire engineer] sat on deck in the evening coolness and smoked profoundly and marvelled at Brazil. They were six days up the Amazon, some hundreds of miles from the ocean, and east and west of him there was a horizon like the sea, and to the south nothing but a sand-bank island with some tufts of scrub. The water was always running like a sluice, thick with dirt, animated with crocodiles and hovering birds, and fed by some inexhaustible source of tree trunks; and the waste of it, the headlong waste of it, filled his soul. The town of Alemquer, with its meagre church, its thatched sheds for houses, its discoloured ruins of ampler days, seemed a little thing lost in this wilderness of Nature, a sixpence dropped on Sahara. He was a young man, this was his first sight of the tropics, he came straight from England, where Nature is hedged, ditched, and drained, into the perfection of submission, and he had suddenly discovered the insignificance of man. For six days they had been steaming up from the sea by unfrequented channels; and man had been as rare as a rare butterfly. One saw one day a canoe, another day a distant station, the next no men at all. He began to perceive that man is indeed a rare animal, having but a precarious hold upon this land.

H. G. Wells (1866–1946)

Graceful But Unspellable

From *Journal*, 1866

June 30:

Thunderstorms all day, great claps and lightning running up and down. When it was bright betweentimes great towering clouds behind which the sun put out his shaded horns very clearly and a longish way. Level curds and whey sky after sunset. – Graceful growth of Etzkoltzias or however those unhappy flowers are spelt. Yews and evergreen trees now very thin and putting out their young pale shoots.

Gerard Manley Hopkins (1844–1889)

JULY

To Ramble Through Beautiful Fields

Silence

From *Chronicles of the Hedges*, 1880

The country in July is much less animated to appearance than would be imagined at a time when the length of the days seems favourable to bird and animal life. Yet those who may chance to walk among meadows and cornfields thinking to find more than usual to interest them may possibly return without seeing anything. July conceals so much. The foliage of the trees, just further thickened by the second or summer shoot adding another layer of leaves, hides the lesser birds which frequent them. By waiting and watching, of course, they can be seen, but just in walking past they are invisible. If they have not yet ceased to sing, their notes are not heard so continually. There is, comparatively, silence, and you may go some distance along the hedge without hearing a sound.

Richard Jefferies (1848–1887)

Shepherd's Needle *(Scandix pecten)*

From *Wild Flowers*, 1855

There is something very pleasing in the old English names of many of our wild flowers. They are connected with rural haunts and habits, and bear with the remembrances of those old simplers and herbalists, who, though they might have greatly overrated the virtues of plants, yet found out many things respecting them which have proved of use to succeeding generations. Very often, too, they are significant of some obvious feature of the plant, or some property which distinguishes it. Thus, the Shepherd's Purse which has its seeds in little heart-shaped pouches, formed like the purses of olden times; and the Shepherd's Weather-glass foretells the rain by closing up its petals; and our Shepherd's Needle has very peculiar seed-vessels, growing in clusters of five or six, long, and tapering to a point, and each as large, in some specimens, as a packing needle. The plant has in an earlier stage small clusters of tiny white flowers, and is very abundant in corn-fields in June and July.

Anne Pratt (1806–1893)

Fresh Cut Flowers

From *The Lark*, 1922

Jane's grand plan:

'We will get our living by selling flowers out of the garden. Ourselves. To people who go by and admire. No sending our flowers to market to be sold all crushed and bruised and disheartened. 'Fresh flowers sold here' – that's what's going on the board. No, 'Fresh cut flowers sold here.' I shall paint the board to-morrow. Why, the board for the gate, of course, to show the world what we sell. Let's count the money. I make it fifteen and eight pence.'

'It is fifteen and ninepence halfpenny,' said Lucilla, and added slowly, 'it's quite a good idea, Jane.'

'Out with it,' said Jane, adjusting the little silver tower of her eleven sixpences. 'What's the dreadful drawback?'

'I hate to throw cold water,' said Lucilla, 'but how long will the flowers in our garden last if we sell them like this? You'll be 'sold out,' as the shops say, before the paint's dry on your board.'

'But more flowers will come out.'

'Not fast enough.'

'We could buy flowers at Covent Garden and sell those.'

'Then they wouldn't precisely be fresh-cut, would they?'

'True. How right you always are!'

E. Nesbit (1858–1924)

Lake Wiandermer

From *The Journeys of Celia Fiennes*, 1698

This great water seemes to flow and wave about with the wind or in one motion but it does not ebb and flow like the sea with the tyde, neither does it run so as to be perceivable, tho' at the end of it a little rivulet trills from it into the sea, but it seemes to be a standing lake encompass'd with vast high hills, that are perfect rocks and barren ground of a vast height, from which many little springs out of the rock does bubble up and descend down and fall into this water; notwithstanding great raines the water does not seem much increased, tho' it must be so, then it does draine off more at the end of the Lake; these hills which they call Furness Fells a long row continued some miles, and some of them are call'd Donum Fells and soe from the places they adjoyne to are named, but they hold the whole length of the water which is 10 mile.

Celia Fiennes (1662–1741)

Desertion for a Field

From *A Victorian Poacher: James Hawker's Journal*, 1858

The poacher enlists:

The Aldershot Camp was my home until July 1858. During my stay there I proved beyond doubt that I Could never be trained to Kill Peasants, but Pheasants were another matter. I knew that the Class what trained me to shoot Peasants would kill me or at least imprison me for Killing what God sent for everyman – the pheasants.

So I made up my mind to Desert. Once more I longed to ramble through the Beautiful Fields.

James Hawker (1836–1921)

The Reason Flowers Don't Talk

From *Through the Looking-Glass*, 1871

This time she [Alice] came upon a large flower-bed, with a border of daisies, and a willow-tree growing in the middle.

'O Tiger-lily,' said Alice, addressing herself to one that was waving gracefully about in the wind, 'I *wish* you could talk!'

'We *can* talk,' said the Tiger-lily: 'when there's anybody worth talking to.'

Alice was so astonished that she could not speak for a minute: it quite seemed to take her breath away. At length, as the Tiger-lily only went on waving about, she spoke again, in a timid voice – almost in a whisper. 'And can *all* the flowers talk?'

'As well as *you* can,' said the Tiger-lily. 'And a great deal louder.'

'It isn't manners for us to begin, you know,' said the Rose, 'and I really was wondering when you'd speak! Said I to myself, 'Her face has got *some* sense in it, though it's not a clever one!' Still, you're the right colour, and that goes a long way.'

'I don't care about the colour,' the Tiger-lily remarked. 'If only her petals curled up a little more, she'd be all right.'

Alice didn't like being criticised, so she began asking questions. 'Aren't you sometimes frightened at being planted out here, with nobody to take care of you?'

'There's the tree in the middle,' said the Rose: 'what else is it good for?'

'But what could it do, if any danger came?' Alice asked.
'It says "Bough-wough!"' cried a Daisy: 'that's why its branches are called boughs!'

'Didn't you know *that*?' cried another Daisy, and here they all began shouting together, till the air seemed quite full of little shrill voices.

'Silence, every one of you!' cried the Tiger-lily, waving itself passionately from side to side, and trembling with excitement. 'They know I can't get at them!' it panted, bending its quivering head towards Alice, 'or they wouldn't dare to do it!'

'Never mind!' Alice said in a soothing tone, and stooping down to the daisies, who were just beginning again, she whispered, 'If you don't hold your tongues, I'll pick you!'

There was silence in a moment, and several of the pink daisies turned white.

'That's right!' said the Tiger-lily. 'The daisies are worst of all. When one speaks, they all begin together, and it's enough to make one wither to hear the way they go on!'

'How is it you can all talk so nicely?' Alice said, hoping to get it into a better temper by a compliment. 'I've been in many gardens before, but none of the flowers could talk.'

'Put your hand down, and feel the ground,' said the Tiger-lily. 'Then you'll know why.'

Alice did so. 'It's very hard,' she said, 'but I don't see what that has to do with it.'

'In most gardens,' the Tiger-lily said, 'they make the beds too soft – so that the flowers are always asleep.'

Lewis Carroll (1832–1898)

Clouds at Sunset

From *Rambles Beyond Railways*, 1851

The sky had partially cleared, and the rain had ceased; but huge fantastic masses of cloud, tinged with lurid copper-colour by the setting sun, still towered afar off over the horizon, and were reflected in a deeper hue on the calm surface of the sea, with a perfectness and grandeur that I never remember to have witnessed before.

Wilkie Collins (1824–1889)

White Owls

From *The Natural History and Antiquities of Selborne*, Letter XV to
The Honourable Daines Barrington

Selborne, July 8, 1773

White owls seem not (but in this I am not positive) to hoot
at all: all that clamorous hooting appears to me to come from
the wood kinds. The white owl does indeed snore and hiss in a
tremendous manner; and these menaces well answer the intention
of intimidating: for I have known a whole village up in arms on
such an occasion, imagining the church-yard to be full of goblins
and spectres. White owls also often scream horribly as they fly
along; from this screaming probably arose the common people's
imaginary species of screech-owl, which they superstitiously think
attends the windows of dying persons. The plumage of the remiges
of the wings of every species of owl that I have yet examined is
remarkably soft and pliant. Perhaps it may be necessary that the
wings of these birds should not make much resistance or rushing,
that they may be enabled to steal through the air unheard upon a
nimble and watchful quarry.

Gilbert White (1720–1793)

Flowers in an Orchard

From *A New Orchard and Garden*, 1618

What can your eye desire to see, your ears to heare, your mouth to tast, or your nose to smell, that is not to be had in an Orchard, with abundance of variety? What more delightsome than an infinite variety of sweet smelling flowers? Decking with sundry colours, the green mantle of the earth, the universall mother of us all, so by them bespotted, so dyed, that all the world cannot sample them, and wherein it is more fit to admire the dyer, then imitate his workmanship, colouring not onely the earth, but decking the aire, and sweetening every breath and spirit.

The Rose red, damask, velvet, and double double province Rose, the sweet musk Rose, double and single, the double and single white Rose; The fair and sweet scenting woodbine, double and single, and double double. Purple Cowslip, and double Cowslips; Primrose double and single. The Violet nothing behind the best, for smelling sweetly. A thousand more will provoke your content.

William Lawson (c. 1554–1635)

The Stars

From 'Nature', 1836

If the stars should appear one night in a thousand years, how would men believe and adore; and preserve for many generations the remembrance of the city of God which had been shown! But every night come out these envoys of beauty, and light the universe with their admonishing smile.

The stars awaken a certain reverence, because though always present, they are inaccessible; but all natural objects make a kindred impression, when the mind is open to their influence.

Ralph Waldo Emerson (1803–1882)

the looking-glass. Heaven be praised, he was a dog of birth and breeding! His head was smooth; his eyes were prominent but not gozzled; his feet were feathered; he was the equal of the best-bred cocker in Wimpole Street. He noted with approval the purple jar from which he drank – such are the privileges of rank; he bent his head quietly to have the chain fixed to his collar – such are its penalties. When about this time Miss Barrett observed him staring in the glass, she was mistaken. He was a philosopher, she thought, meditating the difference between appearance and reality. On the contrary, he was an aristocrat considering his points.

Virginia Woolf (1882–1941)

Dogs Are Not Equal

From *Flush: A Biography*, 1933

At Three Mile Cross Flush had mixed impartially with tap-room dogs and the Squire's greyhounds; he had known no difference between the tinker's dog and himself. Indeed it is probable that the mother of his child, though by courtesy called Spaniel, was nothing but a mongrel, eared in one way, tailed in another. But the dogs of London, Flush soon discovered, are strictly divided into different classes. Some are chained dogs; some run wild. Some take their airings in carriages and drink from purple jars; others are unkempt and uncollared and pick up a living in the gutter. Dogs therefore, Flush began to suspect, differ; some are high, others low; and his suspicions were confirmed by snatches of talk held in passing with the dogs of Wimpole Street. 'See that scallywag? A mere mongrel!

An Eclipse

From *Kilvert's Diary*, 1870

12 July

After tea we all strolled out into the garden and stood on the high terrace to see the eclipse. It had just begun. The shadow was slowly steadily stretching over the large bright moon and had eaten away a small piece at the lower left side. It was very strange and solemn to see the shadow stealing gradually on till half the moon was obscured. As the eclipse went on the bright fragment of the moon seemed to change colour, to darken and redden. We were well placed for seeing the eclipse and the night was beautiful, and most favourable, not a cloud in the way. We watched the eclipse till all that was left of the moon was a point of brightness like a large three-cornered star. Then it vanished altogether. Some people said they could discern the features of the moon's face through the black shadow.

Francis Kilvert (1840–1879)

The Fall of the Swallow

From *Wild Wales*, 1862

The Fall of the Swallow is not a majestic single fall, but a succession of small ones. First there are a number of little foaming torrents, bursting through rocks about twenty yards above the promontory on which I stood. Then come two beautiful rolls of white water, dashing into a pool a little way above the promontory; then there is a swirl of water round its corner into a pool below on its right, black as death, and seemingly of great depth; then a rush through a very narrow outlet into another pool, from which the water clamours away down the glen. Such is the Rhaiadr y Wennol, or Swallow Fall; called so from the rapidity with which the waters rush and skip along.

George Borrow (1803–1881)

Archimedes

From *The Sword in the Stone*, 1938

Merlyn took off his pointed hat when he came into this extraordinary chamber, because it was too high for the roof, and immediately there was a scamper in one of the dark corners and a flap of soft wings, and a young tawny owl was sitting on the black skull-cap which protected the top of his head.

'Oh, what a lovely owl!' cried the Wart.

But when he went up to it and held out his hand, the owl grew half as tall again, stood up as stiff as a poker, closed its eyes so that there was only the smallest slit to peep through, as one is in the habit of doing when told to shut one's eyes at hide-and-seek, and said in a doubtful voice:

'There is no owl.'

Then it shut its eyes entirely and looked the other way.

'It's only a boy,' said Merlyn.

'There is no boy,' said the owl hopefully, without turning round.

T. H. White (1906–1964)

The Rain

From *Observations on the River Wye, and Several Parts of South Wales, &c. Relative Chiefly to Picturesque Beauty; made in the Summer of the Year 1770*

I must however premise, how ill-qualified I am to do justice to the banks of the Wye, were it only from having seen them under the circumstance of a continued rain; which began early in the day, before one third of our voyage was performed.

It is true, scenery *at hand* suffers less under such a circumstance, than scenery at a distance; which it totally obscures.

The picturesque eye also, in quest of beauty, finds it almost in every incident, and under every appearance of nature. Her works, and all her works, must ever, in some degree, be beautiful. Even the rain gave a gloomy grandeur to many of the scenes; and by throwing a veil of obscurity over the removed banks of the river, introduced, now and then, something like a pleasing distance. Yet still it hid greater beauties; and we could not help regretting the loss of those broad lights, and deep shadows, which would have given so much lustre to the whole; and which, ground like this, is, in a peculiar manner, adapted to receive.

William Gilpin (1724–1804)

Conclusion

From *The Origin of Species*, 6th edition, 1872

It is interesting to contemplate a tangled bank, clothed with many plants of many kinds, with birds singing on the bushes, with various insects flitting about, and with worms crawling through the damp earth, and to reflect that these elaborately constructed forms, so different from each other, and dependent upon each other in so complex a manner, have all been produced by laws acting around us. These laws, taken in the largest sense, being Growth with Reproduction; Inheritance which is almost implied by reproduction; Variability from the indirect and direct action of the conditions of life, and from use and disuse; a Ratio of Increase so high as to lead to a Struggle for Life, and as a consequence to Natural Selection, entailing Divergence of Character and the Extinction of less improved forms. Thus, from the war of nature, from famine and death, the most exalted object which we are capable of conceiving, namely, the production of the higher animals, directly follows. There is grandeur in this view of life, with its several powers, having been originally breathed by the Creator into a few forms or into one; and that, whilst this planet has gone circling on according to the fixed law of gravity, from so simple a beginning endless forms most beautiful and most wonderful have been, and are being evolved.

Charles Darwin (1809–1882)

War Against Donkeys

From *David Copperfield*, 1850

David's aunt protects her green:

To this hour I don't know whether my aunt had any lawful right of way over that patch of green; but she had settled it in her own mind that she did, and it was all the same to her. The one great outrage of her life, demanding to be constantly avenged, was the passage of a donkey over the immaculate spot. In whatever occupation she was engaged, however interesting to her the conversation in which she was taking part, the donkey turned the current of her ideas in a moment, and she was upon him straight. Jugs of water, and watering-pots, were kept in secret places, ready to be discharged on the offending boys; sticks were laid in ambush behind the door; sallies were made at all hours; and incessant war prevailed. Perhaps this was an agreeable excitement to the donkey-boys; or perhaps the more sagacious of the donkeys, understanding how the case stood, delighted with constitutional obstinacy in coming that way.

Charles Dickens (1812–1870)

A Small and Outraged Dog

From *The Irish R.M.*, 1928

Mrs. Knox's woolly dog was the sole occupant of the dining-room when I entered it; he was sitting on his mistress's chair, with all the air of outrage peculiar to a small and self-important dog when routine has been interfered with.

Somerville & Ross
(Edith Somerville, 1858–1949,
and Martin Ross / Violet Florence Martin, 1862–1915)

Cormorants

From *The Peverel Papers*, August, 1923

Presently a pair of cormorants winged heavily out from the river, settled themselves upon two stakes a few yards out to sea, and commenced their toilet. First one, then the other, would open a sooty wing, stretch it out to its full width, and fan it gently in the warm air to dry it. Evidently they had been upriver with the tide, and had good success with their fishing, for there was an unmistakable air of well-content about their attitude as they sat, alternately drowsing and preening, in the sun.

At close quarters the cormorant is even more sinister looking than in flight. With its hunched figure, like that of a deformed black giant among the innocent whiteness of the gulls, its hooked claws and eagle beak, it looks the very emblem of the evil it was once supposed to be.

There is something primitive looking, too, about its appearance; it seems a survival of some ruder, wilder era.

Flora Thompson (1876–1947)

From *The Charm of Birds*, 1927

Cormorants have a peculiar habit with their wings: they will stand on a rock for a long time with the wings outspread and motionless, as if they represented something in heraldry.

Sir Edward Grey (1862–1933)

A Pure Crystalline Stream

From *The Compleat Angler*, Part II, 1676

[The river *Dove*] is so called from the swiftness of its current, and that swiftness occasion'd by the declivity of its course, and by being so straitned in that course betwixt the Rocks; by which, and those very high ones, it is, hereabout, for four or five Miles, confin'd into a very narrow stream. A River that from a contemptible Fountain (which I can cover with my Hat) by the confluence of other Rivers, Rivulets, Brooks, and Rills, is swell'd, (before it falls into *Trent*, a little below *Eggington*, where it loses the name) to such a breadth and depth as to be in most places navigable, were not the passage frequently interrupted with Fords and Wires; and has as fertile Bancks as any River in *England*, none excepted. And this River, from its head for a Mile or two, is a black water (as all the rest of the *Derby-shire* Rivers of note originally are, for they all spring from the Mosses); but is in a few Miles travel so clarified by the addition of several clear, and very great springs (bigger than it self) which gush out of the Lime-stone Rocks, that before it comes to my House, which is but six, or seven Miles from its source, you will find it one of the purest Chrystalline streams you have seen.

Charles Cotton (1630–1687)

The Snail

From 'Kew Gardens', 1919

In the oval flower bed the snail, whose shell had been stained red, blue, and yellow for the space of two minutes or so, now appeared to be moving very slightly in its shell, and next began to labour over the crumbs of loose earth which broke away and rolled down as it passed over them. It appeared to have a definite goal in front of it, differing in this respect from the singular high stepping angular green insect who attempted to cross in front of it, and waited for a second with its antennæ trembling as if in deliberation, and then stepped off as rapidly and strangely in the opposite direction. Brown cliffs with deep green lakes in the hollows, flat, blade-like trees that waved from root to tip, round boulders of grey stone, vast crumpled surfaces of a thin crackling texture – all these objects lay across the snail's progress between one stalk and another to his goal.

. . . .

The snail had now considered every possible method of reaching his goal without going round the dead leaf or climbing over it. Let alone the effort needed for climbing a leaf, he was doubtful whether the thin texture which vibrated with such an alarming crackle when touched even by the tip of his horns would bear his weight; and this determined him finally to creep beneath it, for there was a point where the leaf curved high enough from the ground to admit him.

Virginia Woolf (1882–1941)

Common Lizard (*Lacerta vivipara*)

From *Animal Life of the British Isles*, 1921

Sitting on a sunny, heather-clad hillside it will not be long, probably, before we see the active little Common Lizard peeping at us from under cover or leaping swiftly over the crowded plants. Its movements are so rapid that it is not at all easy to follow them in detail, or even to catch one for closer examination. It can run nimbly enough with a gliding motion, for the body and tail are scarcely lifted from the ground; but the principal mode of progression is to shoot forwards horizontally from one tuft of herbage to the next. They run with as much facility over the shoots of heather or heath, and their long, delicate fingers and toes secure them as sure a landing as that of the Squirrel leaping from branch to branch. When we have hit upon a spot and seen several Lizards thus active a good plan is to sit down quietly for a time, and keep our eyes on a patch of sand that is fully exposed to sunshine. In a little while a Lizard, maybe two or three Lizards, will appear from under the heather or other plants and bask in the sun.

Edward Step (1855–1931)

Two Roads

From *Silent Spring*, 1962

We stand now where two roads diverge. But unlike the roads in Robert Frost's familiar poem, they are not equally fair. The road we have long been travelling is deceptively easy, a smooth superhighway on which we progress with great speed, but at its end lies disaster. The other fork of the road – the one 'less travelled by' offers our last, our only chance to reach a destination that assures the preservation of our earth.

The choice, after all, is ours to make. If, having endured much, we have at last asserted our 'right to know', and if, knowing, we have concluded that we are being asked to take senseless and frightening risks, then we should no longer accept the counsel of those who tell us that we must fill our world with poisonous chemicals; we should look about and see what other course is open to us.

Rachel Carson (1907–1964)

The View From Moosewood Lake

From *The Maine Woods*, The Allegash and East Branch, 1857

The clouds breaking away a little, we had a glorious wild view, as we ascended, of the broad lake with its fluctuating surface and numerous forest-clad islands, extending beyond our sight both north and south, and the boundless forest undulating away from its shores on every side, as densely packed as a rye-field, and enveloping nameless mountains in succession; but above all, looking westward over a large island, was visible a very distant part of the lake, though we did not then suspect it to be Moosehead, – at first a mere broken white line seen through the tops of the island trees, like hay-caps, but spreading to a lake when we got higher. Beyond this we saw what appears to be called Bald Mountain on the map, some twenty-five miles distant, near the sources of the Penobscot. It was a perfect lake of the woods. But this was only a transient gleam, for the rain was not quite over.

Looking southward, the heavens were completely overcast, the mountains capped with clouds, and the lake generally wore a dark and stormy appearance, but from its surface just north of Sugar Island, six or eight miles distant, there was reflected upward to us through the misty air a bright blue tinge from the distant unseen sky of another latitude beyond. They probably had a clear sky then at Greenville, the south end of the lake. Standing on a mountain in the midst of a lake, where would you look for the first sign of approaching fair weather?

Not into the heavens, it seems, but into the lake.

Henry David Thoreau (1817–1862)

Francie's Walk

From *The Real Charlotte*, 1894

In front of her spread a long, low wood, temptingly cool and green, with a gate pillared by tall fir-trees, from which, as she lifted the latch, a bevy of wood-pigeons dashed out startling her with the sudden frantic clapping of their wings. It was a curious wood – very old, judging by its scattered knots of hoary, weather-twisted pine-trees; very young, judging by the growth of ash saplings and slender larches that made dense every inch of space except where rides had been cut through them for the woodcock shooting. Francie walked along the quiet path, thinking little of the beauty that surrounded her, but unconsciously absorbing its rich harmonious stillness. The little grey rabbits did not hear her coming, and hopped languidly across the path, 'for all the world like toys from Robinson's,' thought Francie; the honeysuckle hung in delicious tangle from tree to tree; the wood-pigeons crooned shrilly in the fir-trees, and every now and then a bumble-bee started from a clover blossom in the grass with a deep resentful note, as when one plucks the lowest string of a violoncello.

Somerville & Ross
(Edith Somerville, 1858–1949,
and Martin Ross / Violet Florence Martin, 1862–1915)

The Lizard

From *Rambles Beyond Railways*, 1851

On each side of us, precipice over precipice, cavern within cavern, rose the great cliffs protecting the land against the raging sea. Three hundred feet beneath, the foam was boiling far out over a reef of black rocks. Above and around, flocks of sea-birds flew in ever lengthening circles, or perched flapping their wings and sunning their plumage, on ledges of riven stone below us. Every object forming the wide sweep of the view was on the vastest and most majestic scale. The wild varieties of form in the jagged line of rocks stretched away eastward and westward, as far as the eye could reach; black shapeless masses of mist scowled over the whole landward horizon; the bright blue sky at the opposite point was covered with towering white clouds which moved and changed magnificently; the tossing and raging of the great bright sea was sublimely contrasted by the solitude and tranquillity of the desert, overshadowed land – while ever and ever, sounding as they first sounded when the morning stars sang together, the rolling waves and the rushing wind pealed out their primeval music over the whole scene!

Wilkie Collins (1824–1889)

After Rain

From *A Month in the Country*, 1980

Tom Birkin's first morning at Oxgodby:

The rain had ceased and dew glittered on the graveyard grass, gossamer drifted down air-currents, a pair of blackbirds picked around after insects, a thrush was singing where I could see him in one of the ash trees. And beyond lay the pasture I had crossed on my way from the station (with a bell-tent pitched near a stream) then more fields rising towards a dark rim of hills. And, as it lightened, a vast and magnificent landscape unfolded. I turned away; it was immensely satisfying.

J. L. Carr (1912–1994)

The Season for Heffalumps

From *Winnie-the-Pooh*, 1926

One day when Christopher Robin and Winnie-the-Pooh and Piglet were all talking together, Christopher Robin finished the mouthful he was eating and said carelessly: 'I saw a Heffalump to-day, Piglet.'

'What was it dong?' asked Piglet.

'Just lumping along,' said Christopher Robin. 'I don't think it saw me.'

'I saw one once,' said Piglet. 'At least I think I did,' he said. 'Only perhaps it wasn't.'

'So did I,' said Pooh, wondering what a Heffalump was like.

'You don't often see them,' said Christopher Robin carelessly.

'Not now,' said Piglet.

'Not at this time of year,' said Pooh.

A. A. Milne (1882–1956)

The Swift (*Cypselus apus*)

From *British Birds in their Haunts*, 1909

The Swift is, perhaps, the strongest and swiftest, not merely of the Swallow tribe, but of all birds; hence a voyage from Southern Africa to England is performed without overtaxing its strength. It stands in no need of rest after this prodigious flight, but immediately on its arrival starts with a right good will on its pursuit of food, as if its journey had been but a pleasant course of training for its daily vocation.

With respect to temperature, however, its powers of endurance are limited; it never proceeds far northwards, and occasionally even suffers from unseasonably severe weather in the temperate climates where it fixes its summer residence. Mr F. Smith, of the British Museum, related in the *Zoologist*, that, at Deal, on the eighth of July, 1856, after a mild but wet day, the temperature suddenly fell till it became disagreeably cold. The Swifts were sensibly affected by the atmospheric change; they flew unsteadily, fluttered against the walls of the houses, and some even flew into open windows.

Rev. C. A. Johns (1811–1874)

Feverfew

From *The Herball*, 1597

Feverfew bringeth forth many little round stalkes, divided into certaine branches. The leaves are tender, diversely torne and jagged, and nickt on the edges like the first and nethermost leaves of Coriander, but greater. The floures stand on the tops of the branches, with a small pale of white leaves, set round about a yellow ball or button, like the wild field Daisie. The root is hard and tough: the whole plant is of a light whitish greene colour, of a strong smell, and bitter taste.

The common single Feverfew growth in hedges, gardens, and about old wals, it joyeth to grow among rubbish. There is oftentimes found when it is digged up a little cole under the strings of the root, and never without it, whereof *Cardane* in his booke of Subtilties setteth down divers vaine and trifling things.

Feverfew dried and made into a pouder, and two drams of it taken with hony or sweet wine, purgeth by siege melancholy and flegme; wherefore it is very good for them that are giddie in the head, or which have the turning called *Vertigo*, that is, a swimming and turning in the head. Also it is good for such as be melancholike, sad, pensive, and without speech.

John Gerard (1545–1612)

The River

From *The Last of the Mohicans*, 1826

The vast canopy of woods spread itself to the margin of the river, overhanging the water, and shadowing its dark current with a deeper hue. The rays of the sun were beginning to grow less fierce, and the intense heat of the day was lessened, as the cooler vapors of the springs and fountains rose above their leafy beds, and rested in the atmosphere.

James Fenimore Cooper (1789–1851)

AUGUST

A Glimpse of Heathery Mountains

A Humble-bee

From *Bevis: The Story of a Boy*, 1882

The sunburnt woodbine, the oaks dotted with coppery leaves
where the second shoot appeared, the ash-poles rising from the
hollow stoles, and whose pale sprays touching above formed a
green surface, hazel with white nuts, stiff, ragged thistles on the
stream bank, burrs with brown-tipped hooks, the hard dry ground,
all silent, fixed, held in the light.

The sun slipped through the sky like a yacht under the shore
where the light wind coming over a bank just fills the sails, but
leaves the surface smooth. Through the smooth blue the sun
slipped silently, and no white fleck of foam cloud marked his
speed. But in the deep narrow channel of the streamlet there was
a change – the tiny trickle of water was no longer illumined by the
vertical beams, a slight slant left it to run in shadow.

Burr! came a humble-bee whose drone was now put out as
he went down among the grass and leaves, now rose again as he
travelled. Burr! The faintest breath of air moved without rustling
the topmost leaves of the oaks. The humble-bee went on, and
disappeared behind the stoles.

Richard Jefferies (1848–1887)

The Young Goshawk

From *H is for Hawk*, 2014

The feathers down her front are the colour of sunned newsprint, of tea-stained paper, and each is marked darkly towards its tip with a leaf-bladed spearhead, so from her throat to her feet she is patterned with a shower of falling raindrops. Her wings are the colour of stained oak, their covert feathers edges in palest teak, barred flight-feathers folded quietly beneath. And there's a strange grey tint to her that is felt, rather than seen, a kind of silvery light like a rainy sky reflected from the surface of a river. She looks new. Looks as if the world cannot touch her. As if everything that exists and is observed rolls off her like drops of water from her oiled and close-packed feathers. And the more I sit with her, the more I marvel at how reptilian she is. The lucency of her pale, round eyes. The waxy skin about her Bakelite-black beak. The way she snakes her small head from side to side to focus on distant objects. Half the time she seems as alien as a snake, a thing hammered of metal and scales and glass. But then I see the ineffably birdlike things about her, familiar qualities that turn her into something lovable and close. She scratches her fluffy chin with one awkward taloned foot; sneezes when bits of errant down get up her nose. And when I look up again she seems neither bird nor reptile, but a creature shaped by a million years of evolution for a life she's not yet lived.

Helen Macdonald (1970–)

oad?

From *Martin Chuzzlewit*, 1844

Montague Tigg, or Tigg Montague, takes the footpath:

The last rays of the sun were shining in, aslant, making a path of golden light along the stems and branches in its range, which, even as he looked, began to die away, yielding gently to the twilight that came creeping on. It was so very quiet that the soft and stealthy moss about the trunks of some old trees, seemed to have grown out of the silence, and to be its proper offspring. Those other trees which were subdued by blasts of wind in winter time, had not quite tumbled down, but being caught by others, lay all bare and scathed across their leafy arms, as if unwilling to disturb the general repose by the crash of their fall. Vistas of silence opened everywhere, into the heart and innermost recesses of the wood; beginning with the likeness of an aisle, a cloister, or a ruin open to the sky; then tangling off into a deep green rustling mystery, through which gnarled trunks, and twisted boughs, and ivy-covered stems, and trembling leaves, and bark-stripped bodies of old trees stretched out at length, were faintly seen in beautiful confusion.

As the sunlight died away, and evening fell upon the wood, he entered it. Moving, here and there a bramble or a drooping bough which stretched across his path, he slowly disappeared.

Charles Dickens (1812–1870)

Wayfarers All

From *The Wind in the Willows*, 1908

The Water Rat was restless, and he did not exactly know why. To all appearance the summer's pomp was still at fullest height, and although in the tilled acres green had given way to gold, though rowans were reddening, and the woods were dashed here and there with a tawny fierceness, yet light and warmth and colour were still present in undiminished measure, clean of any chilly premonitions of the passing year. But the constant chorus of the orchards and hedges had shrunk to a casual evensong from a few yet unwearied performers; the robin was beginning to assert himself once more; and there was a feeling in the air of change and departure. The cuckoo, of course, had long been silent; but many another feathered friend, for months a part of the familiar landscape and its small society, was missing too, and it seemed that the ranks thinned steadily day by day. Rat, ever observant of all winged movement, saw that it was taking daily a southing tendency; and even as he lay in bed at night he thought he could make out, passing in the darkness overhead, the beat and quiver of impatient pinions, obedient to the peremptory call.

Nature's Grand Hotel has its Season, like the others. As the guests one by one pack, pay, and depart, and the seats at the *table-d'hôte* shrink pitifully at each succeeding meal; as suites of rooms are closed, carpets taken up, and waiters sent away; those boarders who are staying on, *en pension*, until the next year's full re-opening, cannot help being somewhat affected by all these flittings and farewells, this eager discussion of plans, routes, and fresh quarters, this daily shrinkage in the stream of comradeship. One gets unsettled, depressed, and inclined to be querulous. Why this craving for change? Why not stay on quietly here, like us, and be jolly? You don't know this hotel out of the season, and what fun we have among ourselves, we fellows who remain and see the whole interesting year out. All very true, no doubt, the others always reply; we quite envy you – and some other year perhaps – but just now we have engagements – and there's the bus at the door – our time is up! So they depart, with a smile and a nod, and we miss them, and feel resentful. The Rat was a self-sufficing sort of animal, rooted to the land, and, whoever went, he stayed; still, he could not help noticing what was in the air, and feeling some of its influence in his bones.

. . . .

Footsteps fell on his ear, and the figure of one that walked somewhat wearily came into view; and he saw that it was a Rat, and a very dusty one. The wayfarer, as he reached him, saluted

with a gesture of courtesy that had something foreign about it –
hesitated a moment – then with a pleasant smile turned from the
track and sat down by his side in the cool herbage. He seemed
tired, and the Rat let him rest unquestioned, understanding
something of what was in his thoughts; knowing, too, the value all
animals attach at times to mere silent companionship, when the
weary muscles slacken and the mind marks time.

The wayfarer was lean and keen-featured, and somewhat bowed
at the shoulders; his paws were thin and long, his eyes much
wrinkled at the corners, and he wore small gold ear rings in his
neatly-set well-shaped ears. His knitted jersey was of a faded
blue, his breeches, patched and stained, were based on a blue
foundation, and his small belongings that he carried were tied up
in a blue cotton handkerchief.

Kenneth Grahame (1859–1932)

The Room of Roots

From *Titus Groan*, 1946

The twins, the Ladies Cora and Clarice, invite Steerpike
to their chambers:

If the name of the room was unusual there was no doubt about it
being apt. It was certainly a room of roots. Not of a few simple,
separate formations, but of a thousand branching, writhing,
coiling, intertwining, diverging, converging, interlacing limbs
whose origin even Steerpike's quick eyes were unable for some
time to discover.

He found eventually that the thickening stems converged at
a tall, narrow aperture on the far side of the room, through the
upper half of which the sky was pouring a grey, amorphous light.
It seemed at first as though it would be impossible to stir at all
in this convoluting meshwork, but Steerpike was amazed to see
that the twins were moving about freely in the labyrinth. Years
of experience had taught them the possible approaches to the
window. They had already reached it and were looking out into the
evening. Steerpike made an attempt at following them, but was
soon inextricably lost in the writhing maze. Wherever he turned he
was faced with a network of weird arms that rose and fell, dipped
and clawed, motionless yet alive with serpentine rhythms.

Yet the roots were dead. Once the room must have been filled with earth, but now, suspended for the most part in the higher reaches of the chamber, the thread-like extremities clawed impotently at the air. Nor was it enough that Steerpike should find a room so incongruously monopolized, but that every one of these twisting terminals should be hand-painted was even more astonishing. The various main limbs and their wooden tributaries, even down to the minutest rivulet of root, were painted in their own especial colours, so that it appeared as though seven coloured boles had forced their leafless branches through the window, yellow, red and green, violet and pale blue, coral pink and orange. The concentration of effort needed for the execution of this work must have been considerable, let alone the most almost superhuman difficulties and vexations that must have resulted from the efforts to establish among the labyrinthic entanglements of the finer roots, which tendril belonged to which branch, which branch to which limb, and which limb to which trunk, for only after discovering its source could its correct colour be applied.

The idea had been that birds on entering should choose those roots whose colours most nearly approximated to their own plumage, or if they preferred it to nest among roots whose hue was complementary to their own.

Mervyn Peake (1911–1968)

The Fall of Fiers

From *Journey to the Western Islands of Scotland*, 1773, published 1775

Towards evening we crossed, by a bridge, the river which makes the celebrated fall of Fiers. The country at the bridge strikes the imagination with all the gloom and grandeur of Siberian solitude. The way makes a flexure, and the mountains, covered with trees, rise at once on the left hand and in the front. We desired our guides to shew us the fall, and dismounting, clambered over very rugged crags, till I began to wish that our curiosity might have been gratified with less trouble and danger. We came at last to a place where we could overlook the river, and saw a channel torn, as it seems, through black piles of stone, by which the stream is obstructed and broken, till it comes to a very steep descent, of such dreadful depth, that we were naturally inclined to turn aside our eyes.

But we visited the place at an unseasonable time, and found it divested of its dignity and terror. Nature never gives every thing at once. A long continuance of dry weather, which made the rest of the way easy and delightful, deprived us of the pleasure expected from the fall of Fiers. The river having now no water but what the springs supply, showed us only a swift current, clear and shallow, fretting over the asperities of the rocky bottom, and we were left to exercise our thoughts, by endeavouring to conceive the effect of a thousand streams poured from the mountains into one channel, struggling for expansion in a narrow passage, exasperated by rocks rising in their way, and at last discharging all their violence of waters by a sudden fall through the horrid chasm.

Samuel Johnson (1709–1784)

The Devil's Jumps

From *Rural Rides*, 1823

August 7th

At Churt I had, upon my left, three hills out upon the common, called the Devil's Jumps. The Unitarians will not believe in the Trinity, because they cannot account for it. Will they come here to Churt, go and look at these 'Devil's Jumps,' and account to me for the placing of these three hills, in the shape of three rather squat sugar-loaves, along in a line upon this heath, or the placing of a rock-stone upon the top of one of them as big as a church tower? For my part, I cannot account for this placing of these hills. That they should have been formed by mere chance is hardly to be believed. How could waters rolling about have formed such hills? How could such hills have bubbled up from beneath? But, in short, it is all wonderful alike: the stripes of loam running down through the chalk-hills; the circular parcels of loam in the midst of chalk-hills; the lines of flint running parallel with each other horizontally along the chalk-hills; the flints placed in circles as true as a hair in the chalk-hills; the layers of stone at the bottom of hills of loam; the chalk first soft, then some miles further on, becoming chalk-stone; then, after another distance, becoming burr-stone, as they call it; and at last becoming hard, white stone, fit for any buildings; the sand-stone at Hindhead becoming harder and harder till it becomes very nearly iron in Herefordshire, and quite iron in Wales; but, indeed, they once dug iron out of this very Hindhead. The clouds, coming and settling upon the hills, sinking down and creeping along, at last coming out again in springs, and those becoming rivers. Why, it is all equally wonderful.

William Cobbett (1763–1835)

The Scene Without

From *Mansfield Park*, 1814

The scene without, where all that was solemn and soothing, and
lovely, appeared in the brilliancy of an unclouded night, and the
contrast of the deep shade of the woods. Fanny spoke her feelings.
'Here's harmony!' said she; 'Here's repose! Here's what may leave
all Painting and all Music behind, and what Poetry only can
attempt to describe! Here's what may tranquillize every care, and
lift the heart to rapture! When I look out on such a night as this,
I feel as if there could be neither wickedness nor sorrow in the
world; and there certainly would be less of both if the sublimity of
Nature were more attended to, and people were carried more out
of themselves by contemplating such a scene.'

Jane Austen (1775–1817)

Water-bugs

From *The Story of My Boyhood and Youth*, 1913

We were great admirers of the little black water-bugs. Their whole lives seemed to be play, skimming, swimming, swirling, and waltzing together in little groups on the edge of the lake and in the meadow springs, dancing to music we never could hear. The long-legged skaters, too, seemed wonderful fellows, shuffling about on top of the water, with air-bubbles like little bladders tangled under their hairy feet; and we often wished that we also might be shod in the same way to enable us to skate on the lake in summer as well as in icy winter. Not less wonderful were the boatmen, swimming on their backs, pulling themselves along with a pair of oar-like legs.

John Muir (1838–1914)

A Charm of Starlings

From *Wild Life in a Southern County*, 1879

In the thick foliage of this belt of firs the starlings love to roost. If you should be passing along any road – east, north, west, or south – a mile or two distant, as the sun is sinking and evening approaching, suddenly there will come a rushing sound in the air overhead: it is a flock of starlings flying in their determined manner straight for the distant copse. From every direction these flocks converge upon it: some large, some composed only of a dozen birds, but all with the same intent. If the country chances to be open, the hedges low, and the spectator on a rise so as to see over some distance, he may observe several such flights at the same time. Rooks, in returning to roost fly in long streams, starlings in numerous separate divisions. This is especially noticeable in summer, when the divisions are composed of fewer birds: in winter the starlings congregate in larger bodies.

It would appear that after the young birds are able to fly they flock together in parties by themselves, the old birds clubbing together also, but all meeting at night. The parties of young birds are easily distinguished by their lighter colour. This may not be an invariable rule (for the birds to range themselves according to age), but it is the case frequently. Viewed from a spot three or four fields away, the copse in the evening seems to be overhung by a long dark cloud like a bar of mist, while the sky is clear and no dew has yet risen. The resemblance to a cloud is so perfect that anyone – not thinking of such things – may for the time be deceived, and wonder why a cloud should descend and rest over that particular spot. Suddenly, the two ends of the extended black bar contract and the middle swoops down in the shape of an inverted cone, much resembling a waterspout, and in a few seconds the cloud pours itself into the trees. Another minute, and a black streak shoots upwards, spreads like smoke, parts in two, and wheels round back into the firs again.

On approaching it this apparent cloud is found to consist of thousands of starlings, the noise of whose calling to each other is indescribable – the country folk call it a 'charm,' meaning a noise made up of innumerable lesser sounds, each interfering with the other. The vastness of these flocks is hardly credible until seen; in winter the bare trees on which they alight become suddenly quite black.

Richard Jefferies (1848–1887)

Prologue

From *Land's End: A Walk Through Provincetown*, 2002

There is a short interval on clear summer evenings in Provincetown, after the sun has set, when the sky is deep blue but the hulls of the boats in the harbor retain a last vestige of light that is visible nowhere else. They become briefly phosphorescent in a dim blue world. Last summer as I stood on the beach of the harbor, watching the boats, I found a coffee cup in the shallows. It's not unusual to find bits of crockery on this beach (Provincetown's harbor, being shaped like an enormous ladle, catches much of what the tides stir landward from the waters that surround Cape Cod), but a whole cup is rare. It was not, I'm sorry to say, the perfect white china cup that poetry demands. It was in fact a cheap thing, made in the seventies I suppose, a graceless shallow oval, plastic (hence its practical but unflattering ability to survive intact), covered with garish orange and yellow daisies; the official flower of the insistent, high-gloss optimism I remember from my adolescence, as talk of revolution dimmed and we all started, simply, to dance. It wasn't much of a cup, though it would outlast many of humankind's more vulnerable attempts to embody the notion of hope in everyday objects. It had gotten onto the beach in one piece, while its lovelier counterparts, concoctions of clay and powdered bone, white as moons, lay in fragments on the ocean floor. This cup contained a prim little clamshell, pewter-colored, with a tiny flourish of violet at its broken hinge, and a scattering of iridescent, mica-ish grit, like tea leaves, at its shallow bottom. I held it up, as if I expected to drink from it, as the boats put out their light.

Michael Cunningham (1952–)

The Crater

From *The Innocents Abroad*, 1869

Vesuvius:

The crater itself – the ditch – was not so variegated in coloring, but yet, in its softness, richness, and unpretentious elegance, it was more charming, more fascinating to the eye. There was nothing 'loud' about its well-bred and well-creased look. Beautiful? One could stand and look down upon it for a week without getting tired of it. It had the semblance of a pleasant meadow, whose slender grasses and whose velvety mosses were frosted with a shining dust, and tinted with palest green that deepened gradually to the darkest hue of the orange leaf, and deepened yet again into gravest brown, then faded into orange, then into brightest gold, and culminated in the delicate pink of a new-blown rose. Where portions of the meadow had sunk, and where other portions had been broken up like an ice-floe, the cavernous openings of the one, and the ragged upturned edges exposed by the other, were hung with a lace-work of soft-tinted crystals of sulphur that changed their deformities into quaint shapes and figures that were full of grace and beauty.

The walls of the ditch were brilliant with yellow banks of sulphur and with lava and pumice-stone of many colors. No fire was visible any where, but gusts of sulphurous steam issued silently and invisibly from a thousand little cracks and fissures in the crater, and were wafted to our noses with every breeze. But so long as we kept our nostrils buried in our handkerchiefs, there was small danger of suffocation.

Mark Twain (1835–1910)

The Rope-bound Cliff

From *Yorkshire Legends and Traditions*, 1889

The village of Austwick:

This was, perhaps, the most successful of the villagers' efforts. One of the tall limestone cliffs, which abound near their village, was deemed to be in great danger of separating from the mountain-side, and hurling itself upon the devoted village. Frequent councils were held to devise some effectual means of preventing such a catastrophe. On top of the projecting mass grew a large oak-tree, and the result of the long debates of the 'carles' was that a number of stout ropes should be procured, and with these, passed round the face of the cliff, it should be firmly bound to the tree which stood upon its top. The device was carried out, and answered its purpose most effectually, for the cliff, with the tree on the top, still overlooks and smiles upon the village.

Rev. Thomas Parkinson (1864–1922)

Great Snapdragon *(Antirrhinum majus)*

From *Flowers of the Field*, 1885

A handsome plant, with numerous leafy stems, each of which bears
a spike of large, erect, personate flowers of a purple hue sporting
to rose-colour or white. Specimens are common in gardens, the
tints of which vary considerably; the most beautiful is of a rich
crimson; one of a delicate lemon-colour is also frequent.
Children derive much amusement from pinching the flowers
between the finger and thumb, when the palate opens, as if in
imitation of the fabulous monster from which it derives its name.

Fl. June–August.

Rev. C. A. Johns (1811–1874)

Thinking in Deep Time

From *Underland*, 2019

To think in deep time can be a means not of escaping our troubled present, but rather of re-imagining it; countermanding its quick greeds and furies with older, slower stories of making and unmaking. At its best, a deep time awareness might help us to see ourselves as part of a web of gift, inheritance and legacy stretching over millions of years past and millions to come, bringing us to consider what we are leaving behind for the epochs and beings that will follow us.

When viewed in deep time, things come alive that seem inert. New responsibilities declare themselves. A conviviality of being leaps to mind and eye. The world becomes eerily various and vibrant again. Ice breathes. Rock has tides. Mountains ebb and flow. Stone pulses. We live on a restless Earth.

Robert Macfarlane (1976–)

Dogs and Cats

From *Akenfield*, 17. The Vet, Dr Tim Swift, aged fifty-five, veterinary surgeon, 1969

There are lots of dogs in the village. The pet population of England is fantastic. Of course, it is different in the country. All our village animals are economic, with the exception of the dog. The difference between a town veterinary practice and a country one is that in town you are dealing with pets which have become members of human families, lovers, partners – anything you like – so when they are sick you can charge their owners anything you like. They will spend fantastic sums. In a village you only treat an animal up to the economic level. Cats don't rate as high in the country as in the town, although they are intensely useful. You see a farm where the cat population has been wiped out by enteritis and then you'll see something! The rats and mice arriving – in armies! A farm will have as many as a dozen cats queened over by some great 'Betty-cat' who is mother and great-grandmother of them all. They live pleasant, active, unsentimental lives. They are lucky.

Ronald Blythe (1922–)

Directions: Of Leaves and Trees

From *The English Physician*, 1653

1. Of leaves, choose such only as are green, and full of juice; pick them carefully, and cast away such as are any way declining, for they will putrify the rest. So shall one handful be worth ten of those you buy in any of the shops.

2. Note what places they most delight to grow in, and gather them there: for betony that grows in the shade is far better than that which grows in the sun, because it delights in the shade; so also such herbs as delight to grow near the water, should be gathered near it, though haply you may find some of them upon dry ground: the treatise will inform you where every herb delights to grow.

3. The leaves of such herbs, as run up to seed, are not so good when they are in flower as before, (some few excepted, the leaves of which are seldom or never used) in such cases, if through negligence forgotten, you had better take the top and the flowers than the leaf.

4. Dry them well in the sun, and not in the shade, as the saying of physicians is; for if the sun draw away the virtues of the herb, it must needs do the like by hay, by the same rule, which the experience of every country farmer will explode for a notable piece of nonsense.

Nicholas Culpeper (1616–1654)

New Arrivals

From *Wilding: The Return of Nature to a British Farm*, 2018

It is often assumed that a new species will inevitably take over
the niche of another. But ecosystems, even on islands, do not
necessarily work this way. The space may not be 'full', the niche
may be new. New arrivals may simply add to the diversity. The
picture, too, is often blurred by other causes of ecosystem change.
Are exotics responsible, or are they merely taking advantage
of instabilities caused by pollution, climate change and habitat
degradation? When a flock of ring-necked parakeets squawked
over our heads in the Southern Block a few years into the project,
we persuaded ourselves to keep an open mind. In the event, they
vanished after a couple of weeks, seen off, perhaps, by our growing
population of raptors. Maybe these colourful escapees have
succeeded in establishing in Richmond Park and Kew Gardens
precisely because there are fewer species there to harry them.

Isabella Tree (1964–)

The Wild Still Lingered

From *White Fang*, 1906

He remained somehow different from other dogs. He knew the law even better than did the dogs that had known no other life, and he observed the law more punctiliously; but still there was about him a suggestion of lurking ferocity, as though the Wild still lingered in him and the wolf in him merely slept.

He never chummed with other dogs. Lonely he had lived, so far as his kind was concerned, and lonely he would continue to live. In his puppyhood, under the persecution of Lip-lip and the puppy-pack, and in his fighting days with Beauty Smith, he had acquired a fixed aversion for dogs. The natural course of his life had been diverted, and, recoiling from his kind, he had clung to the human.

Besides, all Southland dogs looked upon him with suspicion. He aroused in them their instinctive fear of the Wild, and they greeted him always with snarl and growl and belligerent hatred. He, on the other hand, learned that it was not necessary to use his teeth upon them. His naked fangs and writhing lips were uniformly efficacious, rarely failing to send a bellowing on-rushing dog back on its haunches.

Jack London (1876–1916)

Strawberries

From *The History of the Worthies of England*, Devonshire, 1662

In Latin *fraga*, most toothsome to the palate (I mean if with claret wine or sweet cream), and so plentiful in this county, that a traveller may gather them, sitting on horseback, in their hollow highways. They delight to grow on the north side of a bank, and are great coolers. These, small and sour, as growing wild (having no other gardener than nature) quickly acquire greatness and sweetness if transplanted into gardens, and become as good as those at Porbery in Somersetshire, where twenty pounds per annum (thank the vicinity of Bristol) have been paid for the tithe thereof. I would not wish this county the increase of these berries, according to the proverb; 'Cut down an oak, and set up a strawberry'.

Thomas Fuller (1608–1661)

Of the Camelopardal

From *The History of Four-footed Beasts*, Volume I, 1607

The head thereof is like to a Camels, the neck to a Horses, the body to a Harts; and his cloven hoof is the same with a Camels; the colour of this Beast is for the most part red and white, mixed together, therefore very beautifull to behold, by reason of the variable and interchangeable skin, being full of spots: but yet they are not alway of one colour. He hath two little horns growing on his head of the colour of iron, his eyes rowling and frowing, his mouth but small like a Harts, his tongue is neer three foot long, and with that he will so speedily gather in his meat, that the eyes of a man will fail to behold his hast, and his neck diversly coloured, is fifteen foot long, which he holdeth up higher then a Camels, and far above the proportion of his other parts. His forefeet are much longer then his hinder and therefore his back declineth towards his buttocks, which are very like an Asses. The pace of this beast differeth from all other in the world, for he doth not move his right and left foot one after another, but both together, and so likewise the other, whereby his whole body is removed at every step or strain.

. . . .

It is a solitary beast, and keepeth altogether in woods, if it be not taken when it is young: they are very tractable and easie to be handled, so that a child may lead them with a small line or cord about their head, and when any come to see them, they willingly and of their own accord turn themselves round as it were of purpose to shew their soft hairs, and beautiful colour, being as it were proud to ravish the eyes of the beholders.

Edward Topsell (1572–1625)

A Fishing Trip

From *The Tale of Jeremy Fisher*, 1906

Once upon a time there was a frog called Mr. Jeremy Fisher; he lived in a little damp house amongst the buttercups at the edge of a pond. The water was all slippy-sloppy in the larder and in the back passage. But Mr. Jeremy liked getting his feet wet; nobody ever scolded him, and he never caught a cold!

He was quite pleased when he looked out and saw large drops of rain, splashing in the pond –

'I will get some worms and go fishing and catch a dish of minnows for my dinner,' said Mr. Jeremy Fisher. 'If I catch more than five fish, I will invite my friends Mr. Alderman Ptolemy Tortoise and Sir Isaac Newton. The Alderman, however, eats salad.'

Mr. Jeremy put on a macintosh, and a pair of shiny goloshes; he took his rod and basket, and set off with enormous hops to the

He had the dearest little red float. His rod was a tough stalk of grass, his line was a fine long white horse-hair, and he tied a little wriggling worm at the end. The rain trickled down his back, and for nearly an hour he stared at the float.

'This is getting tiresome, I think I should like some lunch,' said Mr. Jeremy Fisher.

He punted back again amongst the water-plants, and took some lunch out of his basket.

'I will eat a butterfly sandwich, and wait till the shower is over,' said Mr. Jeremy Fisher.

Beatrix Potter (1866–1943)

Seeing Nature

From 'Nature', 1836

To speak truly, few adult persons can see nature. Most persons do not see the sun. At least they have a very superficial seeing. The sun illuminates only the eye of the man, but shines into the eye and the heart of the child. The lover of nature is he whose inward and outward senses are still truly adjusted to each other; who has retained the spirit of infancy even into the era of manhood. His intercourse with heaven and earth, becomes part of his daily food. In the presence of nature, a wild delight runs through the man, in spite of real sorrows. Nature says, – he is my creature, and maugre all his impertinent griefs, he shall be glad with me. Not the sun or the summer alone, but every hour and season yields its tribute of delight; for every hour and change corresponds to and authorizes a different state of the mind, from breathless noon to grimmest midnight. Nature is a setting that fits equally well a comic or a mourning piece. In good health, the air is a cordial of incredible virtue. Crossing a bare common, in snow puddles, at twilight, under a clouded sky, without having in my thoughts any occurrence of special good fortune, I have enjoyed a perfect exhilaration. I am glad to the brink of fear. In the woods too, a man casts off his years, as the snake his slough, and at what period soever of life, is always a child. In the woods, is perpetual youth.

. . . .

For, nature is not always tricked in holiday attire, but the same scene which yesterday breathed perfume and glittered as for the frolic of the nymphs, is overspread with melancholy today. Nature always wears the colors of the spirit.

Ralph Waldo Emerson (1803–1882)

Common Borage (Borago officinalis)

From *Flowers of the Field*, 1885

The stems are about 2 feet high, and, as well as the leaves, are thickly covered with stiff whitish bristles; the flowers, which are large, deep blue, and very handsome, grow in terminal drooping clusters, and may readily be distinguished from any other plant in the order by their prominent black anthers.

The juice has the smell and flavour of cucumber, and is an ingredient in a beverage called 'cool tankard'.

Fl. June–September.

Rev. C. A. Johns (1811–1874)

Pluto

From 'The Black Cat', 1843

We had birds, gold-fish, a fine dog, rabbits, a small monkey, and a cat.

This latter was a remarkably large and beautiful animal, entirely black, and sagacious to an astonishing degree. In speaking of his intelligence, my wife, who at heart was not a little tinctured with superstition, made frequent allusion to the ancient popular notion, which regarded all black cats as witches in disguise. Not that she was ever serious upon this point – and I mention the matter at all for no better reason than that it happens, just now, to be remembered.

Pluto – this was the cat's name – was my favourite pet and playmate. I alone fed him, and he attended me wherever I went about the house. It was even with difficulty that I could prevent him from following me through the streets.

Edgar Allan Poe (1809–1849)

Petals in the Breeze

From 'Kew Gardens', 1919

From the oval-shaped flower-bed there rose perhaps a hundred stalks spreading into heart-shaped or tongue-shaped leaves half way up and unfurling at the tip red or blue or yellow petals marked with spots of colour raised upon the surface; and from the red, blue or yellow gloom of the throat emerged a straight bar, rough with gold dust and slightly clubbed at the end.

The petals were voluminous enough to be stirred by the summer breeze, and when they moved, the red, blue and yellow lights passed one over the other, staining an inch of the brown earth beneath with a spot of the most intricate colour. The light fell either upon the smooth, grey back of a pebble, or, the shell of a snail with its brown, circular veins, or falling into a raindrop, it expanded with such intensity of red, blue and yellow the thin walls of water that one expected them to burst and disappear. Instead, the drop was left in a second silver grey once more, and the light now settled upon the flesh of a leaf, revealing the branching thread of fibre beneath the surface, and again it moved on and spread its illumination in the vast green spaces beneath the dome of the heart-shaped and tongue-shaped leaves.

Virginia Woolf (1882–1941)

Mountainous and Wild

From *Journey to the Western Islands of Scotland*, 1773, published 1775

Regions mountainous and wild, thinly inhabited, and little cultivated, make a great part of the earth, and he that has never seen them, must live unacquainted with much of the face of nature, and with one of the great scenes of human existence.

Samuel Johnson (1709–1784)

Rikki-tikki

From *The Jungle Book*, 1894

An English family rescues Rikki-tikki from the flood:

It is the hardest thing in the world to frighten a mongoose, because he is eaten up from nose to tail with curiosity. The motto of all the mongoose family is, 'Run and find out'; and Rikki-tikki was a true mongoose. He looked at the cotton-wool, decided it was not good to eat, ran all round the table, sat up and put his fur in order, and jumped on the small boy's shoulder.

Rudyard Kipling (1865–1936)

Helvellyn

From *The Journal of a Disappointed Man*, 1915

August 29

Climbed a windy eminence on the other side of the Lake and had a splendid view of Helvellyn – like a great hog's back. It is fine to walk over the elastic turf with the wind bellowing into each ear and swirling all around me in a mighty sea of air until I was as clean-blown and resonant as a sea-shell. I moved along as easily as a disembodied spirit and felt free, almost transparent. The old earth seemed to have soaked me up into itself, I became dissolved into it, my separate body was melted away from me, and Nature received me into her deepest communion – until. *UNTIL* I got on the lee side of a hedge where the calm brought me back my gaol of clay.

W. N. P. Barbellion (1889–1919)

Loch Ness

From *The Journal of a Tour to the Hebrides with Samuel Johnson, LL.D.*, 1773, published 1785

August 30th

It was a delightful day. Lochness, and the road upon the side of it, shaded with birch trees, and the hills above it, pleased us much. The scene was as sequestered and agreeably wild as could be desired, and for a time engrossed all our attention.

James Boswell (1740–1795)

Ants and a Heron

From *The Return of the Native*, 1878

Mrs Yeobright's weary walk home:

In two hours she reached a slope about three-fourths the whole distance from Alderworth to her own home, where a little patch of shepherd's-thyme intruded upon the path; and she sat down upon the perfumed mat it formed there. In front of her a colony of ants had established a thoroughfare across the way, where they toiled a never-ending and heavy-laden throng. To look down upon them was like observing a city street from the top of a tower. She remembered that this bustle of ants had been in progress for years at the same spot – doubtless those of the old times were the ancestors of these which walked there now. She leant back to obtain more thorough rest, and the soft eastern portion of the sky was as great a relief to her eyes as the thyme was to her head. While she looked a heron arose on that side of the sky and flew on with his face towards the sun. He had come dripping wet from some pool in the valleys, and as he flew the edges and lining of his wings, his thighs and his breast were so caught by the bright sunbeams that he appeared as if formed of burnished silver. Up in the zenith where he was seemed a free and happy place, away from all contact with the earthly ball to which she was pinioned; and she wished that she could arise uncrushed from its surface and fly as he flew then.

Thomas Hardy (1840–1928)

SEPTEMBER

Airy Spheres of Thistledown

Mountains

From *The Journal of a Tour to the Hebrides with Samuel Johnson, LL.D.*, 1773, published 1785

September 1st

We passed through Glensheal, with prodigious mountains on each side. We saw where the battle was fought in the year 1719. Dr Johnson owned he was now in a scene of as wild nature as he could see; but he corrected me sometimes in my inaccurate observations.

'There, (said I,) is a mountain like a cone.'

Johnson. 'No, sir. It would be called so in a book; and when a man comes to look at it, he sees it is not so. It is indeed pointed at the top; but one side of it is larger than the other.'

Another mountain I called immense.

Johnson. 'No; it is no more than a considerable protuberance.'

James Boswell (1740–1795)

The Colour of the Sea

From *Cape Cod*, 1865

Commonly, in calm weather, for half a mile from the shore, where the bottom tinges it, the sea is green, or greenish, as are some ponds; then blue for many miles, often with purple tinges, bounded in the distance by a light almost silvery stripe; beyond which there is generally a dark-blue rim, like a mountain-ridge in the horizon, as if, like that, it owed its color to the intervening atmosphere. On another day it will be marked with long streaks, alternately smooth and rippled, light-colored and dark, even like our inland meadows in a freshet, and showing which way the wind sets.

Henry David Thoreau (1817–1862)

Happiness and the Sea

From *To the Lighthouse*, 1927

She had known happiness, exquisite happiness, intense happiness, and it silvered the rough waves a little more brightly, as daylight faded, and the blue went out of the sea and it rolled in waves of pure lemon which curved and swelled and broke upon the beach and the ecstasy burst in her eyes and waves of pure delight raced over the floor of her mind and she felt, It is enough! It is enough!

Virginia Woolf (1882–1941)

The Summit of Carrock

From *The Lazy Tour of Two Idle Apprentices*, 1857

Francis Goodchild (Charles Dickens) and Thomas Idle (Wilkie Collins) climb Carrock in the Lake District, guided by their landlord:

At first the ascent was delusively easy, the sides of the mountain sloped gradually, and the material of which they were composed was a soft spongy turf, very tender and pleasant to walk upon. After a hundred yards or so, however, the verdant scene and the easy slope disappeared, and the rocks began. Not noble, massive rocks, standing upright, keeping a certain regularity in their positions, and possessing, now and then, flat tops to sit upon, but little irritating, comfortless rocks, littered about anyhow, by Nature; treacherous, disheartening rocks of all sorts of small shapes and small sizes, bruisers of tender toes and trippers-up of wavering feet. When these impediments were passed, heather and slough followed. Here the steepness of the ascent was slightly mitigated; and here the exploring party of three turned round to look at the view below them. The scene of the moorland and the fields was like a feeble water-colour drawing half sponged out.

The mist was darkening, the rain was thickening, the trees were dotted about like spots of faint shadow, the division-lines which mapped out the fields were all getting blurred together, and the lonely farm-house where the dog-cart had been left, loomed spectral in the grey light like the last human dwelling at the end of the habitable world. Was this a sight worth climbing to see? Surely – surely not!

. . . .

Up and up and up again, till a ridge is reached and the outer edge of the mist on the summit of Carrock is darkly and drizzingly near. Is this the top? No, nothing like the top. It is an aggravating peculiarity of all mountains, that, although they have only one top when they are seen (as they ought always to be seen) from below, they turn out to have a perfect eruption of false tops whenever the traveller is sufficiently ill-advised to go out of his way for the purpose of ascending them. Carrock is but a trumpery little mountain of fifteen hundred feet, and it presumes to have false tops, and even precipices, as if it were Mont Blanc.

Wilkie Collins (1824–1889) and Charles Dickens (1812–1870)

A Country Running

From *My Ántonia*, 1918

The road from the post-office came directly by our door, crossed the farmyard, and curved round this little pond, beyond which it began to climb the gentle swell of unbroken prairie to the west. There, along the western sky-line it skirted a great cornfield, much larger than any field I had ever seen. This cornfield, and the sorghum patch behind the barn, were the only broken land in sight. Everywhere, as far as the eye could reach, there was nothing but rough, shaggy, red grass, most of it as tall as I.

North of the house, inside the ploughed fire-breaks, grew a thick-set strip of box-elder trees, low and bushy, their leaves already turning yellow. This hedge was nearly a quarter of a mile long, but I had to look very hard to see it at all. The little trees were insignificant against the grass. It seemed as if the grass were about to run over them, and over the plum-patch behind the sod chicken-house.

As I looked about me I felt that the grass was the country, as the water is the sea. The red of the grass made all the great prairie the colour of wine-stains, or of certain seaweeds when they are first washed up. And there was so much motion in it; the whole country seemed, somehow, to be running.

Willa Cather (1873–1947)

The Weald of Kent

From *Rural Rides*, 1823

September 6th

Not far from BOUGH-BEACH, I saw two oak trees, one of which was, they told me, more than thirty feet round, and the other more than twenty-seven; but they have been hollow for half a century. They are not much bigger than the oak upon Tilford Green, if any. I mean in the trunk; but they are hollow, while that tree is sound in all its parts, and growing still.

I have had a most beautiful ride through the Weald. The day is very hot; but I have been in the shade; and my horse's feet very often in the rivulets and wet lanes. In one place I rode above a mile completely arched over by the boughs of the underwood, growing in the banks of the lane. What an odd taste that man must have who prefers a turnpike-road to a lane like this!

William Cobbett (1763–1835)

The Remnants

From *A Sand County Almanac and Sketches Here and There*, Wilderness, 1949

Many of the diverse wildernesses out of which we have hammered America have already gone; hence in any practical program the unit areas to be preserved must vary greatly in size and in degree of wildness.

No living man will see again the long-grass prairie, where a sea of prairie flowers lapped at the stirrups of the pioneer. We shall do well to find a forty here and there on which the prairie plants can be kept alive as species. There were a hundred such plants, many of exceptional beauty. Most of them are quite unknown to those who have inherited their domain.

Aldo Leopold (1887–1948)

Daubenton's Bat *(Myotis daubentonii)*

From *Animal Life of the British Isles*, 1921

Daubenton's or the Water bat was formerly considered one of our rarest bats, but is now known to be one of the most widely distributed and plentiful species. It had probably been mistaken for the Common Bat or Pipistrelle to which it comes near in point of size, though its habits are different. It keeps close to water, especially to some alder-sheltered pool in the river where there are plenty of caddis-flies and other insects. There from an hour before sunset it flies slowly in circles, frequently dipping its muzzle into the water to pick up surface insects. In such places the evening fly-fisher sometimes finds this Bat caught on his hook. It appears to be on the wing all night. It was probably to this Bat that Gilbert White referred in his eleventh letter to Pennant, when he said: 'As I was going, some years ago, pretty late, in a boat from Richmond to Sunbury, on a warm summer's evening, I think I saw myriads of Bats between the two places; the air swarmed with them all along the Thames, so that hundreds were in sight at a time.' This was long before it had been distinguished as a distinct species, and when it would probably have been regarded as the common Bat.

Edward Step (1855–1931)

Bats: Tame and Wild

From *The Natural History and Antiquities of Selborne*, Letter XI to
Thomas Pennant, esquire

Selborne, September 9, 1767

I was much entertained last summer with a tame bat, which would take flies out of a person's hand. If you gave it anything to eat, it brought its wings round before the mouth, hovering and hiding its head in the manner of birds of prey when they feed. The adroitness it showed in shearing off the wings of the flies, which were always rejected, was worthy of observation, and pleased me much. Insects seem to be most acceptable, though it did not refuse raw flesh when offered: so that the notion that bats go down chimneys and gnaw men's bacon, seems no improbable story. While I amused myself with this wonderful quadruped, I saw it several times confute the vulgar opinion, that bats when down on a flat surface cannot get on the wing again, by rising with great ease from the floor. It ran, I observed, with more dispatch than I was aware of; but in a most ridiculous and grotesque manner.

Bats drink on the wing, like swallows, by sipping the surface, as they play over pools and streams. They love to frequent waters, not only for the sake of drinking, but on account of insects, which are found over them in the greatest plenty. As I was going, some years ago, pretty late, in a boat from Richmond to Sunbury, on a warm summer's evening, I think I saw myriads of bats between the two places: the air swarmed with them all along the Thames, so that hundreds were in sight at a time.

Gilbert White (1720–1793)

Common Agrimony (*Agrimonia eupatoria*)

From *Wild Flowers*, 1855

There are few of our wild plants which are in more esteem with the village herbalist than the Agrimony. Every gatherer of 'simples' knows it well, and the author has often seen the dried bundles of the plant hung up not only by the cottage fireplace, but in shops, in several of the towns of France, where it is exposed for sale. It is still retained in the London Materia Medica; but though once esteemed an important medicine, it is seldom or never prescribed by our modern physicians.

The leaves are slightly bitter and aromatic, and the flowers have, while growing, an odour commonly said to resemble the apricot, but which might rather be described as like that of the lemon. They are of a yellow colour, growing in a long spike, about a third part down the stem, which is usually one or two feet high. The leaflets are deeply notched at the edges, and have intermediate small ones, cleft into three, four or five segments. The plant imparts a greenish yellow colour to water, and a deep green tint to spirituous liquors. It has also been used for dressing leather, and when just coming into flower it will dye wool of a fine nankeen hue, but if gathered in the month of September, it yields a deeper yellow. Most cattle refuse it, but the sheep and goat will eat its foliage.

Anne Pratt (1806–1893)

The American Forests

From *Our National Parks*, 1901

The forests of America, however slighted by man, must have been a great delight to God; for they were the best he ever planted. The whole continent was a garden, and from the beginning it seemed to be favored above all the other wild parks and gardens of the globe. To prepare the ground, it was rolled and sifted in seas with infinite loving deliberation and fore-thought, lifted into the light, submerged and warmed over and over again, pressed and crumpled into folds and ridges, mountains, and hills, subsoiled with heaving volcanic fires, ploughed and ground and sculptured into scenery and soil with glaciers and rivers, – every feature growing and changing from beauty to beauty, higher and higher. And in the fullness of time it was planted in groves, and belts, and broad, exuberant, mantling forests, with the largest, most varied, most fruitful, and most beautiful trees in the world. Bright seas made its border, with wave embroidery and icebergs; gray deserts were outspread in the middle of it, mossy tundras on the north, savannas on the south, and blooming prairies and plains; while lakes and rivers shone through all the vast forests and openings, and happy birds and beasts gave delightful animation. Everywhere, everywhere over all the blessed continent, there were beauty and melody and kindly, wholesome, foodful abundance.

John Muir (1838–1914)

A Camel is Not Jumpable

From *The Innocents Abroad*, 1869

From Tabor to Nazareth:

As it was an uncommonly narrow, crooked trail, we necessarily met all the camel trains and jackass caravans between Jericho and Jacksonville in that particular place and nowhere else. The donkeys do not matter so much, because they are so small that you can jump your horse over them if he is an animal of spirit, but a camel is not jumpable. A camel is as tall as any ordinary dwelling-house in Syria – which is to say a camel is from one to two, and sometimes nearly three feet taller than a good-sized man. In this part of the country his load is oftenest in the shape of colossal sacks – one on each side. He and his cargo take up as much room as a carriage. Think of meeting this style of obstruction in a narrow trail. The camel would not turn out for a king. He stalks serenely along, bringing his cushioned stilts forward with the long, regular swing of a pendulum, and whatever is in the way must get out of the way peaceably, or be wiped out forcibly by the bulky sacks. It was a tiresome ride to us, and perfectly exhausting to the horses. We were compelled to jump over upwards of eighteen hundred donkeys, and only one person in the party was unseated less than sixty times by the camels.

Mark Twain (1835–1910)

Harvest Festival

From *The Vicar of Morwenstow*, 1876

Now there is scarcely a church in England in which a harvest thanksgiving service is not held. But probably the first to institute such a festival in the Anglican Church was the vicar of Morwenstow in 1843.

In that year he issued a notice to his parishioners to draw their attention to the duty of thanking God for the harvest, and of announcing that he would set apart a Sunday for such a purpose.

To the Parishioners of Morwenstow.
When the sacred Psalmist inquired what he should render unto the Lord for all the benefits that He had done unto him, he made answer to himself, and said: 'I will receive the cup of salvation, and call upon the name of the Lord.' Brethren, God has been very merciful to us this year also. He hath filled our garners with increase, and satisfied our poor with bread. He opened His hand, and filled all things living with plenteousness. Let us offer a sacrifice of thanksgiving among such as keep Holy Day. Let us gather together in the chancel of our church on the first Sunday of the next month, and there receive, in the bread of the new corn, that blessed sacrament which was ordained to strengthen and refresh our souls. As it is written, 'He rained down manna also upon them for to eat, and gave them food from heaven.' And

again, 'In the hand of the Lord there is a cup, and the wine is red.' Furthermore, let us remember, that, as a multitude of grains of wheat are mingled into one loaf, so we, being many, are intended to be joined together into one, in that holy sacrament of the Church of Jesus Christ. Brethren, on the first morning of October call to mind the word, that, wheresoever the body is, thither will the eagles be gathered together. 'Let the people praise thee, O God, yea, let all the people praise thee! Then shall the earth bring forth her increase, and God, even our own God, shall give us His blessing. God shall bless us, and all the ends of the earth shall fear Him.'

The Vicar.

The Vicarage, Morwenstow, Sept. 13, 1843.

Rev. Sabine Baring-Gould (1834–1924)

Modestine

From *Travels with a Donkey in the Cévennes*, 1878

Robert Louis Stevenson gets ready to depart:

It remained to choose a beast of burden. Now, a horse is a fine lady among animals, flighty, timid, delicate in eating, of tender health; he is too valuable and too restive to be left alone, so that you are chained to your brute as to a fellow galley-slave; a dangerous road puts him out of his wits; in short, he's an uncertain and exacting ally, and adds thirty-fold to the troubles of the voyager. What I required was something cheap and small and hardy, and of a stolid and peaceful temper; and all these requisites pointed to a donkey.

Robert Louis Stevenson (1850–1894)

A Town at One With Nature

From *The Mayor of Casterbridge*, 1886

When Elizabeth-Jane opened the hinged casement next morning the mellow air brought in the feel of imminent autumn almost as distinctly as if she had been in the remotest hamlet. Casterbridge was the complement of the rural life around, not its urban opposite. Bees and butterflies in the cornfields at the top of the town, who desired to get to the meads at the bottom, took no circuitous course, but flew straight down High Street without any apparent consciousness that they were traversing strange latitudes. And in autumn airy spheres of thistledown floated into the same street, lodged upon the shop fronts, blew into drains, and innumerable tawny and yellow leaves skimmed along the pavement, and stole through people's doorways into their passages with a hesitating scratch on the floor, like the skirts of timid visitors.

Thomas Hardy (1840–1928)

The Time to Visit

From *Guide to the Lakes*, 1835

To the sincere admirer of Nature, who is in good health and spirits, and at liberty to make a choice, the six weeks following the first of September may be recommended in preference to July and August. For there is no inconvenience arising from the season which, to such a person, would not be amply compensated by the *autumnal* appearance of any of the more retired valleys, into which discordant plantations and unsuitable buildings have not yet found entrance. – In such spots, at this season, there is an admirable compass and proportion of natural harmony in colour, through the whole scale of objects; in the tender green of the after-grass upon the meadows, interspersed with islands of grey or mossy rock, crowned by shrubs and trees; in the irregular enclosures of standing corn, or stubble-fields, in like manner broken; in the mountain-sides glowing with fern of divers colours; in the calm blue lakes and river-pools; and in the foliage of the trees, through all the tints of autumn, – from the pale and brilliant yellow of the birch and ash, to the deep greens of the unfaded oak and alder, and of the ivy upon the rocks, upon the trees, and the cottages.

William Wordsworth (1770–1850)

No Heat, No Hurry

From *The White Peacock*, 1911

I was born in September, and love it best of all the months. There is no heat, no hurry, no thirst and weariness in corn harvest as there is in the hay. If the season is late, as is usual with us, then mid-September sees the corn still standing in stook. The mornings come slowly. The earth is like a woman married and fading; she does not leap up with a laugh for the first fresh kiss of dawn, but slowly, quietly, unexpectantly lies watching the waking of each new day. The blue mist, like memory in the eyes of a neglected wife, never goes from the wooded hill, and only at noon creeps from the near hedges.

D. H. Lawrence (1885–1930)

Strawberry Tree (*Arbutus unedo*)

From *Flowers of the Field*, 1885

A beautiful evergreen tree, with a rough, reddish bark, large deep-green leaves, and numerous terminal clusters of *greenish-white* flowers. The *berries*, which ripen in the following autumn, are nearly globular, scarlet, and rough with minute, hard grains. They are eatable, but so much less attractive to the taste than to the eye, as to have originated the name 'Unedo', 'One-I-eat', as if no one would choose to try a second. The flowers are in full perfection at the time when the fruit, formed in the preceding year, is ripening; and then of course, the tree presents its most beautiful appearance.

Fl. September, October.

Rev. C. A. Johns (1811–1874)

Ant and Dove

From *The Fables of Aesop*, retold by Rev. Thomas James (1809–1863), 1848

An Ant went to a fountain to quench his thirst, and tumbling in, was almost drowned. But a Dove that happened to be sitting on a neighbouring tree saw the Ant's danger, and plucking off a leaf, let it drop into the water before him, and the Ant mounting upon it, was presently wafted safe ashore. Just at that time a Fowler was spreading his net, and was in the act of ensnaring the Dove, when the Ant, perceiving his object, bit his heel. The start which the man gave made him drop his net, and the Dove, aroused to a sense of her danger, flew safe away.

One good turn deserves another.

Aesop (620–564 BC)

The Coming of Autumn

From *Nature Rambles*, 1930

When does autumn begin? The astronomers, followed by the almanac-makers, begin it in the third week of September, when the day and night become equal in length, and continue until a few days short of Christmas. Many people are guided entirely by the weather of the year, and find usually that what they had thought to be early autumn is followed by another spell of summer. The rambling naturalist knows that you cannot fix dates to our seasons before they come: that they merge one into another gradually, and that a few miles north or south or the two sides of a range of hills may show a marked difference.

Some of our bird visitors left us before we began to think of autumn; but when the last of the Swifts have gone, the Lapwings flock and the Starlings move to some other district, we know the season is about to change, and we watch for signs like the thinning of the Limes, the yellowing of the Elms and the browning of the Beeches. As a rule, these changes are gradual; and there is still much of summer shown by the flowers and insects when the wild fruits are getting their tints of ripeness and the early fungi are beginning to appear.

Edward Step (1855–1931)

The Wind

From *The Journal of a Disappointed Man*, 1911

September 21

A cool, breezy autumn day. The beach was covered with patches
of soapy foam that shook tremulously in the wind – all the rocks
and everything were drenched with water, and the spray came off
the breaking waves like steam. A red sun went lower and lower
and the shadows cast by the rocks grew very long and grotesque.
Underneath the breaking waves, the hollows were green and dark
like sea caverns. Herring Gulls played about in the air balancing
themselves as they faced the breeze, then sweeping suddenly
around and downwards with the wind behind them. We all sat
down on the rocks and were very quiet, almost monosyllabic. We
pointed out a passing vessel to one another or chucked a bit of
shingle into the sea. You would have said we were bored. Yet deep
down in ourselves we were astir and all around us we could hear
the rumours of divine passage, soft and mysterious as the flight of
birds migrating in the dark.

The wind rose and tapped the line against the flag-staff at the
Coastguard Station. It roared through my hair and past my ears
for an hour on end till I felt quite windswept and bleak. On the
way home we saw the wind darting hither and thither over the
long grass like a lunatic snake. The wind! Oh! the wind – I have
an enormous faith in the curative properties of the wind. I feel
better already.

W. N. P. Barbellion (1889–1919)

Within the Deep Churning

First published 2021

Within the deep churning there is no need for limits and/or coordinates: language finds no tongue here: a liquid topography of light and/or no light; a terrain threaded by unmapped motion.

Joel Knight (1975–)

True Saffron

From *The Herball*, 1597

The floure of Saffron doth first rise out of the ground nakedly in September, and his long smal grassie leaves shortly after, never bearing floure and leafe at once. The floure consisteth of six small blew leaves tending to purple, having in the middle many small yellow strings or threds; among which are two, three or more thicke fat chives of a fierie colour somewhat reddish, of a strong smell when they be dried, which doth stuffe and trouble the head.

Common or best knowne Saffron growth plentifully in Cambridge-shire, Saffron-Walden, and other places thereabout, as corne in the fields. Saffron beginneth to floure in September, and presently after spring up the leaves, and remaine greene all the Winter long.

John Gerard (1545–1612)

The Bay at Evening

From *To the Lighthouse*, 1927

'It suddenly gets cold. The sun seems to give less heat,' she said, looking about her, for it was bright enough, the grass still a soft deep green, the house starred in its greenery with purple passion flowers, and rooks dropping cool cries from the high blue. But something moved, flashed, turned a silver wing in the air. It was September after all, the middle of September, and past six in the evening. So off they strolled down the garden in the usual direction, past the tennis lawn, past the pampas grass, to that break in the thick hedge, guarded by red hot pokers like braziers of clear burning coal, between which the blue waters of the bay looked bluer than ever.

They came there regularly every evening drawn by some need. It was as if the water floated off and set sailing thoughts which had grown stagnant on dry land, and gave to their bodies even some sort of physical relief. First, the pulse of colour flooded the bay with blue, and the heart expanded with it and the body swam, only the next instant to be checked and chilled by the prickly blackness on the ruffled waves. Then, up behind the great black rock, almost every evening spurted irregularly, so that one had to watch for it and it was a delight when it came, a fountain of white water; and then, while one waited for that, one watched, on the pale semicircular beach, wave after wave shedding again and again smoothly, a film of mother-of-pearl.

Virginia Woolf (1882–1941)

The First Peregrine

From *The Peregrine*, 1967

I saw my first peregrine day at the estuary ten years ago. The sun reddened out of the white river mist, fields glittered with rime, boats were encrusted with it; only the gently lapping water moved freely and shone. I went across the high river-wall towards the sea. The stiff crackling white grass became limp and wet as the sun rose through a clear sky into dazzling mist. Frost stayed all day in shaded places, the sun was warm and there was no wind.

I rested at the foot of the wall and watched dunlin feeding at the tide-line. Suddenly they flew upstream, and hundreds of finches fluttered overhead, whirling away with a 'hurr' of desperate wings. Too slowly it came to me that something was happening which I ought not to miss. I scrambled up, and saw that the stunted hawthorns on the inland slope of the wall were full of fieldfares. Their sharp bills pointed to the north-east, and they clacked and spluttered in alarm. I followed their point, and saw a falcon flying towards me. It veered to the right, and passed inland. It was like a kestrel, but bigger and yellower, with a more bullet-shaped head, longer wings, and greater zest of buoyancy and flight. It did not glide till it saw starlings feeding in stubble, then it swept down and was hidden among them as they rose. A minute later it rushed overhead and was gone in a breath into the sunlit mist. It was flying much higher than before, flinging and darting forwards, with its sharp wings angled back and flicking like a snipe's.

That was my first peregrine.

J. A. Baker (1926–1987)

Good Advice

From *Black Beauty*, 1877

Duchess gives advice to Darkie, later Black Beauty:

'I wish you to pay attention to what I am going to say to you. The colts who live here are very good colts, but they are carthorse colts, and, of course, they have not learned manners. You have been well bred and well born; your father has a great name in these parts, and your grandfather won the cup two years ago at the Newmarket races; your grandmother has the sweetest temper of any horse I ever knew, and I think you have never seen me kick or bite. I hope you will grow up gentle and good, and never learn bad ways; do your work with a good will, lift your feet up well when you trot, and never bite or kick, even in play.'

I have never forgotten my mother's advice; I knew she was a wise old horse, and our master thought a great deal of her. Her name was Duchess, but he often called her Pet.

Anna Sewell (1820–1878)

The Choral Copse

From *A Sand County Almanac and Sketches Here and There,* September, 1949

By September, the day breaks with little help from the birds. A song sparrow may give a single half-hearted song, a woodcock may twitter overhead en route to his daytime thicket, a barred owl may terminate the night's argument with one last wavering call, but few other birds have anything to say or sing about.

It is on some, but not all, of these misty autumn daybreaks that one may hear the chorus of the quail. The silence is suddenly broken by a dozen contralto voices, no longer able to restrain their praise of the day to come. After a brief minute or two, the music closes as suddenly as it began.

There is a particular virtue in the music of elusive birds. Songsters that sing from top-most boughs are easily seen and as easily forgotten; they have the mediocrity of the obvious. What one remembers is the invisible hermit thrush pouring silver clouds from impenetrable shadows; the soaring crane trumpeting from behind a cloud; the prairie chicken booming from the mists of nowhere; the quail's Ave Maria in the hush of dawn. No naturalist

Pure Nature

From *The Maine Woods*, Ktaadn, 1846

Perhaps I most fully realized that this was primeval, untamed, and forever untamable Nature, or whatever else men call it, while coming down this part of the mountain. We were passing over 'Burnt Lands' burnt by lightning, perchance, though they showed no recent marks of fire, hardly so much as a charred stump, but looked rather like a natural pasture for the moose and deer, exceedingly wild and desolate, with occasional strips of timber crossing them, and low poplars springing up, and patches of blueberries here and there. I found myself traversing them familiarly, like some pasture run to waste, or partially reclaimed by man; but when I reflected what man, what brother or sister or kinsman of our race made it and claimed it, I expected the proprietor to rise up and dispute my passage. It is difficult to conceive of a region uninhabited by man. We habitually presume his presence and influence everywhere. And yet we have not seen pure Nature, unless we have seen her thus vast and drear and inhuman, though in the midst of cities. Nature was here something savage and awful, though beautiful. I looked with awe at the ground I trod on, to see what the Powers had made there, the form and fashion and material of their work. This was that Earth of which we have heard, made out of Chaos and Old Night. Here was no man's garden, but the unhandseled globe.

Henry David Thoreau (1817–1862)

The Track of Autumn

From *The Woman in White*, 1859

The track of the golden autumn wound its bright way visibly through the green summer of the trees.

Wilkie Collins (1824–1889)

British Dogges

From *The Natural History of Wiltshire*, 1656–1691

The British dogges were in great esteeme in the time of the
Romans; as appeares by Gratius, who lived in Augustus Caesar's
time, and Oppian, who wrote about two ages after Gratius, in
imitation of him. Gratii Cynegeticon, translated by Mr. Chr.
Wace, 1654:

'What if the Belgique current you should view,
And steer your course to Britain's utmost shore!
Though not for shape, and much deceiving show,
The British hounds no other blemish know:
When fierce work comes, and courage must be shown,
And Mars to extreme combat leads them on,
Then stout Molossians you will lesse commend;
With Athemaneans these in craft contend.'

John Aubrey (1626–1697)

OCTOBER

Acorns Cracking Underfoot

The Thrill of Octobers

From *Anne of Green Gables*, 1908

October was a beautiful month at Green Gables, when the birches in the hollow turned as golden as sunshine and the maples behind the orchard were royal crimson and the wild cherry trees along the lane put on the loveliest shades of dark red and bronzy green, while the fields sunned themselves in aftermaths.

Anne reveled in the world of color about her.

'Oh, Marilla,' she exclaimed one Saturday morning, coming dancing in with her arms full of gorgeous boughs, 'I'm so glad I live in a world where there are Octobers. It would be terrible if we just skipped from September to November, wouldn't it? Look at these maple branches. Don't they give you a thrill – several thrills? I'm going to decorate my room with them.'

· · · · · · · · · ·

It was October again when Anne was ready to go back to school – a glorious October, all red and gold, with mellow mornings when the valleys were filled with delicious mists as if the spirit of autumn had poured them in for the sun to drain – amethyst, pearl, silver, rose, and smoke-blue. The dews were so heavy that the fields glistened like cloth of silver and there were such heaps of rustling leaves in the hollows of many-stemmed woods to run crisply through. The Birch Path was a canopy of yellow and the ferns were sear and brown all along it. There was a tang in the very air that inspired the hearts of small maidens tripping, unlike snails, swiftly and willingly to school.

L. M. Montgomery (1874–1942)

A Richly Coloured Rug

From *Cape Cod*, 1865

Before sunset, having already seen the mackerel fleet returning into the Bay, we left the sea-shore on the north of Provincetown, and made our way across the Desert to the eastern extremity of the town. From the first high sand-hill, covered with beach-grass and bushes to its top, on the edge of the desert, we overlooked the shrubby hill and swamp country which surrounds Provincetown on the north, and protects it, in some measure, from the invading sand. Notwithstanding the universal barrenness, and the contiguity of the desert, I never saw an autumnal landscape so beautifully painted as this was. It was like the richest rug imaginable spread over an uneven surface; no damask nor velvet, nor Tyrian dye or stuffs, nor the work of any loom, could ever match it. There was the incredibly bright red of the Huckleberry, and the reddish brown of the Bayberry, mingled with the bright and living green of small Pitch-Pines, and also the duller green of the Bayberry, Boxberry, and Plum, the yellowish green of the Shrub-oaks, and the various golden and yellow and fawn-colored tints of the Birch and Maple and Aspen, – each making its own figure, and, in the midst, the few yellow sand-slides on the sides of the hills looked like the white floor seen through rents in the rug. Coming from the country as I did, and many autumnal woods as I had seen, this was perhaps the most novel and remarkable sight that I saw on the Cape. Probably the brightness of the tints was enhanced by contrast with the sand which surrounded this tract.

Henry David Thoreau (1817–1862)

The Sky Scenery of Wisconsin

From *The Story of My Boyhood and Youth*, 1913

We reveled in the glory of the sky scenery as well as that of the woods and meadows and rushy, lily-bordered lakes. The great thunder-storms in particular interested us, so unlike any seen in Scotland, exciting awful, wondering admiration. Gazing awe-stricken, we watched the upbuilding of the sublime cloud-mountains, – glowing, sun-beaten pearl and alabaster cumuli, glorious in beauty and majesty and looking so firm and lasting that birds, we thought, might build their nests amid their downy bosses; the black-browed storm-clouds marching in awful grandeur across the landscape, trailing broad gray sheets of hail and rain like vast cataracts, and ever and anon flashing down vivid zigzag lightning followed by terrible crashing thunder. We saw several trees shattered, and one of them, a punky old oak, was set on fire, while we wondered why all the trees and everybody and everything did not share the same fate, for oftentimes the whole sky blazed. After sultry storm days, many of the nights were darkened by smooth black apparently structureless cloud-mantles which at short intervals were illumined with startling suddenness to a fiery glow by quick, quivering lightning-flashes, revealing the landscape in almost noonday brightness, to be instantly quenched in solid blackness.

John Muir (1838–1914)

No Ordinary Bird

From *Jonathan Livingston Seagull*, 1972

It was morning, and the new sun sparkled gold across the ripples of a gentle sea.

A mile from shore a fishing boat chummed the water, and the word for Breakfast Flock flashed through the air, till a crowd of a thousand seagulls came to dodge and fight for bits of food. It was another busy day beginning.

But way off alone, out by himself beyond the boat and shore, Jonathan Livingston Seagull was practicing. A hundred feet in the sky he lowered his webbed feet, lifted his beak, and strained to hold a painful hard twisting curve through his wings. The curve meant that he would fly slowly, and now he slowed till the wind was a whisper in his face, until the ocean stood still beneath him. He narrowed his eyes in fierce concentration, held his breath, forced one ... single ... more ... inch ... of ... curve ... Then his feathers ruffled, he stalled and fell.

Seagulls, as you know, never alter, never stall. To stall in the air is for them disgrace, and it is dishonour.

But Jonathan Livingston Seagull, unashamed, stretching his wings again in that trembling hard curve – slowing, slowing, and stalling once more – was no ordinary bird.

Richard Bach (1936–)

The Wild Land

From *O Pioneers!*, 1913

Alexandra drew her shawl closer about her and stood leaning against the frame of the mill, looking at the stars which glittered so keenly through the frosty autumn air. She always loved to watch them, to think of their vastness and distance, and of their ordered march. It fortified her to reflect upon the great operations of nature, and when she thought of the law that lay behind them, she felt a sense of personal security. That night she had a new consciousness of the country, felt almost a new relation to it. Even her talk with the boys had not taken away the feeling that had overwhelmed her when she drove back to the Divide that afternoon. She had never known before how much the country meant to her. The chirping of the insects down in the long grass had been like the sweetest music. She had felt as if her heart were hiding down there, somewhere, with the quail and the plover and all the little wild things that crooned or buzzed in the sun. Under the long shaggy ridges, she felt the future stirring.

Willa Cather (1873–1947)

Corn Blue-bottle (*Centaurea cyanus*)

From *Flowers of the Field*, 1885

One of the prettiest flowers, and well meriting the distinctive name, often given to it of *Corn-flower*. The flowers are bright blue, with dark anthers, and when mixed with Poppies and yellow Ox-daisies, form as brilliantly-coloured a bouquet as can be imagined.

Children often string the outer florets by the help of a needle and thread, and bringing the ends together, press them in a book, to form a wreath, which retains its colour for a long while. Recently expanded flowers should be chosen, or their colour will fade.

The juice of the flowers, expressed and mixed with cold alum-water, may be used in water-colour drawings. Rose-coloured, white and dark purple varieties are commonly to be met with in gardens, and the last are occasionally found in a wild slate.

Fl. July, August; and, in turnip-fields, again in October and November.

Rev. C. A. Johns (1811–1874)

A Nymph-child

From *The Scarlet Letter*, 1850

The child Pearl waits while her mother talks with the clergyman:

The great black forest – stern as it showed itself to those who
brought the guilt and troubles of the world into its bosom –
became the playmate of the lonely infant, as well as it knew how.
Sombre as it was, it put on the kindest of its moods to welcome
her. It offered her the partridge-berries, the growth of the
preceding autumn, but ripening only in the spring, and now red
as drops of blood upon the withered leaves. These Pearl gathered,
and was pleased with their wild flavor. The small denizens of the
wilderness hardly took pains to move out of her path. A partridge,
indeed, with a brood of ten behind her, ran forward threateningly,
but soon repented of her fierceness, and clucked to her young ones
not to be afraid. A pigeon, alone on a low branch, allowed Pearl to
come beneath, and uttered a sound as much of greeting as alarm.
A squirrel, from the lofty depths of his domestic tree, chattered
either in anger or merriment, – for a squirrel is such a choleric and
humorous little personage, that it is hard to distinguish between
his moods, – so he chattered at the child, and flung down a nut
upon her head. It was a last year's nut, and already gnawed by his

sharp tooth. A fox, startled from his sleep by her light footstep on the leaves, looked inquisitively at Pearl, as doubting whether it were better to steal off, or renew his nap on the same spot. A wolf, it is said, – but here the tale has surely lapsed into the improbable, – came up, and smelt of Pearl's robe, and offered his savage head to be patted by her hand. The truth seems to be, however, that the mother-forest, and these wild things which it nourished, all recognized a kindred wildness in the human child.

And she was gentler here than in the grassy-margined streets of the settlement, or in her mother's cottage. The flowers appeared to know it; and one and another whispered as she passed, 'Adorn thyself with me, thou beautiful child, adorn thyself with me!' – and, to please them, Pearl gathered the violets, and anemones, and columbines, and some twigs of the freshest green, which the old trees held down before her eyes. With these she decorated her hair, and her young waist, and became a nymph-child, or an infant dryad, or whatever else was in closest sympathy with the antique wood.

Nathaniel Hawthorne (1804–1864)

Cathedral Birds

From *In Pursuit of Spring*, 1914

The Cathedral and Palace at Wells:

Two gateways lead out of one side of the market-place to the cathedral and the palace grounds. Taking the right-hand one, I came to the palace, and the moat that flows along one side, between a high wall climbed by fruit trees and ivy, and a walk lined with old pollard elms. Rooks inhabited the elm tops, and swans the water. Rooks are essential to a cathedral anywhere, but Wells is perfected by swans. On the warm palace roof behind the wall – a roof smouldering mellow in the sun – pigeons lay still ecclesiastically. Sometimes one cooed sleepily, as if to seal it canonical that silence is better; the rooks cawed; the water foamed down into the moat at one end between bowery walls. Away from the cathedral on that side to the foot of the Mendips expanded low, green country.

Edward Thomas (1878–1917)

Preservation

From *Guide to the Lakes*, 1835

In truth, no one can now travel through the more frequented tracts, without being offended, at almost every turn, by an introduction of discordant objects, disturbing that peaceful harmony of form and colour, which had been through a long lapse of ages most happily preserved.

All gross transgressions of this kind originate, doubtless, in a feeling natural and honourable to the human mind, viz. the pleasure which it receives from distinct ideas, and from the perception of order, regularity, and contrivance. Now, unpractised minds receive these impressions only from objects that are divided from each other by strong lines of demarcation; hence the delight with which such minds are smitten by formality and harsh contrast. But I would beg of those who are eager to create the means of such gratification, first carefully to study what already exists; and they will find, in a country so lavishly gifted by nature, an abundant variety of forms marked out with a precision that will satisfy their desires. Moreover, a new habit of pleasure will be formed opposite to this, arising out of the perception of the fine gradations by which in nature one thing passes away into another, and the boundaries that constitute individuality disappear in one instance only to be revived elsewhere under a more alluring form.

William Wordsworth (1770–1850)

Mists and Snow

From *The Grasmere Journals*, 1800

Friday 10th October

In the morning when I arose the mists were hanging over the opposite hills, and the tops of the highest hills were covered with snow. There was a most lively combination at the head of the vale of the yellow autumnal hills wrapped in sunshine, and overhung with partial mists, the green and yellow trees, and the distant snow-topped mountains. It was a most heavenly morning.

Dorothy Wordsworth (1771–1855)

A Picturesque View

From *Sense and Sensibility*, 1811

Edward tells Marianne that he knows nothing of the picturesque:

'You must not enquire too far, Marianne – remember I have
no knowledge in the picturesque, and I shall offend you by my
ignorance and want of taste if we come to particulars. I shall call
hills steep, which ought to be bold; surfaces strange and uncouth,
which ought to be irregular and rugged; and distant objects out of
sight, which ought only to be indistinct through the soft medium
of a hazy atmosphere. You must be satisfied with such admiration
as I can honestly give. I call it a very fine country – the hills are
steep, the woods seem full of fine timber, and the valley looks
comfortable and snug – with rich meadows and several neat farm
houses scattered here and there. It exactly answers my idea of a
fine country, because it unites beauty with utility – and I dare
say it is a picturesque one too, because you admire it; I can easily
believe it to be full of rocks and promontories, grey moss and
brush wood, but these are all lost on me. I know nothing of the
picturesque.'

Jane Austen (1775–1817)

The Hedgehog

From *Natural History*, Book VIII, AD 77
Translated by Henry T. Riley (1816–1878) and John Bostock (1773–1846), first published 1855

Hedgehogs also prepare food for winter, and fixing fallen apples on their spines by rolling on them and holding one more in their mouth carry them to hollow trees. The same animals foretell a change of wind from North to South by retiring to their lair. But when they perceive someone hunting them they draw together their mouth and feet and all their lower part, which has thin and harmless down on it, and roll up into the shape of a ball, so that it may not be possible to take hold of any part of them except the prickles.

Pliny the Elder (AD c. 23–79)

From *The History of Four-footed Beasts*, Volume I, 1607

His meat is Apples, Wormes, or Grapes; When he findeth apples or grapes on the earth, he rowleth himself upon them, untill he have filled all his prickles, and then carryeth them home to his den, never bearing above one in his mouth. And if it fortune that one of them fall off by the way, he likewise shaketh off all the residue, and walloweth upon them afresh, untill they be all setled upon his back again, so forth he goeth, making a noise like a cart wheele. And if he have any young ones in his nest, they pull off his load wherewithal he is loaded, eating thereof what they please, and laying up the residue for the time to come.

Edward Topsell (1572–1625)

The Sea Hedgehog

From *Survey of Cornwall*, 1602

The Sea-hedge-hogge, of like or more goodnesse, is enclosed in a round shell, fashioned as a loafe of bread, handsomely wrought and pincked, and guarded by an utter skinne full of prickles, as the land Urchin.

Richard Carew (1555–1620)

Rain and Horses

From *The Irish R.M.*, 1928

My landlord was there on horseback, and with him there was a man standing at the head of a stout grey animal. I recognised with despair that I was about to be compelled to buy a horse.

'Good afternoon, Major,' said Mr. Knox in his slow, sing-song brogue; 'it's rather soon to be paying you a visit, but I thought you might be in a hurry to see the horse I was telling you of.'

I could have laughed. As if I were ever in a hurry to see a horse! I thanked him, and suggested that it was rather wet for horse-dealing.

'Oh, it's nothing when you're used to it,' replied Mr. Knox. His gloveless hands were red and wet, the rain ran down his nose, and his covert coat was soaked to a sodden brown. I thought that I did not want to become used to it. My relations with horses have been of a purely military character, I have endured the Sandhurst riding-school, I have galloped for an impetuous general, I have been steward at regimental races, but none of these feats have altered my opinion that the horse, as a means of locomotion, is obsolete. Nevertheless, the man who accepts a resident magistracy in the south-west of Ireland voluntarily retires into the prehistoric age; to institute a stable became inevitable.

'You ought to throw a leg over him,' said Mr. Knox, 'and you're welcome to take him over a fence or two if you like. He's a nice flippant jumper.'

Even to my unexacting eye the grey horse did not seem to promise flippancy, nor did I at all desire to find that quality in him. I explained that I wanted something to drive, and not to ride.

'Well, that a fine raking horse in harness,' said Mr. Knox, looking at me with his serious grey eyes, 'and you'd drive him with a sop of hay in his mouth. Bring him up here, Michael.'

Michael abandoned his efforts to kick the grey horse's forelegs into a becoming position, and led him up to me.

I regarded him from under my umbrella with a quite unreasonable disfavour. He had the dreadful beauty of a horse in a toy-shop, as chubby, as wooden, and as conscientiously dappled, but it was unreasonable to urge this as an objection, and I was incapable of finding any more technical drawback. Yielding to circumstance, I 'threw my leg' over the brute, and after pacing gravely round the quadrangle that formed the yard, and jolting to my entrance gate and back, I decided that as he had neither fallen down nor kicked me off, it was worth paying twenty-five pounds for him, if only to get in out of the rain.

Somerville & Ross
(Edith Somerville, 1858–1949,
and Martin Ross / Violet Florence Martin, 1862–1915)

Spindle

From *The Peverel Papers*, October, 1924

The yew, at least, must be a thousand years old, for it is past its prime, and, although the lower boughs are red-rinded and dark-leaved, the upper trunk and branches stand stark against the sky. Against the dusky background of the yew the spindle is quite Japanese in its contortions; the boughs, with their twisted grey-green bark, seem positively to writhe, and the leaves and berries are sprinkled so sparsely that they seem to decorate rather than clothe its antiquity.

A few feet from the earth the branches of the two trees mingle, and the flame-coloured leaves and pink and orange berries of the spindle-wood glow like clusters of some strange exotic flower against the drooping blackness of the yew. There is something strangely unfamiliar about these berries of the spindle-wood – berries which open out into dull pink segments, like petals, and expose a bright orange centre, which is really a seed.

. . . .

There was a time, not so many generations ago, when even a woman who knew nothing of trees in general, and cared less, being wholly taken up with her housekeeping, would have recognised the spindle-wood tree at a glance. In those days, when the spinning wheel flashed beside every hearth, and everything possible was made at home, the tough, close-grained wood of the tree was in constant demand, and many a pair of lovers must have come to such a tree as this to choose a branch and cut it, to make a spindle for the lady's use.

Flora Thompson (1876–1947)

Snailes

From *The Natural History of Wiltshire*, 1656–1691

Snailes are everywhere; but upon our downes, and so in Dorset, and I believe in Hampshire, at such degree east and west, in the summer time are abundance of very small snailes on the grasse and corne, not much bigger, or no bigger than small pinnes heads. Though this is no strange thing among us, yet they are not to be found in the north part of Wilts, nor on any northern wolds. When I had the honour to waite on King Charles I* and the Duke of York to the top of Silbury hill, his Royal Highnesse happened to cast his eye on some of these small snailes on the turfe of the hill. He was surprised with the novelty, and commanded me to pick some up, which I did, about a dozen or more, immediately; for they are in great abundance. The next morning as he was abed with his Dutches at Bath he told her of it, and sent Dr. Charleton to me for them, to shew her as a rarity.

John Aubrey (1626–1697)

* This should be 'Charles II' who visited Avebury and Silbury Hill, in company with his brother, afterwards James II, in the autumn of the year 1663, when Aubrey attended them by the King's command. [John Britton, editor of the 1847 edition.]

The Borderland of Nature

From *Wild Life in a Southern County*, 1879

There is a frontier line to civilisation in this country yet, and not far outside its great centres we come quickly even now on the borderland of nature. Modern progress, except where it has exterminated them, has scarcely touched the habits of bird or animal; so almost up to the very houses of the metropolis the nightingale yearly returns to her former haunts. If we go a few hours' journey only, and then step just beyond the highway – where the steam ploughing engine has left the mark of its wide wheels on the dust – and glance into the hedgerow, the copse, or stream, there are nature's children as unrestrained in their wild, free life as they were in the veritable backwoods of primitive England.

Richard Jefferies (1848–1887)

The Speaking Cat

From 'Tobermory', *The Chronicles of Clovis*, 1911

Mr Cornelius Appin, guest at Lady Blemley's house-party, announces that he has made a momentous discovery:

'And do you really ask us to believe,' Sir Wilfrid was saying, 'that you have discovered a means for instructing animals in the art of human speech, and that dear old Tobermory has proved your first successful pupil?'

'It is a problem at which I have worked for the last seventeen years,' said Mr. Appin, 'but only during the last eight or nine months have I been rewarded with glimmerings of success. Of course I have experimented with thousands of animals, but latterly only with cats, those wonderful creatures which have assimilated themselves so marvellously with our civilization while retaining all their highly developed feral instincts. Here and there among cats one comes across an outstanding superior intellect, just as one does among the ruck of human beings, and when I made the acquaintance of Tobermory a week ago I saw at once that I was in contact with a 'Beyond-cat' of extraordinary intelligence. I had gone far along the road to success in recent experiments; with Tobermory, as you call him, I have reached the goal.'

Mr. Appin concluded his remarkable statement in a voice which he strove to divest of a triumphant inflection. No one said 'Rats,' though Clovis's lips moved in a monosyllabic contortion which probably invoked those rodents of disbelief.

'And do you mean to say,' asked Miss Resker, after a slight pause, 'that you have taught Tobermory to say and understand easy sentences of one syllable?'

'My dear Miss Resker,' said the wonder-worker patiently, 'one teaches little children and savages and backward adults in that piecemeal fashion; when one has once solved the problem of making a beginning with an animal of highly developed intelligence one has no need for those halting methods. Tobermory can speak our language with perfect correctness.'

This time Clovis very distinctly said, 'Beyond-rats!' Sir Wilfrid was more polite, but equally sceptical.

'Hadn't we better have the cat in and judge for ourselves?' suggested Lady Blemley.

Sir Wilfrid went in search of the animal, and the company settled themselves down to the languid expectation of witnessing some more or less adroit drawing-room ventriloquism.

In a minute Sir Wilfrid was back in the room, his face white beneath its tan and his eyes dilated with excitement.

'By Gad, it's true!'

His agitation was unmistakably genuine, and his hearers started forward in a thrill of awakened interest.

Collapsing into an armchair he continued breathlessly: 'I found him dozing in the smoking-room and called out to him to come for his tea. He blinked at me in his usual way, and I said, 'Come on, Toby; don't keep us waiting'; and, by Gad! he drawled out in a most horribly natural voice that he'd come when he dashed well pleased! I nearly jumped out of my skin!'

Appin had preached to absolutely incredulous hearers; Sir Wilfred's statement carried instant conviction. A Babel-like chorus of startled exclamation arose, amid which the scientist sat mutely enjoying the first fruit of his stupendous discovery.

In the midst of the clamour Tobermory entered the room and made his way with velvet tread and studied unconcern across to the group seated round the tea-table.

A sudden hush of awkwardness and constraint fell on the company. Somehow there seemed an element of embarrassment in addressing on equal terms a domestic cat of acknowledged mental ability.

'Will you have some milk, Tobermory?' asked Lady Blemley in a rather strained voice.

'I don't mind if I do,' was the response, couched in a tone of even indifference. A shiver of suppressed excitement went through the listeners, and Lady Blemley might be excused for pouring out the saucerful of milk rather unsteadily.

'I'm afraid I've spilt a good deal of it,' she said apologetically.

'After all, it's not my Axminster,' was Tobermory's rejoinder.

Another silence fell on the group, and then Miss Resker, in her best district-visitor manner, asked if the human language had been difficult to learn. Tobermory looked squarely at her for a moment and then fixed his gaze serenely on the middle distance. It was obvious that boring questions lay outside his scheme of life.

'What do you think of human intelligence?' asked Mavis Pellington lamely.

'Of whose intelligence in particular?' asked Tobermory coldly.

'Oh, well, mine for instance,' said Mavis, with a feeble laugh.

'You put me in an embarrassing position,' said Tobermory, whose tone and attitude certainly did not suggest a shred of embarrassment. 'When your inclusion in this house-party was suggested, Sir Wilfrid protested that you were the most brainless woman of his acquaintance, and that there was a wide distinction between hospitality and the care of the feeble-minded. Lady Blemley replied that your lack of brain-power was the precise quality which had earned you your invitation, as you were the only person she could think of who might be idiotic enough to buy their old car. You know, the one they call 'The Envy of Sisyphus,' because it goes quite nicely up-hill if you push it.'

Lady Blemley's protestations would have had greater effect if she had not casually suggested to Mavis only that morning that the car in question would be just the thing for her down at her Devonshire home.

Major Barfield plunged in heavily to effect a diversion.

'How about your carryings-on with the tortoise-shell puss up at the stables, eh?'

The moment he had said it every one realized the blunder.

'One does not usually discuss these matters in public' said Tobermory frigidly. 'From a slight observation of your ways since you've been in this house I should imagine you'd find it inconvenient if I were to shift the conversation on to your own little affairs.'

The panic which ensued was not confined to the Major.

'Would you like to go and see if cook has got your dinner ready?' suggested Lady Blemley hurriedly, affecting to ignore the fact that it wanted at least two hours to Tobermory's dinner-time.

'Thanks,' said Tobermory, 'not quite so soon after my tea. I don't want to die of indigestion.'

'Cats have nine lives, you know,' said Sir Wilfrid heartily.

'Possibly,' answered Tobermory; 'but only one liver.'

Saki / Hector Hugh Munro (1870–1916)

Crab Apple *(Pyrus malus)*

From *Wild Flowers*, 1855

Few, indeed, are the wild fruit-trees of our land, and fewer still are those which can claim to be true natives of our soil, for some of those now growing wild were introduced by the Romans. The Crab Apple, however, is a truly British plant, and its richly tinted blossoms grace our spring woodlands, and the fruit is ornamental at a later season of the year. Our wild apple is of little use, save that its juice forms the verjuice of commerce; yet the harsh austere crab of the wild tree is the origin of all the valuable apples, the blossoms of which render the orchard grounds of some countries so beautiful.

Besides the many uses which we, in modern days, make of the Apple, it was employed for many others by our ancestors. Thus, a cosmetic was formerly made from the juice, and in some diseases physicians prescribed, as a remedy, that the patient should hold, both sleeping and waking, a sweet apple in his hand, as its odour was considered healthful. The old herbalist, Gerarde, also tells us of a valuable ointment made in his time of the pulp of apples, lard, and rosewater, which was called pomatum, from pomum, an apple, and was used to beautify the skin.

Anne Pratt (1806–1893)

The Bountiful Year

From *The Woodlanders*, 1887

The gorgeous autumn landscape of White-Hart Vale:

Surrounded by orchards lustrous with the reds of apple-crops, berries, and foliage, the whole intensified by the gilding of the declining sun. The earth this year had been prodigally bountiful, and now was the supreme moment of her bounty. In the poorest spots the hedges were bowed with haws and blackberries; acorns cracked underfoot, and the burst husks of chestnuts lay exposing their auburn contents as if arranged by anxious sellers in a fruit-market.

Thomas Hardy (1840–1928)

On the Prognosticks of the Weather

From *The Pocket Encyclopaedia of Natural Phenomena*, 1827

Perhaps one of the most useful purposes to which meteorology can be applied, is that when accurately studied with reference to the prognosticative import of particular phenomena, it enables us to predict with greater certainty the future changes of the weather. Soon after my attention was directed to atmospherical science I observed that mariners, shepherds, husbandmen, and others whose employment kept them constantly out of doors, could foretel with more certainty what sorts of weather were coming than the more scientific meteorologists could do; they seemed to me to have a sort of code of prognosticks of their own, founded partly on tradition and partly on experience: they used numberless trite sayings and proverbial adages respecting the weather which were handed down from the remotest antiquity, but which, in the long run, seldom failed to be right.

. . . .

Bats flitting about late in the evening in spring and autumn, at which seasons they are most commonly seen, foretell a fine day on the morrow, as do dorbeetles, and some other insects.

On the contrary, when bats return soon to their hiding places, and send forth loud cries, bad weather may be expected.

. . . .

Cats are said, when they wash their faces, or when they seem sleepy and dull, to foretell rain. The same is said of them when they appear irritable and restless, and play with their tails.

. . . .

Cattle, when they gambol about in their pastures more than ordinary, foreshew rain, and in general a change of weather.

. . . .

Dogs, before rain, grow sleepy and dull, and lay drowsily before the fire, and are not easily aroused. They also often eat grass, which indicates that their stomachs, like ours, are apt to be disturbed before change of weather. It is also said to be a sign of change of weather when dogs howl and bark much in the night; they certainly do this much at the full moon, which has given rise to the saying relative to the Dogs that bay at the moon.

. . . .

Ducks. The loud and clamorous quackling of ducks, geese, and other waterfowl, is a sign of rain. It is also a sign of rain when they wash themselves, and flutter about in the water more than usual.

. . . .

Frogs, by their clamorous croaking, indicate rainy weather; as does likewise their coming abroad in great numbers of an evening.

. . . .

Larks, when they fly high, and remain singing a long while in the air, forbode fine weather.

. . . .

Moles often afford us a prognostic of rain, by working and throwing up the earth into molehills more than usual.

. . . .

Raven. When the raven is observed early in the morning at a great height in the air, soaring round and round, and uttering a hoarse croaking sound, we may be sure the day will be fine, and may conclude the weather is about to clear and become fair.

. . . .

Urchins of the Sea, a sort of fish, when they thrust themselves into the mud, and try to cover their bodies with sand, foreshew a storm.

Thomas Furley Forster (1761–1825)

A Crocodile

From *The Diary of John Evelyn*, 1684

October 22

At the same time, I went to see a living Crocodile, brought from some of the W: Indian Ilands, in every respect resembling the Egyptian Crocodile, it was not yet fully 2 yards from head to taile, very curiously scaled and beset with impenetrable studs of a hard horny substance, and most beautifully ranged in works, especially on the ridge of the back and the sides, of a dusky greene Colour, save the belly, which being tender, and onely vulnerable, was of a lively and lovely greene, as lizards are, whose shape it exactly kept: The Eyes were sharp and piercing, over which it could at pleasure draw up a thin cobweb skinn: the rictus was exceeding deepe set with a terrible rank of sharp and long teeth: We could not discerne any tongue, but a small lump of flesh at the very bottome of its throate, which I suppose helped his swallowing: the feete were divided into long fingers as the Lizards, and he went forward waddling, having a chaine about the neck: seemed to be very tame; I made its keeper take up his upper jaw which he affirmed did onely move, and so Pliny and others confidently report; but it did not appeare so plaine to me, whither his keeper did not use some dexterity in opening his mouth and placing his head so as to make it seeme that the upper chap, was loose; since in that most ample and perfect skeleton in our Repositarie at the R: Socoety, it is manifestly fixed to the neck and Vertebrae: the nether jaw onely loose: They kept the beast or Serpent in a longish Tub of warme Water, and fed him with flesh etc.: If he grow, it will be a dangerous Creature.

John Evelyn (1620–1706)

Fallen Leaves

From *The Books That Bind*, 2018

In Hatchards Bookshop:

We wander down to the ground floor, where a few lost leaves are briefly gathered by a gust of wind on the pavement and perform a balletic twirl before landing in the bookshop. They can sense memories of wood, trees, home. They long for attachment again. They don't realise how beautiful they are as they lay dead. Their life was always about the fall. But they burnt bright once, and they held hands with the wood of future books that would one day spark the imagination, to paper over the cracks ... leafing through.

Mark Staples (1980–)

On Extinction

From *The Origin of Species*, 6th edition, 1872

Both single species and whole groups of species last for very unequal periods; some groups, as we have seen, have endured from the earliest known dawn of life to the present day; some have disappeared before the close of the palaeozoic period. No fixed law seems to determine the length of time during which any single species or any single genus endures. There is reason to believe that the extinction of a whole group of species is generally a slower process than their production: if their appearance and disappearance be represented, as before, by a vertical line of varying thickness the line is found to taper more gradually at its upper end, which marks the progress of extermination, than at its lower end, which marks the first appearance and the early increase in number of the species. In some cases, however, the extermination of whole groups, as of ammonites, towards the close of the secondary period, has been wonderfully sudden.

The extinction of species has been involved in the most gratuitous mystery. Some authors have even supposed that, as the individual has a definite length of life, so have species a definite duration.

Charles Darwin (1809–1882)

Not Seeing

From *The Snow Leopard*, 1973

October 25:

By firelight, we talk about the snow leopard. Not only is it rare, so says GS [George Schaller], but it is wary and elusive to a magical degree, and so well camouflaged in the places it chooses to lie that one can stare straight at it from yards away and fail to see it. Even those who know the mountains rarely take it by surprise.

November 13:

If all else fails, GS will send Jang-bu to Saldang to buy an old goat as leopard bait. I long to see the snow leopard, yet to glimpse it by camera flash, at night, crouched on a bait, is not to see it. If the snow leopard should manifest itself, then I am ready to see the snow leopard. If not, then somehow (and I don't understand this instinct, even now) I am not ready to perceive it, in the same way that I am not ready to resolve my *koan*; and in the not-seeing, I am content. I think I must be disappointed, having come so far, and yet I do not feel that way. I am disappointed, and also, I am not disappointed. That the snow leopard is, that it is here, that its frosty eyes watch us from the mountain – that is enough.

Peter Matthiessen (1927–2014)

Laura's Last Morning

From *Candleford Green*, 1943

On the last morning of her postwoman's round, when she came
to the path between trees where she had seen the birds' footprints
on the snow, she turned and looked back upon the familiar
landmarks. It was a morning of ground mist, yellow sunshine, and
high rifts of blue, white-cloud-dappled sky. The leaves were still
thick on the trees, but dew-spangled gossamer threads hung on the
bushes and the shrill little cries of unrest of the swallows skimming
the green open spaces of the park told of autumn and change.

. . . .

As she went on her way, gossamer threads, spun from bush to
bush, barricaded her pathway, and as she broke through one after
another of these fairy barricades she thought, 'They're trying to
bind and keep me'. But the threads which were to bind her to her
native county were more enduring than gossamer. They were spun
of love and kinship and cherished memories.

Flora Thompson (1876–1947)

The Puff-ball

From *Nature Rambles*, 1930

Let us look at that grassy patch over there, for what looks like a large, rounded stone may be something very different. Yes: it is the largest of our Puffballs – a group of fungi of which we have a number of species, all of them good to eat if you can find them when they are young. This one, which must be seven or eight inches across – and is sometimes very much larger – has a creamy-white, smooth skin that feels like the soft kid-leather of which the finest gloves are made. There are several others around, so we will break this one open, to show you that the inside is a close mass of very fine white sponge. Later on, this will break up into loose cobwebby stuff, and the spaces will be filled with olive-coloured dust, which consists really of millions of minute spores. Here is an older one which has become dark in colour, with the outer skin flaking off in patches, which have left two or three openings. Keep away for a moment, whilst I tap it with my stick. You see the small clouds that puff out on the slightest touch. The Puffball by slight contractions does this for itself when left alone: it is its way of getting air movements to carry the light spores far away. In playing with the Puffball as we have done, we must be careful not to inhale the spore-dust, for it has been found to set up irritation in the air-passages.

Edward Step (1855–1931)

Mushroom

From *The English Physician*, 1653

The poison of mushrooms has been much talked of by several persons but there seems to be no certain account of any body's having ever been injured by eating the common mushroom; though there are perhaps some kinds of them that are truly poisonous. The ancients have taken great pains to distinguish the several kinds of them, that the world might know the hurtful from the safe. The *boletus*, mentioned by Juvenal, on account of the death of Claudius, is sufficiently described by Pliny. Clusius, among the moderns, has described a vast number of different species, every where distinguishing the esculent and wholesome from the poisonous and pernicious kinds. The several authors who have treated of them since the time of Clusius, have all mentioned the effects of some or other of the poisonous kinds, and there are numerous instances of the mischief done by them at one time or other. The true eatable mushroom is distinguished from the poisonous and unpleasant kinds by these marks: when young it appears of a roundish form, like a button, the stalk as well as the button being white, and the fleshy part very white when broken, the gills within being livid. As they grow larger, they expand their heads by degrees into a flat form, and the gills underneath are of a pale flesh colour; but, as they stand long, become blackish.

Nicholas Culpeper (1616–1654)

The Great Glass Sea Snail

From *The Voyages of Doctor Dolittle*, 1922

The Doctor: 'Er – who, or what, is the Great Glass Sea Snail?'

The Fidgit: 'He is an enormous salt-water snail, one of the winkle family, but as large as a big house. He talks quite loudly – when he speaks, but this is not often. He can go to any part of the ocean, at all depths because he doesn't have to be afraid of any creature in the sea. His shell is made of transparent mother-o'-pearl so that you can see through it; but it's thick and strong. When he is out of his shell and he carries it empty on his back, there is room in it for a wagon and a pair of horses. He has been seen carrying his food in it when traveling.'

The Doctor: 'I feel that that is just the creature I have been looking for. He could take me and my assistant inside his shell and we could explore the deepest depths in safety. Do you think you could get him for me?'

The Fidgit: 'Alas! no. I would willingly if I could; but he is hardly ever seen by ordinary fish. He lives at the bottom of the Deep Hole, and seldom comes out – And into the Deep Hole, the lower waters of which are muddy, fishes such as we are afraid to go.'

The Doctor: 'Dear me! That's a terrible disappointment. Are there many of this kind of snail in the sea?'

The Fidgit: 'Oh no. He is the only one in existence, since his second wife died long, long ago. He is the last of the Giant Shellfish. He belongs to past ages when the whales were land-animals and all that. They say he is over seventy thousand years old.'

Hugh Lofting (1886–1947)

Nature Reclaims The Wilderness

From *The Wild Places*, 2007

Twenty-five feet up in a sycamore:

From there I was able to look down on the Wilderness and to
get some sense of the land's lie. The ditch was a moat; this much
was clear. It ran in a squashed circle round the central area,
which looked to be about an acre in size. I could see evidence of
earthworks and more exposed areas of brickwork, suggesting walls
and palisades. And beyond the moat in every direction were bands
of thistles and waist-high nettles. These were the new fortifications
of this area, keeping people out, preserving the land for the
creatures that lived there.

My guess was that the name on the map was a late eighteenth-
century relic: that a big house, perhaps Elizabethan, had once
stood here, and had then been taken over by an early Romantic
landowner who, following the picturesque taste of the time, had
created for his estate a 'Wilderness': an area of rough country,
regulated for its irregularity – often with artificial waterfalls
and faux rock outcrops – which could be excitingly strayed
into by visitors.

But the name had proved a prophecy: two or more centuries
later, The Wilderness had become a wild place, properly reclaimed,
only a few hundred yards from the road. The building that had
once stood here had dilapidated, and had then been steadily and
thoroughly reoccupied by nature: by nettle, thistle, elder, hazel,
fox, badger and bird.

Robert Macfarlane (1976–)

The Element of Air

From *The Compleat Angler*, Part I, 1653–1676

Auceps, the falconer, praises the air:

Auceps. This Element of Air which I profess to trade in, the worth of it is such, and it is of such necessity, that no creature whatsoever – not only those numerous creatures that feed on the face of the Earth, but those various creatures that have their dwelling within the waters, every creature that hath life in its nostrils, stands in need of my element. The Waters cannot preserve the Fish without Air, witness the not breaking of Ice in an extream Frost; the reason is, for that if the inspiring and expiring Organ of any animal be stopt, it suddenly yields to Nature, and dies. Thus necessary is Air, to the existence both of Fish and Beasts, nay, even to Man himself; that Air, or breath of life, with which God at first inspired Mankind, he, if he wants it, dies presently, becomes a sad object to all that loved and beheld him, and in an instant turns to putrefaction.

Nay more; the very birds of the air (those that be not Hawks) are both so many and so useful and pleasant to mankind, that I must not let them pass without some observations:

. . . .

Those little nimble Musicians of the air, that warble forth their curious Ditties, with which Nature hath furnished them to the shame of Art.

Izaak Walton (1593–1683)

NOVEMBER

A Powdering of Hoar-frost

Late Blackberries

From *The Peverel Papers*, November, 1925

Although browns and greys are the predominating colours of the month, they still form a background for the splashes of brighter hues. The flowers, though few, have not wholly gone; the garden still yields a bunch of chrysanthemums and starwort; the smaller gorse is blooming against the sere brown of the heath, and in the sheltered recesses of the woods a tree here and there stands out in its red or yellow.

Beside the field paths, at least a dozen late lingerers may be found – yellow toadflax with its butter and egg tints; pimpernel, charlock, and the last of the rose-mallow, and a few belated poppies, with petals all crinkled and blanched to a pale pink by the rain and the cold. Of such things it would be possible to gather quite a respectable nosegay, but for the most part they are passed over; the faded beauties of a deserted season have lost their charm, and the hedges hold a more seasonal selection – hips, haws, and brightly-tinted leaves with long straw-coloured trails of crimson berried bryony.

Against the grey humidity of the atmosphere these late autumn treasures stand out more vivid in contrast. The bramble alone should save the month from the reproach of colourlessness, long trails of its crimson and yellow veined leaves still thread the wet grass, and its branches are still heavy with overlooked fruit.

These late autumn blackberries are as large and juicy as those of September; but, tempting as they look, they tempt no one, for the local legend runs that upon Old Michaelmas Day the devil drags his tail over the bushes, and after that the fruit is unfit for human food.

Flora Thompson (1876–1947)

The River Doon

From *Our Old Home*, 1863

We leaned over the parapet [of the new bridge] to admire the beautiful Doon, flowing wildly and sweetly between its deep and wooded banks. I never saw a lovelier scene; although this might have been even lovelier, if a kindly sun had shone upon it. The ivy-grown, ancient bridge, with its high arch, through which we had a picture of the river and the green banks beyond, was absolutely the most picturesque object, in a quiet and gentle way, that ever blessed my eyes. Bonny Doon, with its wooded banks, and the boughs dipping into the water!

The memory of them, at this moment, affects me like the song of birds, and Burns crooning some verses, simple and wild, in accordance with their native melody.

Nathaniel Hawthorne (1804–1864)

Recherche Donkeys

From *The Innocents Abroad*, 1869

The donkeys were all good, all handsome, all strong and in good condition, all fast and all willing to prove it. They were the best we had found any where, and the most recherche. I do not know what recherche is, but that is what these donkeys were, anyhow. Some were of a soft mouse-color, and the others were white, black, and vari-colored. Some were close-shaven, all over, except that a tuft like a paint-brush was left on the end of the tail. Others were so shaven in fanciful landscape garden patterns, as to mark their bodies with curving lines, which were bounded on one side by hair and on the other by the close plush left by the shears. They had all been newly barbered, and were exceedingly stylish. Several of the white ones were barred like zebras with rainbow stripes of blue and red and yellow paint. These were indescribably gorgeous. Dan and Jack selected from this lot because they brought back Italian reminiscences of the 'old masters.'

Mark Twain (1835–1910)

Even Yet

First published 2021

Even yet (past dark boles where whispers lay) our hooves—not quite cloven—found weight on dampened gorse, as keen mouths with hardened lips voiced unseen cries above us.

The sleeping houses—moon sheathed and watchless—recoiled from our passing: pale bodies in motion, and even yet gathering a silent pace.

Joel Knight (1975–)

The Phoenix Rises From the Fire

From *The Phoenix and the Carpet*, 1904

The egg was now red-hot, and inside it something was moving. Next moment there was a soft cracking sound; the egg burst in two, and out of it came a flame-coloured bird. It rested a moment among the flames, and as it rested there the four children could see it growing bigger and bigger under their eyes.

Every mouth was a-gape, every eye a-goggle.

The bird rose in its nest of fire, stretched its wings, and flew out into the room. It flew round and round, and round again, and where it passed the air was warm. Then it perched on the fender. The children looked at each other. Then Cyril put out a hand towards the bird. It put its head on one side and looked up at him, as you may have seen a parrot do when it is just going to speak, so that the children were hardly astonished at all when it said, 'Be careful; I am not nearly cool yet.'

They were not astonished, but they were very, very much interested.

They looked at the bird, and it was certainly worth looking at. Its feathers were like gold. It was about as large as a bantam, only its beak was not at all bantam-shaped. 'I believe I know what it is,' said Robert. 'I've seen a picture –'

He hurried away. A hasty dash and scramble among the papers on father's study table yielded, as the sum-books say, 'the desired result'. But when he came back into the room holding out a paper, and crying, 'I say, look here,' the others all said 'Hush!' and he hushed obediently and instantly, for the bird was speaking.

'Which of you,' it was saying, 'put the egg into the fire?'

'He did,' said three voices, and three fingers pointed at Robert.

The bird bowed; at least it was more like that than anything else.

'I am your grateful debtor,' it said with a high-bred air.

The children were all choking with wonder and curiosity – all except Robert. He held the paper in his hand, and he knew. He said so. He said – 'I know who you are.'

And he opened and displayed a printed paper, at the head of which was a little picture of a bird sitting in a nest of flames.

'You are the Phoenix,' said Robert; and the bird was quite pleased.

E. Nesbit (1858–1924)

The Phoenix

From *Pseudodoxia Epidemica*, Chap. XII, Of the Phoenix, 1650

That there is but one Phoenix in the World, which after many hundred years burneth it self, and from the ashes thereof ariseth up another, is a conceit not new or altogether popular, but of great Antiquity; not only delivered by humane Authors, but frequently expressed also by holy Writers.

. . . .

All which notwithstanding, we cannot presume the existence of this Animall; nor dare we affirm there is any Phoenix in Nature. For, first there wants herein the definitive confirmator and test of things uncertain, that is, the sense of man. For though many Writers have much enlarged hereon, yet is there not any ocular describer, or such as presumeth to confirm it upon aspection.

. . . .

Nor are men only at variance in regard of the Phoenix it self, but very disagreeing in the accidents ascribed thereto: for some affirm it liveth three hundred, some five, others six, some a thousand, others no lesse then fifteen hundred years; some say it liveth in Æthiopia, others in Arabia, some in Ægypt, others in India, and some in Utopia.

Sir Thomas Browne (1605–1682)

The Rulers of East and West

From *The Mirror of the Sea*, 1913

There is no part of the world of coasts, continents, oceans, seas, straits, capes, and islands which is not under the sway of a reigning wind, the sovereign of its typical weather.

As a ruler, the East Wind has a remarkable stability; as an invader of the high latitudes lying under the tumultuous sway of his great brother, the Wind of the West, he is extremely difficult to dislodge, by the reason of his cold craftiness and profound duplicity.

The narrow seas around these isles, where British admirals keep watch and ward upon the marches of the Atlantic Ocean, are subject to the turbulent sway of the West Wind. Call it north-west or south-west, it is all one – a different phase of the same character, a changed expression on the same face. In the orientation of the winds that rule the seas, the north and south directions are of no importance. There are no North and South Winds of any account upon this earth. The North and South Winds are but small princes in the dynasties that make peace and war upon the sea. They never assert themselves upon a vast stage. They depend upon local causes – the configuration of coasts, the shapes of straits, the accidents of bold promontories round which they play their little part. In the polity of winds, as amongst the tribes of the earth, the real struggle lies between East and West.

Joseph Conrad (1857–1924)

The Setting Sun

From *North and South*, 1854

There was a filmy veil of soft dull mist obscuring, but not hiding, all objects, giving them a lilac hue, for the sun had not yet fully set; a robin was singing, – perhaps, Margaret thought, the very robin that her father had so often talked of as his winter pet, and for which he had made, with his own hands, a kind of robin-house by his study-window. The leaves were more gorgeous than ever; the first touch of frost would lay them all low on the ground. Already one or two kept constantly floating down, amber and golden in the low slanting sun-rays.

Elizabeth Gaskell (1810–1865)

Snakes

From *Wild Life in a Southern County*, 1879

There is no subject upon which they [farm labourers] make such extraordinary statements, evidently believing what they say, as about snakes. A man told me once that he had been pursued by a snake, which rushed after him at such a speed that he could barely escape; the snake not only glided but actually leaped over the ground. Now this must have been pure imagination: he fancied he saw an adder, and fled, and in his terror thought himself pursued. They constantly state that they have seen adders; but I am confident that no viper exists in this district, nor for some miles round. That they do elsewhere of course is well known, but not here; neither is the slow-worm ever seen.

The belief that snakes can jump – or coil themselves up and spring – is, however, very prevalent. They all tell you that a snake can leap across a ditch. This is not true. A snake, if alarmed, will make for the hedge; and he glides much faster than would be supposed. On reaching the shore or edge of the ditch he projects his head over it, and some six or eight inches of the neck, while the rest of the body slides down the slope. If it happens to be a steep-sided ditch he often loses his balance and rolls to the bottom; and that is what has been mistaken for leaping. As he rises up the mound he follows a zigzag course, and presently enters some small hole or a cavity in a decaying stole. After creeping in some distance he often meets with an obstruction, and has to remain half in and half out till he can force his way. He usually takes possession of a mouse-hole, and does not seem to be able to enlarge it for additional convenience.

Richard Jefferies (1848–1887)

Fog

From *Bleak House*, 1853

Fog everywhere. Fog up the river, where it flows among green aits and meadows; fog down the river, where it rolls defiled among the tiers of shipping and the waterside pollutions of a great (and dirty) city. Fog on the Essex marshes, fog on the Kentish heights. Fog creeping into the cabooses of collier-brigs; fog lying out on the yards and hovering in the rigging of great ships; fog drooping on the gunwales of barges and small boats. Fog in the eyes and throats of ancient Greenwich pensioners, wheezing by the firesides of their wards; fog in the stem and bowl of the afternoon pipe of the wrathful skipper, down in his close cabin; fog cruelly pinching the toes and fingers of his shivering little 'prentice boy on deck. Chance people on the bridges peeping over the parapets into a nether sky of fog, with fog all round them, as if they were up in a balloon and hanging in the misty clouds.

Charles Dickens (1812–1870)

Crystals of Shining Silver

From *Nature Rambles*, 1930

If we are out early in the day after a misty evening followed by a very cold night, we shall find the land transformed: the bushes and the ground vegetation that was yesterday a matter mainly of dead stems are all changed into a scene of great beauty. Tall, dry stalks of Cow Parsnip are coated with crystals of shining silver, the dead bents of tall grass bear knobs of the same glistening material, and the reddened leaves of the Brambles are outlined with a silver edging. More striking, perhaps, are the rosettes of wayside Thistles under this powdering of hoar-frost; every lobe and prickle is silvered and bright. All the dead leaves on the ground that are loose have similar glory sprinkled over them. This wonderful sight must be enjoyed early in the day, for an hour or so of winter sunshine will dissolve all the ice-crystals.

Edward Step (1855–1931)

Defenders of Wilderness

From *A Sand County Almanac and Sketches Here and There,* The Upshot, 1949

Wilderness is a resource which can shrink but not grow. Invasions can be arrested or modified in a manner to keep an area usable for either recreation, or for science, or for wildlife, but the creation of new wilderness in the full sense of the world is impossible.

It follows, then, that any wilderness program is a rearguard action, through which retreats are reduced to a minimum. The Wilderness Society was organized in 1935 'for the one purpose of saving wilderness remnants in America.'

It does not suffice, however, to have such a society. Unless there be wilderness-minded men scattered through all the conservation bureaus, the society may never learn of new invasions until the time for action has passed. Furthermore, a militant minority of wilderness-minded citizens must be on watch throughout the nation, and available for action in a pinch.

Aldo Leopold (1887–1948)

The Snow Goose

From *The Snow Goose*, 1941

The bird was a young one, no more than a year old. She was born in a northern land far, far across the seas, a land belonging to England. Flying to the south to escape the snow and ice and bitter cold, a great storm had seized her and whirled and buffeted her about. It was a truly terrible storm, stronger than her great wings, stronger than anything. For days and nights it held her in its grip and there was nothing she could do but fly before it. When finally it had blown itself out and her sure instincts took her south again, she was over a different land and surrounded by strange birds that she had never seen before. At last, exhausted by her ordeal, she had sunk to rest in a friendly green marsh, only to be met by the blast from the hunter's gun.

'A bitter reception for a visiting princess,' concluded Rhayader. 'We will call her 'La Princesse Perdue,' the Lost Princess. And in a few days she will be feeling much better. See!' He reached into his pocket and produced a handful of grain. The snow goose opened its round yellow eyes and nibbled at it.

Paul Gallico (1897–1976)

A Kingfisher

From *Diary*, 1906

November 14:

I saw a Kingfisher fly across the little pool by the road-side below Olton station today. The new Catkins are showing on all the Alder and Hazel trees now.

The sun had a most remarkable appearance just before setting tonight. I never saw it look so large in my life. It was deep crimson, shaded with purple which gave it a globular appearance, and it looked like a huge fire-balloon suspended against a curtain of grey cloud.

Edith Holden (1871–1920)

Nature and Naturalness

From *The Common Ground*, 1980

If we wanted to keep our wildlife, would we have to begin regarding it as another article of trade between countryside and consumer – perhaps even begin paying for it, as we did for bread and beer and newsprint. When it was put that baldly it seemed an alien and offensive suggestion, an infringement of a natural right that would be on a par with having to pay for air or sunshine. It also seemed, in some less definable way, to debase one of the intrinsic values of nature, which is – and it is not a truism to say so – its naturalness.

Nature has always had this double meaning for us, being a matter of style as much as content, a way of being as much a collection of living things. For much of our history the two had run parallel, and the 'natural things' – the bluebells and the butterflies – had appeared 'naturally', without effort or planning. That was part of their appeal. But the radical changes brought about by the new agriculture made us sharply aware that what we had regarded as a natural landscape was a much more complex product of growth and husbandry. The turf of the southern chalk downs, which W. H. Hudson christened 'the living garment', turned out to be the product of intensive sheep-grazing. A good deal of it had once been under the plough and before that the site of Celtic forts and townships. The wild sweeps of moorland in the Scottish Highlands had been created by a massive programme of forest clearance. The Norfolk Broads were the flooded remains of medieval open-cast peat-mines. Heaths and reed-beds would cease to exist if they were not deliberately cut or burnt. Even the new protectiveness itself seems to compromise the natural world with a slight hint of preciousness. Could we really use the word 'natural' about orchids which depended upon artificial pollination for their survival, or butterflies that had been bred in tented enclosures?

These new realizations raised many fundamental questions. If part of what we valued about nature was its wildness and spontaneity, was deliberate nature conservation a contradiction in terms? Was the familiar picture of British wildlife we had inherited, and which was captured so perfectly by Clare, already an anachronism, on a par with the perennial nostalgia for some pastoral Golden Age? Had the time come for us, as products of late-twentieth-century industrialization, to 'grow out' of the natural world? We could always save its bits and pieces in zoos and botanical gardens if we wished. If we preferred to be thoroughly modern we could even make them out of plastic, as was seriously suggested by a senior official in the Department of the Environment [in *The Sunday Times*, 11 June 1978].

Richard Mabey (1941–)

The Legend of the Dog

From *Wild Wales*, 1862

Llywelyn during his contests with the English had encamped with
a few followers in the valley, and one day departed with his men
on an expedition, leaving his infant son in a cradle in his tent,
under the care of his hound Gelert, after giving the child its fill
of goat's milk. Whilst he was absent a wolf from the neighbouring
mountains, in quest of prey, found its way into the tent, and was
about to devour the child, when the watchful dog interfered,
and after a desperate conflict, in which the tent was torn down,
succeeded in destroying the monster. Llywelyn returning at
evening found the tent on the ground, and the dog, covered with
blood, sitting beside it. Imagining that the blood with which
Gelert was besmeared was that of his own son devoured by the
animal to whose care he had confided him, Llywelyn in a paroxysm
of natural indignation forthwith transfixed the faithful creature
with his spear. Scarcely, however, had he done so when his ears
were startled by the cry of a child from beneath the fallen tent, and
hastily removing the canvas he found the child in its cradle, quite
uninjured, and the body of an enormous wolf, frightfully torn and
mangled, lying near. His breast was now filled with conflicting
emotions, joy for the preservation of his son, and grief for the
fate of his dog, to whom he forthwith hastened. The poor animal
was not quite dead, but presently expired, in the act of licking
his master's hand. Llywelyn mourned over him as over a brother,
buried him with funeral honours in the valley, and erected
a tomb over him as over a hero. From that time the valley was
called Beth Gelert.

Such is the legend, which, whether true or fictitious, is
singularly beautiful and affecting.

George Borrow (1803–1881)

Justification

From *The Charm of Birds*, 1927

This book will have no scientific value. Those who have studied birds will not find anything in it that they do not already know; those who do not care for birds will not be interested in the subject. The writing of the book, and still more the publishing of it, require some explanation.

· · · · · · · · · ·

After all, it is not entirely to exchange information that lovers of birds converse together on the subject. An artist will paint the commonest object in order to bring out some aspect that has particularly struck him. So with watchers of birds, some are attracted by one aspect of a well-known species and some by another. Thus even those of us who have nothing new to tell, may have something that is fresh to say.

Sir Edward Grey (1862–1933)

The Elephant

From *Natural History*, Book VIII, AD 77
Translated by Henry T. Riley (1816–1878) and John Bostock (1773–1846), first published 1855

The largest land animal is the elephant, and it is the nearest to
man in intelligence: it understands the language of its country
and obeys orders, remembers duties that it has been taught, is
pleased by affection and by marks of honour, nay more it possesses
virtues rare even in man, honesty, wisdom, justice, also respect for
the stars and reverence for the sun and moon. Authorities state
that in the forests of Mauretania, when the new moon is shining,
herds of elephants go down to a river named Amilo and there
perform a ritual of purification, sprinkling themselves with water,
and after thus paying their respects to the moon return to the
woods carrying before them those of their calves who are tired.
They are also believed to understand the obligations of another's
religion in so far as to refuse to embark on board ships when going
overseas before they are lured on by the mahout's sworn promise
in regard to their return. And they have been seen when exhausted
by suffering (as even those vast frames are attacked by diseases)
to lie on their backs and throw grass up to the heaven, as though
deputing the earth to support their prayers.

Pliny the Elder (AD c. 23–79)

Gos the Goshawk

From *The Goshawk*, 1937

Hawks were the nobility of the air, ruled by the eagle. They were the only creatures for which man had troubled to legislate:

The *Boke of St Albans* had laid down precisely the classes of people to whom any proper-minded member of the Falconidae might belong. An eagle for an emperor, a peregrine for an earl: the list had defined itself meticulously downward to the kestrel, and he, as crowning insult, was allowed to belong to a mere knave – because he was useless to be trained. Well, a goshawk was the proper servant of a yeoman, and I was well content with that.

There are two kinds of these raptors, the long-winged and the short-winged hawks. Long-winged hawks, whose first primary feather was on the whole the longest, were the 'falcons', who were attended by falconers. Short-winged hawks, whose fourth primary was the longest, were the true 'hawks', who were attended by austringers. Falcons flew high and stooped upon their quarry: hawks flew low, and slew by stealth. Gos was chieftain among the latter.

But it was his own personality that gave more pleasure than his lineage. He had a way of looking. Cats can watch a mousehole cruelly, dogs can be seen to watch their masters with love, a mouse watched Robert Burns with fear. It was an alert, concentrated, piercing look. My duty at present was not to return it. Hawks are sensitive to the eye and do not like to be regarded. It is their prerogative to regard.

T. H. White (1906–1964)

The Scent of the City

From *Greyfriars Bobby*, 1912

Bobby makes his way back to Auld Jock's grave:

Suddenly shifting a point, the wind brought to the little dog's nose
a whiff of the acrid coal smoke of Edinburgh three miles away.

Straight as an arrow he ran across country, over roadway and
wall, ploughed fields and rippling burns. He scrambled under
hedges and dashed across farmsteads and cottage gardens. As he
neared the city the hour bells aided him, for the Skye terrier is
keen of hearing. It was growing dark when he climbed up the last
bank and gained Lauriston Place. There he picked up the odours of
milk and wool, and the damp smell of the kirkyard.

Now for something comforting to put into his famished little
body. A night and a day of exhausting work, of anxiety and grief,
had used up the last ounce of fuel. Bobby raced down Forest
Road and turned the slight angle into Greyfriars Place. The lamp
lighter's progress toward the bridge was marked by the double row
of lamps that bloomed, one after one, on the dusk. The little dog
had come to the steps of Mr. Traill's place, and lifted himself to
scratch on the door, when the bugle began to blow. He dropped
with the first note and dashed to the kirkyard gate.

None too soon! Mr. Brown was setting the little wicket gate
inside, against the wall. In the instant his back was turned, Bobby
slipped through. After nightfall, when the caretaker had made his
rounds, he came out from under the fallen table-tomb of Mistress
Jean Grant.

Lights appeared at the rear windows of the tenements, and families sat at supper. It was snell weather again, the sky dark with threat of snow, and the windows were all closed. But with a sharp bark beneath the lowest of them Bobby could have made his presence and his wants known. He watched the people eating, sitting wistfully about on his haunches here and there, but remaining silent. By and by there were sounds of crying babies, of crockery being washed, and the ringing of church bells far and near. Then the lights were extinguished, and huge bulks of shadow, of tenements and kirk, engulfed the kirkyard.

When Bobby lay down on Auld Jock's grave, pellets of frozen snow were falling and the air had hardened toward frost.

Eleanor Atkinson (1863–1942)

Lichens and Mosses

From *The Peverel Papers*, November, 1925

The mosses and lichens are brightening to another blooming. In the woods in winter they may be seen in their full beauty, thriving upon damp and cold as other plants do upon sunshine: the mosses rising, golden-green, feathery or clubbed, from dead leaves and withered herbage; the lichens splashing the rugged bark of trees with orange, rust and smoke-grey, hanging from the leafless thorns like beards, and covering flat stones and naked earth with patterns embossed in black or yellow.

Strange plants! The winter of all other vegetation is their spring; and at the dead of the year, just before and after Christmas, many a bank and hillside will be brightened with their flowering. At that season a small microscope adds greatly to the pleasures of country ramblers. By its aid a thousand unsuspected beauties are revealed; splashes of rust or orange are seen as whole flower gardens within a few square inches, and the sight of the infinitesimal cup or star-shaped florets is bound to lead to the study of the structure and habits of the different varieties.

Flora Thompson (1876–1947)

The Heath

From *The Return of the Native*, 1878

A Saturday afternoon in November was approaching the time of twilight, and the vast tract of unenclosed wild known as Egdon Heath embrowned itself moment by moment. Overhead the hollow stretch of whitish cloud shutting out the sky was as a tent which had the whole heath for its floor.

The heaven being spread with this pallid screen and the earth with the darkest vegetation, their meeting-line at the horizon was clearly marked. In such contrast the heath wore the appearance of an instalment of night which had taken up its place before its astronomical hour was come: darkness had to a great extent arrived hereon, while day stood distinct in the sky. Looking upwards, a furze-cutter would have been inclined to continue work; looking down, he would have decided to finish his faggot and go home. The distant rims of the world and of the firmament seemed to be a division in time no less than a division in matter. The face of the heath by its mere complexion added half an hour to evening; it could in like manner retard the dawn, sadden noon, anticipate the frowning of storms scarcely generated, and intensify the opacity of a moonless midnight to a cause of shaking and dread.

Thomas Hardy (1840–1928)

The Arrival of Mijbil

From *Ring of Bright Water*, 1960

Gavin Maxwell is handed a squirming sack, with the following note attached: 'Here is your otter. Wilfred Thesiger.'

The creature that emerged, not greatly disconcerted, from this sack onto the spacious tiled floor of the Consulate bedroom did not at that moment resemble anything so much as a very small medievally conceived dragon. From the head to the tip of the tail he was coated with symmetrical pointed scales of mud armour, between whose tips was visible a soft velvet fur like that of a chocolate-brown mole. He shook himself, and I half-expected this aggressive camouflage to disintegrate into a cloud of dust, but it remained unaffected by this manoeuvre, and in fact it was not for another month that I contrived to remove the last of it and see him, as it were, in his true colours.

Gavin Maxwell (1914–1969)

Hawkley Hanger

From *Rural Rides*, 1822

November 24th

On we trotted up this pretty green lane; and indeed, we had been coming gently and generally *up hill* for a good while. The lane was between highish banks and pretty high stuff growing on the banks, so that we could see no distance from us, and could receive not the smallest hint of what was so near at hand. The lane had a little turn towards the end; so that, out we came, all in a moment, at the very *edge of the hanger*! And never, in all my life, was I so surprised and so delighted! I pulled up my horse, and sat and looked; and it was like looking from the top of a castle down into the sea, except that the valley was land and not water. I looked at my servant, to see what effect this unexpected sight had upon him. His surprise was as great as mine, though he had been bred amongst the North Hampshire hills. Those who had so strenuously dwelt on the dirt and dangers of this route, had said not a word about beauties, the matchless beauties of the scenery. These hangers are *woods* on the

The Polecat

From *A Victorian Poacher: James Hawker's Journal*, 1906

One word about the Polecat. Many people are under the impression that this animal is a species of the House Cat. I have asked many men if they have ever se one. They generally say yes. But when I ask them to Describe it, they can't. I have seen one alive, two stuffed.

When seven years of age I used to take a Labourer's Dinner – he lived next door – to the Farm I first went to work on. While the old man sat having his Dinner, a Dog he had with him began to scratch at a hole in some standing beans. 'Boy,' cried the labourer, 'go an Find a Bolt hole and Stop it up if you can. He's got a Rat.' I found the Bolt Hole. But instead of stopping it up I began to Dig it out with a Piece of Stick and in a few minutes the Dog had him. The old man say, 'Why boy, it's a Pole cat.' Now after sixty-three years I can smell it. You have heard the remark, 'You stink like a Pole Cat.' There is a good reason for it.

James Hawker (1836–1921)

A Leafy November

From *Chronicles of the Hedges*, 1879

The poplars alone at the opening of the month were bare of leaves. These tall trees, lifting their slender tops so high above the rest, contrasted the more in their leafless state with the thick foliage of the wood beneath them. Rows of elms in the hedges were still green, and of those that did show a yellow tint many upon examination could be seen to be decaying in the trunk or branches. That part of an elm which is slowly dying usually turns yellow first. On some of the oaks the inner leaves were still greenish, while those on the outer boughs were brown, and the mingling of the two tints seen at a little distance under the sunshine produced a remarkable and pleasing colour. Other oak trees had assumed so red a brown as to approach to copper colour. The ash standing in the same hedge was a tender green with the faintest undertone of yellow, and the lowly elder bushes were not less green than at midsummer. Between the dark Scotch firs the foliage of the beeches seemed warm red. The branches of the larch had a fluffy appearance, caused by the yellow needles which had partly separated but had not yet fallen. Horse-chestnuts even retained some leaves; of those that had dropped a few were half yellow and half green, the hues divided by the midrib. Birches, too, except just at the corners of the copses or in isolated positions, were not yet bare. Under the Spanish chestnuts heaps of leaves had collected, in walking through which the foot often exposed the dropped fruit hidden beneath them; but though so many had fallen the branches were not entirely denuded; while whole hedgerows full of maple bushes glowed with orange. The sun shone brilliantly day after day, lighting up the varied hues of the trees and hedges and filling the woodlands with beauty.

Richard Jefferies (1848–1887)

A Moonbow

From *Meadowland*, 2014

27 November

Tonight I see something I have never seen before, something
I never even knew of. It's late, and I have gone for a moon-time
walk around the fields, because I love the solitude of the dark.
While I am looking to the west and the unbroken night of mid-
Wales, an arch of white light suddenly appears in the sky and
spans the earth before me. I feel afraid, as though I have been
singled out for some almighty moment of revelation, that I have
been entrusted with some Damascene vision, and several seconds
pass before I understand what it is I am looking at.

I am looking at a rainbow at night. A moonbow.

John Lewis-Stempel (1961–)

Buck

From *The Call of the Wild*, 1903

Buck's father, Elmo, a huge St. Bernard, had been the Judge's inseparable companion, and Buck bid fair to follow in the way of his father. He was not so large, – he weighed only one hundred and forty pounds, – for his mother, Shep, had been a Scotch shepherd dog. Nevertheless, one hundred and forty pounds, to which was added the dignity that comes of good living and universal respect, enabled him to carry himself in right royal fashion. During the four years since his puppyhood he had lived the life of a sated aristocrat; he had a fine pride in himself, was even a trifle egotistical, as country gentlemen sometimes become because of their insular situation. But he had saved himself by not becoming a mere pampered house-dog. Hunting and kindred outdoor delights had kept down the fat and hardened his muscles; and to him, as to the cold-tubbing races, the love of water had been a tonic and a health preserver.

Jack London (1876–1916)

Hodge

From *The Life of Samuel Johnson*, 1791

I never shall forget the indulgence with which he treated Hodge, his cat: for whom he himself used to go out and buy oysters, lest the servants having that trouble should take a dislike to the poor creature. I am, unluckily, one of those who have an antipathy to a cat, so that I am uneasy when in the room with one; and I own, I frequently suffered a good deal from the presence of this same Hodge. I recollect him one day scrambling up Dr. Johnson's breast, apparently with much satisfaction, while my friend smiling and half-whistling, rubbed down his back, and pulled him by the tail; and when I observed he was a fine cat, saying, 'Why yes, Sir, but I have had cats whom I liked better than this;' and then as if perceiving Hodge to be out of countenance, adding, 'but he is a very fine cat, a very fine cat indeed.'

James Boswell (1740–1795)

The Colours of Starlight

From *The Pocket Encyclopaedia of Natural Phenomena*, 1827

Enough attention has never been paid to the prevailing colours of different stars, a circumstance of some practical importance to astronomical observations:

According to our opinion and observations, the stars should be classed according to their colours into the red, the yellow, the brilliant white, the dull white, and the anomalous. For though each star may differ somewhat from every other, yet we shall be assisted by this general classification.

When observed with a prismatic glass, *Sirius* shows a large brush of extremely beautiful violet colour, and generally speaking, the most refrangible rays in great quantity. The same applies more or less to all the bright white stars.

Procyon is far less beautiful than *Sirius*, and shows rather more of the yellow colour.

Aldebaran, together with many of the other red stars, exhibits only a very small proportion of the more refrangible colours, and has much of the red light.

Arcturus much resembles *Aldebaran*, but differs in the lesser proportion of the red to the yellow rays.

Betalgeus is a very red star, little inferior in magnitude to the two above. This star shows also but little of the more refrangible rays; but the spectrum is always a bad one, and for some unknown cause more liable to fluctuation than the above two.

Lyra and *Spica Virginis*, show much blue light, *Capella* is yellowish, *Alpliard* reddish, *Markab*, *Menkar*, and *Deneb* of the ordinary colour.

Antares, the most extraordinary star of all, contains, like *Aldebaran* and *Arcturus*, much red light; but owing to its greater southern declination as well as to something very peculiar in the composition of its light, we cannot get so perfect a spectrum as might be desirable. This star, too, exhibits in the greatest degree a peculiar and hitherto unexplained phaenomenon which will always interfere with our observations on its permanent spectrum. We allude to the rapid permutations of the colour of its light; every alternate twinkling, if we may so express ourselves, being of an intense reddish crimson colour, and the alternate one of a brilliant white.

Thomas Furley Forster (1761–1825)

DECEMBER

Sloping Drifts of Snow

Everything Has its Own Season

From *Nature Rambles*, 1930

There is one aspect of the gradual close of autumn and the onset of winter of which the rambler should not lose sight. The feeling that is pretty general among people of the average sort is that the country at this season is a place to be avoided: empty, dull, without interest. All the pretty things like flowers and butterflies have disappeared; the birds are silent; the trees are bare poles and the woods are damp and gloomy. This is the accepted notion: but whenever you have the chance for a ramble on a fine day, go forth and prove to yourself how absurd it all is. Some of the details of the wail are true, of course; but the general charge is false. We must not expect to find Snowdrops in October or Blackberries in spring. Everything has its season for display; and we cannot learn the story of the year if we read only eight or nine of its twelve chapters.

Edward Step (1855–1931)

A Perfect Combination

From *The Irish R.M.*, 1928

It was a day when frost and sunshine combined went to one's head like iced champagne.

Somerville & Ross
(Edith Somerville, 1858–1949,
and Martin Ross / Violet Florence Martin, 1862–1915)

The Red Squirrel

From *Walden or Life in the Woods*, 1854

Usually the red squirrel (*Sciurus hudsonius*) waked me in the dawn, coursing over the roof and up and down the sides of the house, as if sent out of the woods for this purpose. In the course of the winter I threw out half a bushel of ears of sweet-corn, which had not got ripe, on to the snow crust by my door, and was amused by watching the motions of the various animals which were baited by it. In the twilight and the night the rabbits came regularly and made a hearty meal. All day long the red squirrels came and went, and afforded me much entertainment by their manœuvres. One would approach at first warily through the shrub-oaks, running over the snow crust by fits and starts like a leaf blown by the wind, now a few paces this way, with wonderful speed and waste of energy, making inconceivable haste with his 'trotters,' as if it were for a wager, and now as many paces that way, but never getting on more than half a rod at a time; and then suddenly pausing with a ludicrous expression and a gratuitous somerset, as if all the eyes in the universe were fixed on him, – for all the motions of a squirrel, even in the most solitary recesses of the forest, imply spectators as much as those of a dancing girl.

Henry David Thoreau (1817–1862)

The Rarest Animal of All

From *The Story of Doctor Dolittle*, 1920

Pushmi-pullyus are now extinct. That means, there aren't any more. But long ago, when Doctor Dolittle was alive there were some of them still left in the deepest jungles of Africa; and even then they were very, very scarce. They had no tail, but a head at each end, and sharp horns on each head. They were very shy and terribly hard to catch. The Africans get most of their animals by sneaking up behind them while they are not looking. But you could not do this with the pushmi-pullyu – because, no matter which way you came towards him, he was always facing you. And besides, only one-half of him slept at a time. The other head was always awake – and watching. This was why they were never caught and never seen in Zoos. Though many of the greatest huntsmen and the cleverest menagerie-keepers spent years of their lives searching through the jungles in all weathers for pushmi-pullyus, not a single one had ever been caught. Even then, years ago, he was the only animal in the world with two heads.

Hugh Lofting (1886–1947)

Chisil Bank

From *The Itinerary of John Leland In or About the Years* 1535–1543

A litle above Abbates-Byri is the hed or point of the Chisil lying north weste, that from thens streachf up 7. miles as a maine narow banke by a right line on to south est, and ther buttith on Portland scant a quarter of a mile above the new castell in Portland.

The nature of this bank of Chisil is such that as often as the wind blowith strene at south est so often the se betith it and losiththe bank [and so] kith thorough it; so that if this winde might most continually blow there this bank should sone be beten away and the se fully enter and devide Portland, making it an isle, as surely in tymes past it hath beene as far as I can by any conjecture gather.

But as much as the south est wind dooth bete and breke of this Chisille bank, so much doth the north west wynd again socor, strengith and augmentith it.

John Leland (c. 1506–1552)

Of the Bear

From *The History of Four-footed Beasts*, Volume I, 1607

First, therefore concerning several kinds of Bears, it is observed, that there is in general two; a greater, and a lesser; and these lesser are more apt to clime trees then the other, neither do they ever grow to so great a stature as the other. Besides there are Bears which are called *Amphibia*, because they live both on the Land and in the Sea, hunting and catching fish like an *Otter* or *Beaver*, and these are white coloured. In the Ocean Islands towards the North, there are Bears of a great stature, fierce and cruel, who with their fore-feet do break up the hardest congealed Ice on the Sea, or other great Waters, and draw out of those holes great abundance of fishes: and so in other frozen Seas are many such like, having black claws, living for the most part upon the Seas, except tempestuous weather drive them to the Land.

Edward Topsell (1572–1625)

Tea in the Garden

From *Elizabeth and Her German Garden*, 1898

Yesterday I sat out of doors near the sun-dial the whole afternoon, with the thermometer so many degrees below freezing that it will be weeks finding its way up again; but there was no wind, and beautiful sunshine, and I was well wrapped up in furs. I even had tea brought out there, to the astonishment of the menials, and sat till long after the sun had set, enjoying the frosty air. I had to drink the tea very quickly, for it showed a strong inclination to begin to freeze. After the sun had gone down the rooks came home to their nests in the garden with a great fuss and fluttering, and many hesitations and squabbles before they settled on their respective trees. They flew over my head in hundreds with a mighty swish of wings, and when they had arranged themselves comfortably, an intense hush fell upon the garden, and the house began to look like a Christmas card, with its white roof against the clear, pale green of the western sky, and lamplight shining in the windows.

Elizabeth von Arnim (1866–1941)

The Great Storm

From *Kilvert's Diary*, 1872

8 December

The morning had been lovely, but during our singing practice after evening Church at about half past four began the Great Storm of 1872. Suddenly the wind rose up and began to roar at the Tower window and shake the panes and lash the glass with torrents of rain. It grew very dark. The storm increased and we struggled home in torrents of rain and tempests of wind so fearful that we could hardly force our way across the Common to the Rectory. All the evening the roaring S.W. wind raged more and more furious. It seemed as if the windows on the west side of the house must be blown in. The glass cracked and strained and bent and the storm shrieked and wailed and howled like multitudes of lost spirits. I went out to see where the cows were, fearing that the large elms in the Avenue might fall and crush them. The trees were writhing, swaying, rocking, lashing their arms wildly and straining terribly in the tempest but I could not see that any were gone yet. The twin firs in the orchard seemed the worst off, they gave the wind such a power and purchase, with their heavy green boughs, and their tops were swaying fearfully and bending nearly double under the tremendous strain. The moon was high and the clouds drove wild and fast across her face. Dark storms and thick black drifts were hurrying up out of the west, where the Almighty was making the clouds His chariot and walking upon the wings of the wind. Now and then the moon looked out for a moment wild and terrified through a savage rent in the storm.

Francis Kilvert (1840–1879)

A Certain Kind of Magpie

From *Natural History*, Book X, AD 77
Translated by Henry T. Riley (1816–1878) and John Bostock (1773–1846), first published 1855

A certain kind of magpie is less celebrated, because it does not come from a distance, but it talks more articulately. These birds get fond of uttering particular words, and not only learn them but love them, and secretly ponder them with careful reflexion, not concealing their engrossment. It is an established fact that if the difficulty of a word beats them this causes their death, and that their memory fails them unless they hear the same word repeatedly, and when they are at a loss for a word they cheer up wonderfully if in the meantime they hear it spoken. Their shape is unusual, though not beautiful: this bird has enough distinction in its power of imitating the human voice.

Pliny the Elder (AD c. 23–79)

A Submerged Forest

The Itinerary of Archbishop Baldwin Through Wales, Book I, Chapter XIII, c. 1188
Translated by Sir Richard Colt Hoare (1758–1838)

The sandy shores of South Wales, being laid bare by the
extraordinary violence of a storm, the surface of the earth, which
had been covered for many ages, re-appeared, and discovered the
trunks of trees cut off, standing in the very sea itself, the strokes
of the hatchet appearing as if made only yesterday. The soil was
very black, and the wood like ebony. By a wonderful revolution,
the road for ships became impassable, and looked, not like a shore,
but like a grove cut down, perhaps, at the time of the deluge, or
not long after, but certainly in very remote ages, being by degrees
consumed and swallowed up by the violence and encroachments
of the sea.

Giraldus Cambrensis / Gerald of Wales (c. 1146–1223)

Snow in the Wild Wood

From *The Wind in the Willows*, 1908

The Otter goes in search of the Mole and the Rat:

'I came straight off here, through the Wild Wood and the snow!
My! it was fine, coming through the snow as the red sun was rising
and showing against the black tree-trunks! As you went along
in the stillness, every now and then masses of snow slid off the
branches suddenly with a flop! making you jump and run for cover.
Snow-castles and snow-caverns had sprung up out of nowhere in
the night – and snow bridges, terraces, ramparts – I could have
stayed and played with them for hours. Here and there great
branches had been torn away by the sheer weight of the snow,
and robins perched and hopped on them in their perky conceited
way, just as if they had done it themselves. A ragged string of
wild geese passed overhead, high on the grey sky, and a few rooks
whirled over the trees, inspected, and flapped off homewards with
a disgusted expression.'

Kenneth Grahame (1859–1932)

Trees in Winter

From *Kilvert's Diary*, 1874

12 December

There is a beauty in the trees peculiar to winter, when their fair delicate slender tracery unveiled by leaves and showing clearly against the sky rises bending with a lofty arch or sweeps gracefully drooping. The crossing and interlacing of the limbs, the smaller boughs and tender twigs make an exquisitely fine network which has something of the severe beauty of sculpture, while the tree in summer in its full pride and splendour and colour of foliage represents the loveliness of painting. The deciduous trees which seem to me most graceful and elegant in winter are the birches, limes, beeches.

Francis Kilvert (1840–1879)

The Redbreast, or Robin
(Erithacus rubecula)

From *British Birds in their Haunts*, 1909

The Redbreast is everywhere invested with a kind of sanctity beyond all other birds. Its wonted habit of making its appearance, no one knows whence, to greet the resting traveller in places the most lonely – its evident predilection for the society of the out-door labourer, whatever his occupation – the constancy with which it affects human habitations – and the readiness with which, without coaxing, or taming, or training, it throws itself on human hospitality – engender an idea that there must be some mysterious connexion between the two – that if there were no men, there would be no Redbreasts. Trust on one side engenders confidence on the other, and mutual attachment is the natural result. There is something, too, beyond the power of explanation in the fact that the Robin is the only bird which frequents from choice the homes of men.

The habits of the Redbreast are so well known, that to describe them would be simply to write down what every one has seen or may see.

Rev. C. A. Johns (1811–1874)

The Redbreast or Robbin Redbreast (Sylvia rubicola)

From *The Pocket Encyclopaedia of Natural Phenomena*, 1827

The Redbreast or Robbin Redbreast *Sylvia rubicola** migrates from the groves and thickets towards the habitation of man in November, and in the frost of the hybernal season comes close to our windows, and even our firesides, when it can find entrance, in search of food.

Thomas Furley Forster (1761–1825)

Hawes Water – A Perfect Lake

From *Can You Forgive Her?* 1864

Alice and Kate take a walk:

A lake should, I think, be small, and should be seen from above, to be seen in all its glory. The distance should be such that the shadows of the mountains on its surface may just be traced, and that some faint idea of the ripple on the waters may be present to the eye. And the form of the lakes should be irregular, curving round from its base among the lower hills, deeper and still deeper into some close nook up among the mountains from which its head waters spring. It is thus that a lake should be seen, and it was

Horns

From *Miscellanies in Prose and Verse*, 1711

Herodotus tells us, that in Cold Countries Beasts very seldom have Horns, but in Hot they have very large ones. This might bear a pleasant Application.

Jonathan Swift (1667–1745)

Tawny Owl (Syrnium aluco)

From *British Birds*, 1930

Owls are not very social birds, and the tawny owl is the most unsocial of all. He inhabits the deep wood, where he lives solitary or with his mate, and he is said to be very jealous of the intrusion of another individual of his species into his hunting-grounds. His chief distinction is his powerful, clear voice: heard in the profound silence of the woods at eventide the sound is wonderfully impressive, and affects us with a sense of mystery. This may be due to imagination, or to some primitive faculty in us, since the feeling is strong only when we are alone. If we are in a merry company, then the wood-owl's *too-whit, too-who*, may even seem to us 'a merry note,' as Shakespeare described it.

W. H. Hudson (1841–1922)

The Starlight Barking

From *The Hundred and One Dalmatians*, 1956

The dogs knew just where they wanted to go. Very firmly, they led the way right across the park, across the road, and to the open space which is called Primrose Hill. This did not surprise the Dearlys as it had always been a favourite walk. What did surprise them was the way Pongo and Missis behaved when they got to the top of the hill. They stood side by side and they barked.

They barked to the north, they barked to the south, they barked to the east and west. And each time they changed their positions, they began barking with three very strange, short, sharp barks.

'Anyone would think they were signalling,' said Mr Dearly.

But he did not really mean it. And they were signalling.

Many people must have noticed how dogs like to bark in the early evening. Indeed, twilight has sometimes been called 'Dogs' Barking Time'. Busy town dogs bark less than country dogs, but all dogs know about the Twilight Barking. It is their way of keeping in touch with distant friends, passing on important news, enjoying a good gossip. But none of the dogs who answered Pongo and Missis expected to enjoy a gossip, for the three short, sharp barks meant: 'Help! Help! Help!'

No dog sends that signal unless the need is desperate. And no dog ever fails to respond.

Within a few minutes, the news of the stolen puppies was travelling across England, and every dog who heard at once turned detective. Dogs living in London's Underworld (hard-bitten characters; also hard-biting) set out to explore sinister alleys where dog thieves lurk. Dogs in Pet Shops hastened to make quite sure all the puppies offered for sale were not Dalmatians in disguise. And dogs who could do nothing else swiftly handed on the news, spreading it through London and on through the suburbs, and on, on to the open country: 'Help! Help! Help! Fifteen Dalmatian puppies stolen. Send news to Pongo and Missis Pongo, of Regent's Park, London. End of message.'

Pongo and Missis hoped all this would be happening. But all they really knew was that they had made contact with the dogs near enough to answer them, and that those dogs would be standing by, at twilight the next evening, to relay any news that had come along.

One Great Dane, over towards Hampstead, was particularly encouraging.

'I have a chain of friends all over England,' he said, in his great booming bark. 'And I will be on duty day and night. Courage, courage, O Dogs of Regent's Park!'

It was almost dark now. And the Dearlys were suggesting – very gently – that they should be taken home. So after a few last words with the Great Dane, Pongo and Missis led the way down Primrose Hill. The dogs who had answered were silent now, but the Twilight Barking was spreading in an ever-widening circle. And tonight it would not end with twilight. It would go on and on as the moon rose high over England.

Dodie Smith (1896–1990)

Survival

From *The South Country*, Chapter III, Hampshire, 1909

How little do we know of the business of the earth, not to speak of the universe; of time, not to speak of eternity. It was not by taking thought that man survived the mastodon. The acts and thoughts that will serve the race, that will profit this commonwealth of things that live in the sun, the air, the earth, the sea, now and through all time, are not known and never will be known. The rumour of much toil and scheming and triumph may never reach the stars, and what we value not at all, are not conscious of, may break the surface of eternity with endless ripples of good. We know not by what we survive.

Edward Thomas (1878–1917)

The Whale

From *Moby-Dick*, 1851

It was not so much his uncommon bulk that so much distinguished him from other Sperm Whales, but, as was elsewhere thrown out – a peculiar snow-white wrinkled forehead, and a high, pyramidical white hump. These were his prominent features; the tokens whereby, even in the limitless, uncharted seas, he revealed his identity, at a long distance, to those who knew him.

The rest of his body was so streaked, and spotted, and marbled with the same shrouded hue, that, in the end, he had gained his distinctive appellation of the White Whale; a name, indeed, literally justified by his vivid aspect, when seen gliding at high noon through a dark blue sea, leaving a milky-way wake of creamy foam, all spangled with golden gleamings.

Nor was it his unwonted magnitude, nor his remarkable hue, nor yet his deformed lower jaw, that so much invested the whale with natural terror, as that unexampled, intelligent malignity which, according to specific accounts, he had over and over again evinced in his assaults. More than all, his treacherous retreats struck more of dismay than perhaps aught else. For, when swimming before his exulting pursuers, with every apparent symptom of alarm, he had several times been known to turn around suddenly, and, bearing down upon them, either stave their boats to splinters, or drive them back in consternation to their ship.

Herman Melville (1819–1891)

An Awesome Responsibility

From *Life on Earth*, 1979

The conclusion:

This last chapter has been devoted to only one species, ourselves. This may have given the impression that somehow man is the ultimate triumph of evolution, that all these millions of years of development have had no purpose other than to put him on the earth. There is no evidence to support such a view and no reason to suppose that our stay will be any more permanent than the dinosaurs'. The processes of evolution are still going on among plants and birds, insects and mammals. So it is more than likely that if men were to disappear from the earth, for whatever reason, there is a modest, unobtrusive creature somewhere that would develop into a new form and take our place.

But although denying that we have a special position in the natural world might seem becomingly modest in the eye of eternity, it might also be used as an excuse for evading our responsibilities. The fact is that no species has ever had such wholesale control over everything on earth, living or dead, as we have now. That lays upon us, whether we like it or not, an awesome responsibility. In our hands now lies not only our own future, but that of all other living creatures with whom we share the earth.

David Attenborough (1926–)

Characteristics of Animals and Man

From *History of Animals*, Book the First, 350 BC
Translated by Richard Cresswell (1815–1882)

Animals exhibit many differences of disposition. Some are gentle, peaceful, and not violent, as the ox. Some are violent, passionate, and intractable, as the wild boar. Some are prudent and fearful, as the stag and the hare. Serpents are illiberal and crafty. Others, as the lion, are liberal, noble, and generous. Others are brave, wild, and crafty, like the wolf. For there is a difference between the generous and the brave – the former means that which comes of a noble race, the latter that which does not easily depart from its own nature.

Some animals are cunning and evil-disposed, as the fox; others, as the dog, are fierce, friendly, and fawning. Some are gentle and easily tamed, as the elephant; some are susceptible of shame, and watchful, as the goose. Some are jealous, and fond of ornament, as the peacock. But man is the only animal capable of reasoning, though many others possess the faculty of memory and instruction in common with him. No other animal but man has the power of recollection.

Aristotle (384–322 BC)

Intolerable Fog

From *English Hours*, An English New Year, 1879

The charms of the capital during the last several weeks have been obscured by peculiarly vile weather. It is of course a very old story that London is foggy, and this simple statement raises no blush on the face of Nature as we see it here. But there are fogs and fogs, and the folds of the black mantle have been during the present winter intolerably thick.

Henry James (1843–1916)

The Christmas Oake

From *The Natural History of Wiltshire*, 1656–1691

In the New Forest, within the trenches of the castle of Molwood (a Roman camp) is an old oake, which is a pollard and short. It putteth forth young leaves on Christmas day, for about a week at that time of the yeare. Old Mr. Hastings, of Woodlands, was wont to send a basket full of them every yeare to King Charles I. I have seen of them severall Christmasses brought to my father.

John Aubrey (1626–1697)

The Marshes

From *Great Expectations*, 1861

Pip steals food and brandy for the convict:

It was a rimy morning, and very damp. I had seen the damp lying on the outside of my little window, as if some goblin had been crying there all night, and using the window for a pocket-handkerchief. Now, I saw the damp lying on the bare hedges and spare grass, like a coarser sort of spiders' webs; hanging itself from twig to twig and blade to blade. On every rail and gate, wet lay clammy, and the marsh mist was so thick, that the wooden finger on the post directing people to our village – a direction which they never accepted, for they never came there – was invisible to me until I was quite close under it. Then, as I looked up at it, while it dripped, it seemed to my oppressed conscience like a phantom devoting me to the Hulks.

The mist was heavier yet when I got out upon the marshes, so that instead of my running at everything, everything seemed to run at me. This was very disagreeable to a guilty mind. The gates and dikes and banks came bursting at me through the mist, as if they cried as plainly as could be, 'A boy with Somebody else's pork pie! Stop him!' The cattle came upon me with like suddenness, staring out of their eyes, and steaming out of their nostrils, 'Halloa, young thief!' One black ox, with a white cravat on, – who even had to my awakened conscience something of a clerical air, – fixed me so obstinately with his eyes, and moved his blunt head round in such an accusatory manner as I moved round, that I blubbered out to him, 'I couldn't help it, sir! It wasn't for myself I took it!' Upon which he put down his head, blew a cloud of smoke out of his nose, and vanished with a kick-up of his hind-legs and a flourish of his tail.

Charles Dickens (1812–1870)

Well-meaning Christmas

From *The Mill on the Floss*, 1860

Snow lay on the croft and river-bank in undulations softer than
the limbs of infancy; it lay with the neatliest finished border on
every sloping roof, making the dark-red gables stand out with a
new depth of colour; it weighed heavily on the laurels and fir-trees,
till it fell from them with a shuddering sound; it clothed the rough
turnip-field with whiteness, and made the sheep look like dark
blotches; the gates were all blocked up with the sloping drifts, and
here and there a disregarded four-footed beast stood as if petrified
'in unrecumbent sadness'; there was no gleam, no shadow, for
the heavens, too, were one still, pale cloud; no sound or motion
in anything but the dark river that flowed and moaned like an
unresting sorrow. But old Christmas smiled as he laid this cruel-
seeming spell on the outdoor world, for he meant to light up home
with new brightness, to deepen all the richness of indoor colour,
and give a keener edge of delight to the warm fragrance of food; he
meant to prepare a sweet imprisonment that would strengthen the
primitive fellowship of kindred, and make the sunshine of familiar
human faces as welcome as the hidden day-star. His kindness fell
but hardly on the homeless, – fell but hardly on the homes where
the hearth was not very warm, and where the food had little
fragrance; where the human faces had had no sunshine in them,
but rather the leaden, blank-eyed gaze of unexpectant want. But
the fine old season meant well; and if he has not learned the secret
how to bless men impartially, it is because his father Time, with
ever-unrelenting unrelenting purpose, still hides that secret in his
own mighty, slow-beating heart.

George Eliot (1819–1880)

Out of Season

From *Love's Labour's Lost* (c. 1595), Act I, scene i

Biron:
At Christmas I no more desire a rose
Than wish a snow in May's new-fangled mirth;
But like of each thing that in season grows.

William Shakespeare (1564–1616)

Snow

From *Dubliners*, The Dead, 1914

A few light taps upon the pane made him turn to the window. It
had begun to snow again. He watched sleepily the flakes, silver and
dark, falling obliquely against the lamplight. The time had come
for him to set out on his journey westward. Yes, the newspapers
were right: snow was general all over Ireland. It was falling on
every part of the dark central plain, on the treeless hills, falling
softly upon the Bog of Allen and, farther westward, softly falling
into the dark mutinous Shannon waves. It was falling, too, upon
every part of the lonely churchyard on the hill where Michael
Furey lay buried. It lay thickly drifted on the crooked crosses and
headstones, on the spears of the little gate, on the barren thorns.
His soul swooned slowly as he heard the snow falling faintly
through the universe and faintly falling, like the descent of their
last end, upon all the living and the dead.

James Joyce (1882–1941)

The Opinion of Cats

From *The Compleat Angler*, Part I, 1653–1676
Translated by Izaak Walton (1593–1683)

When my Cat and I entertain each other with mutual apish tricks (as playing with a garter) who knows but that I make my Cat more sport than she makes me? Shall I conclude her to be simple, that has her time to begin or refuse to play as freely as I myself have? Nay, who knows but that it is a defect of my not understanding her language (for doubtless Cats talk and reason with one another) that we agree no better: and who knows but that she pitties me for being no wiser than to play with her, and laughs and censures my follie for making sport for her, when we two play together?

Michel de Montaigne (1533–1592)

How the World Was Made

From *Cherokee Creation Stories*, 1887–1890

The earth is a great island floating in a sea of water, and suspended at each of the four cardinal points by a cord hanging down from the sky vault, which is of solid rock. When the world grows old and worn out, the people will die and the cords will break and let the earth sink down into the ocean, and all will be water again. The Indians are afraid of this.

When all was water, the animals were above in Gălûñ'lătăĭ, beyond the arch; but it was very much crowded, and the animals wanted more room. They wondered what was below the water, and at last Dȧyuni'sĭ, 'Beaver's Grandchild', the little Water-beetle, offered to go and see if it could find out. It darted in every direction over the surface of the water, but could find no firm place to rest. Then it dived to the bottom and came up with some soft mud, which began to grow and spread on every side until it became the island which we call the earth. It was afterward fastened to the sky with four cords, but no one remembers who did this.

James Mooney (1861–1921)

Stars

From *The Books That Bind*, 2018

Do you know what I think stars are? I think they are little holes in the night sky that hint at eternity. That's why stars burn so bright – we are seeing fragments of forever, other worlds, like sensing silent snowfall on the other side of a curtained window.

Mark Staples (1980–)

INDEX

SOURCES

David Attenborough, *Life on Earth*, © David Attenborough, HarperCollins Publishers.

B. B. (Denys Watkins-Pitchford), *Brendon Chase*, © The Estate of Denys Watkins-Pitchford; reproduced by permission of David Higham Associates Ltd.

Richard Bach, *Jonathan Livingston Seagull*, © Richard Bach, HarperCollins Publishers.

J. A. Baker, *The Peregrine*, © The Estate of J. A. Baker, HarperCollins Publishers.

H. E. Bates, *Through the Woods*. Reproduced with permission of Curtis Brown Group Ltd, London on behalf of The Estate of H. E. Bates. Copyright © H.E. Bates, 1936

Ronald Blythe, *Akenfield*, © Ronald Blythe, Penguin Random House.

Michael Bond, *A Bear Called Paddington*. Reproduced by permission of The Agency (London) Ltd © Michael Bond 1958.

J. L. Carr, *A Month in the Country*, © The Estate of J. L. Carr. United Agents, London.

Rachel Carson, *Two Roads*, © The Estate of Rachel Carson. Peters, Fraser and Dunlop Literary Agents, London.

John Stewart Collis, *Down to Earth: The Wood*, © The Estate of John Stewart Collis. United Agents, London.

ACKNOWLEDGEMENTS

Firstly, a huge thank you to everyone at Hatchards for looking after my books so well.

Thanks to Joel Knight for reminding me that *The Wind in the Willows* is probably one of the most charming books ever written, Richard Bucht for introducing me to the writings of Aldo Leopold, and Julie Apps, Francis Cleverdon, Sue and David Gibb, Sally Hughes, Louy and David Piachaud and Ian Prince for helpful reminders. Joel Knight obligingly moved from poetry to prose and Mark Staples allowed me to include extracts from his magical description of a very special bookshop. Tina Persaud and Nicola Newman are everything that one could wish for in editors, likewise Teresa Chris, my agent. Thanks also to Ruth Ellis for compiling the index so efficiently and recognising the importance of heffalumps, pushmi-pullyus and a certain bear from Darkest Peru. Lastly my thanks as always to Matilda the furry paperweight.

ABOUT THE EDITOR

Jane McMorland Hunter has compiled nine anthologies for Batsford and the National Trust including collections on nature, friendship, London, England and the First World War. She has also worked as a gardener, potter and quilter, writes gardening, cookery and craft books and works at Hatchards Bookshop in Piccadilly. Brought up in the country, she now lives in London, where she has a small but overfull garden.